Praise for *Marketing in t...*

"Vanessa Fox is not only blessed with a brilliant mind, but fantastic perspective into the search marketplace. Her experiences at Google and within the industry, combined with her ability to share those insights in easy-to-understand morsels, makes this book a must-read for anyone with even the slightest interest in what's happening in the online world."

—Richard Zwicky, Founder, Enquisite

"Vanessa Fox grabs your hand, shows you the way into the big black box of search marketing, and flips the lights on. Trying to justify a search-related project? From hard data to helpful checklists, it's all in here. Taking on the challenge of search optimization by yourself? You'll walk away from this book not only *getting* it when it comes to using search to build your business, but knowing how to *do* it."

—Tamara Adlin, cofounder of Fell Swoop and author of *The Essential Persona Lifecycle: Your Guide to Building and Using Personas*

"Finally! A C-level book about smarter search engine marketing. *Marketing in the Age of Google* by Vanessa Fox is undoubtedly the search marketing bible for senior executives looking to maximize business growth through search engine marketing. This is a must-read, and if you don't, your competition certainly will."

—Lee Odden, CEO, TopRank Online Marketing

"Former Googler Vanessa Fox has a unique understanding of search marketing from both sides of the table and has been educating people about the wonderful world of Google and search marketing through speaking and writing for years. Now she compiles all her great knowledge in book form and thoughtfully guides newcomers and the experienced alike past jargon and distractions to focus on the best ways to achieve success in today's searching culture."

—Danny Sullivan, Editor in Chief, *Search Engine Land*

"This tome may be the first book that manages to identify and deconstruct the new search-engine-centric world in which we live. With insights and tips for anyone doing business in the connected world, it's perhaps the first must-read-to-survive business book of the twenty-first century. Highly recommended."

—John C. Dvorak, columnist MarketWatch, *PC Magazine*

"Vanessa is the rare person with big-picture expertise who has spent time deep in the trenches with sleeves rolled up making the magic happen. This book reflects that on every page. Get ready to finally stop marketing on the Web as if it were television!"

—Avinash Kaushik, Google Analytics Evangelist Author of *Web Analytics 2.0: The Art of Online Accountability and Science of Customer Centricity*

"If you are an entrepreneur, Webmaster, designer, or an executive for a Fortune 500 company, *Marketing in the Age of Google* will help you streamline your business strategy based on understanding your customer. I would recommend it as reading material to every project manager within eBay."

—**Dennis Goedegebuure, previously Senior SEO Manager, eBay**

"The connected marketing world should acquire this text by whatever means necessary. Digital marketing isn't just 'digital' anymore. Search isn't just search anymore. If every marketer put these disciplines to use, it would mean billions in revenue almost overnight."

—**Kevin M. Ryan, Motivity Marketing**

"I've been relying on Google to help me drive traffic to my websites for over a decade, and I learned three new (and invaluable) tricks within the first twenty pages. If you have a business on the Web, you'll want Vanessa's book on your shelf."

—**Chris Pirillo, Founder, Lockergnome**

"Charming? Disarmingly so. A smile that melts hearts? Totally. Wicked smart? Abundantly! Vanessa Fox knows all the ins and outs of online marketing and on top of it all, this woman can write. *Marketing in the Age of Google* is amazingly readable. Informative? Without question. Practical? As comfortable shoes. Accessible? A pure pleasure to read and—look—I learned something that will undeniably improve my business. That's rare value."

—**Jim Sterne, Founder, eMetrics Marketing Optimization Summit and Chairman, Web Analytics Association**

"Vanessa is one of the true search experts. This book is full of valuable information that will teach you to develop and execute an effective search plan. No matter if you are a beginner or an expert, set aside some time as you will want to read this book at least twice."

—**Brad Geddes, Author of *Advanced AdWords***

"Marketing your business through search engines is a complex, challenging problem. Thankfully, those new to the field now have this tremendous resource from Vanessa Fox to help guide them through the trials and tribulations of search marketing in a clear and delightfully readable format."

—**Rand Fishkin, CEO, SEOmoz and Author of *The Art of SEO***

"Vanessa is a technical expert in the world of search marketing. Her book will help fill that much needed industry gap of misinformation."

—**Marshall Simmonds, Chief Search Strategist, New York Times Company, CEO and Cofounder, Define Search Strategies**

"Search engines are a crucial component of almost every business. Vanessa Fox is a world-renowned expert in how to optimize your site for search engines. Having worked with her directly on search engine strategies, I know her insights and approaches to this area are unparalleled and can have a major impact on your online business. This book provides you with the tools and insights to optimize your website and ensure you leave your competitors in the dust."

—**Elad Gil, Founder and former CEO, Mixer Labs (acquired by Twitter)**

"With *Marketing in the Age of Google*, Vanessa has succeeded in crafting a comprehensive and engaging introduction to what it means to be 'search aware.' She provides marketers with the starting points to understand not only how to prioritize content (and product) development based on consumer demand, but also how to work with developers to ensure that content will be accessible to search engines. This is artfully accomplished while also providing a solid business case for search efforts. Her book will help agencies and advertisers learn how to bring search engine optimization (SEO) out of the black box and into the creative, collaborative process that has driven smart advertising for decades. This is a necessary addition to all of our reading."

—Jorie Waterman, Senior Vice President and Director of Search, MRM Worldwide

"Eighty-five percent of the clicks on Google's search engine happen in nonpaid results. This book analyzes and explains the rapidly changing landscape of those results and shows you how to leverage them for business. It's an informed and essential contribution to the field."

—Adam Audette, President, AudetteMedia Inc., and Lead SEO for Zappos.com

"Why is a Bing guy giving a quote to a book with Google in the title? Because Vanessa does two things: nails the core truth behind how consumers are using engines today (it's not what you think!) and gives you *actionable* things you can do *today* with free tools to help convert searchers into customers. Finally, a book that combines theory and practice without making me feel like I'm the dumbest guy in the room. Also, Vanessa's impressive citing of quotes from other people and the use of my data (check out Chapters 2 and 3—they are epic) make this book not only believable and an indispensible tool to impress your boss, but a great conversation starter at search conference parties. Believe me, you need it."

—Stefan Weitz, Director, Bing Search

"Fox elegantly explains how search is an essential component of any business's marketing strategy. Her comprehensive statistics should convince even the most skeptical of the need to invest in search."

—Jonathan Hochman, Hochman Consultants

"I have long considered Vanessa Fox the go-to expert on search . . . for everyone from individual publishers to big brands. With her new book *Marketing in the Age of Google*, she's finally doing us all a great service and putting all of that knowledge and strategic insight into one easily digestible place."

—Elisa Camahort Page, Cofounder and COO, BlogHer

"These days, there's a wealth of information available that teaches the techniques necessary to achieve top rankings in search engine results or paid search listings. But few books go beyond tactics to show you how to truly engage with your customers through search and building meaningful relationships that lead not just to results, but to relationships that can last a lifetime. *Marketing in the Age of Google* does just that, making it a unique and invaluable guide to the full spectrum of activities and touch points that are the hallmarks of truly successful search marketing campaigns."

—Chris Sherman, Executive Editor, SearchEngineLand.com,
and President, Searchwise

"I devoured this well-written and very organized book and quickly determined that this information is a game-changer for most companies. Senior management and corporate America no longer have excuses for not understanding search and SEO. Vanessa explains complex search concepts using easy-to-read, real-world examples. Only she could have written this definitive SEO reference manual. This is the type of book that even the most experienced search professional will return to again and again. Whether you are an executive, newbie, or experienced corporate SEO, this book is required reading. I found myself thinking about these search tactics long after I put down the book. Every reader of this book is receiving the highest-level SEO consulting with every turn of the page."

—Rudy De La Garza, Jr., SEO for Bankrate.com,
and Owner, SEOMarketing.com

"Vanessa Fox brings a delightful and insightful approach together to help business owners understand the key tenants of marketing in today's online world of metrics and search—and more important, gives clear guidance on what they need to do to be successful. This book is a must have for every CEO and marketer."

—Natala Menezes, Director, Product Marketing, Gigwalk

"One of the most in-depth, clear reviews of the essence of search marketing and its influence on modern business. Well balanced in its approach and examples, this book is chock full of insights from the brightest minds in search marketing today. From explanations of how we got to where we are, to clarifying future directions business owners should watch, *Marketing in the Age of Google* should be included as part of any business's plan for success on the Internet."

—Duane Forrester, Sr. Program Manager (SEO), Microsoft

"This is a *great* book. I want to recommend it to every client who's ever asked me for search strategy advice! *Marketing in the Age of Google* provides invaluable information about techniques and tools you can use to improve your organic and paid search results—but more important, it explains why your customers' needs, desires, and behaviors should be the central focus of your search marketing strategy. Also, 'Would You Like to Exchange Links with My Site Buy-Cheap-Viagra-While-You-Play-Poker-Online-and-File-a-Mesothelioma-Class-Action-lawsuit.info?' is the best heading ever."

—Debby Levinson, Founder, Nimble Partners

"Search, aim, market. If you want to increase your sales without doubling your sales force, read on. Vanessa Fox opens up the hood of leading search engines and gives us a very insightful tour. Every business manager should know how search works to stay competitive. At the end of the day, running a business without an online strategy is like sending all your online customers to your competitor—you missed the sale because you did not show up."

—Melek Pulatkonak, President and COO, hakia.com

"Vanessa takes what is certainly the most important marketing topic of the decade and makes it not only accessible but concrete. A must-read for marketers; it rises above a mere playbook of tricks and tips to showcase the principles of successful marketing with and through search."

—Randall Lucas, Venture Capitalist, Voyager Capital

"It's hard to succeed on the Internet without understanding the mechanics of search marketing and the technology behind it. Vanessa's book breaks down key technological and marketing elements in a way that's easy to understand and apply regardless of your level of marketing or IT expertise. Do you want more visitors to your website? Do you want to be known as an authority online? If yes, this book will help you understand and take advantage of the marketing opportunities behind search technology. It's a must-read."

—Debra Mastaler, Founder, Alliance-Link

"Vanessa Fox has delivered great search marketing insights with her new book *Marketing in the Age of Google*. She has successfully translated the complex search marketing concepts into easy to understand ideas that can be implemented by everyday business owners who do not have a PhD in computer science."

—Greg Niland, GoodROI

"The building search personas chapter is awesome. I feel like trying everything."

—Devesh Tiwari

"Vanessa Fox does an excellent job of organizing a potentially highly technical topic into an easily accessible format. This is a good book for CMOs, online marketing professionals, agency personnel, and anyone that touches marketing strategy. Her approach is really an excellent framework for marketing, rather than just online or search marketing. At the conclusion of the book, the reader will understand where search fits in the overall marketing plan, how to plan/implement organic search marketing strategies, and which metrics matter for organic search. *Marketing in the Age of Google* is required reading for our consultants."

—Chris Baggott, Cofounder, Compendium

"An excellent read for anyone interested or involved in building a business case for search strategies. . . . [Fox] redirects your focus to the bridge that connects a website, SEO activities, and business strategies with customers. She then catapults you into an overlooked approach to search. . . . Fox provides enough concrete information for you to act, effectively balancing the 'why' of search with the 'how' of using search to improve business. . . . The strategies laid out in this book will give you an edge over the common practices of your competitors as you integrate search into your business and marketing activities."

—Louellen S. Coker, *Journal for the Society of Technical Communication*

"The book is based on the theory of having a Web strategy in place that is aligned to the company's business strategy. If your company has the consumer approach understanding the needs, desires, and motivation why consumers go online to evaluate products and services, then the book is a must-read."

—Martin Meyer-Gossner, The Strategy Web

"Vanessa is different because she understands how Google (search) works from inside out and how it will evolve to better serve the needs of its users. That's what makes her book better than most other books that give you an outside view of how to optimize your site for Google. . . . There are strategies that can help a business understand search and effectively utilize it in order to gain market share."

—Zahid Lilani

"*Marketing in the Age of Google*, written by ex-Googler Vanessa Fox, is the best book that combines the art and science of SEO with the fundamentals of business."

—Conrad Saam, Business Insider

"This is a highly informative, *strategic* overview of search, written for executives who need to understand the business impact of search without unnecessary detail about the mechanics. . . . Beyond making the business case for search, Fox explains—in high-level, non-nerdy terms—how to implement a search strategy, how to get your business strategy and SEO technology in sync, how to separate actionable information from the mass of search and Web traffic data generated by analytics tools, how social media marketing affects search results, and key search trends on the horizon."

—Tom Pick, Webbiquity

"*Marketing in the Age of Google* is not about how to tactically implement search engine optimization, but how to think strategically about search and understand how your business fits into a search-based culture. And yet, those who know there is a financial reward for higher search rankings and a dearth of misinformation being disseminated on the open market, will be gratified to find that each chapter includes a checklist of useful, practical, and actionable steps every website can take to translate their unique value and points of difference into improved search engine visibility."

—Larry Sivitz, Seattle24x7.com

"Fox explains how your company can create and implement an intelligent 'search acquisition strategy.' getAbstract recommends Fox's book as a pivotal SEO guide for marketing managers, website content developers, and online sales professionals."

—getAbstract

MARKETING IN THE AGE OF GOOGLE

MARKETING IN THE AGE OF GOOGLE

YOUR ONLINE STRATEGY IS YOUR BUSINESS STRATEGY

REVISED AND UPDATED

VANESSA FOX

WILEY

John Wiley & Sons, Inc.

Published by John Wiley & Sons, Inc., Hoboken, New Jersey.
Published simultaneously in Canada.

For general information on our other products and services or for technical support, please contact our Customer Care Department within the United States at (800) 762-2974, outside the United States at (317) 572-3993 or fax (317) 572-4002.

Wiley publishes in a variety of print and electronic formats and by print-on-demand. Some material included with standard print versions of this book may not be included in e-books or in print-on-demand. If this book refers to media such as a CD or DVD that is not included in the version you purchased, you may download this material at http://booksupport.wiley.com. For more information about Wiley products, visit www.wiley.com.

Library of Congress Cataloging-in-Publication Data:

Fox, Vanessa, 1972–
    Marketing in the age of Google: your online strategy IS your business strategy / Vanessa Fox. — Rev. and updated
       p.   cm.
    Includes bibliographical references and index.
    ISBN 978-1-118-23193-7 (paper); ISBN 978-1-118-34299-2 (ebk);
    ISBN 978-1-118-34300-5 (ebk); ISBN 978-1-118-34298-5 (ebk)
       1. Internet marketing.   2. Internet searching.   3. Web search engines.   I. Title.
HF5415.1265.F678   2012
658.8'72—dc23

                                                                                        2011052827

Printed in the United States of America

10 9 8 7 6 5 4 3 2 1

To the search marketing community:
You have been welcoming beyond description
since the very beginning. This book
wouldn't exist without you.

Contents

Foreword

There's a special place where customers gather each day, willingly seeking businesses that can help them. They want cars. They want plumbers. They want music downloads. They want vacation rentals, lawn care products, tax advice, and more. You name the product or service, this place has someone looking for it.

This venue is the ultimate destination for those after a prequalified audience. Everyone there is ready to buy or convert in some way. Everyone is explicitly asking to be contacted. Everyone is even willing to take part in market research to help guide a business forward. Here's the best part: As a business, it costs nothing to be admitted.

What's the catch? There isn't one, other than being aware of the opportunity this place provides and tapping into it.

The place? The major search engines used by millions each day—Yahoo!, Microsoft's Bing, and the largest of them all, Google. Consumers increasingly depend on these tools to locate products, services, and information. Search engines continue to usurp more "traditional" means of reaching customers, such as newspapers, phone books, or television. But unlike those traditional means, getting in front of consumers through search engines doesn't require a huge marketing budget.

Search engines mine web pages and other digital content to automatically provide answers to those searching. Becoming one of those answers can require no work at all. Many companies just naturally turn up in the search listings—for free.

With a little savvy, companies can increase their representation. Have you thought about the exact ways people might be searching for your goods? Have you ensured that search engines can properly read your website? Have you considered how you're listed beyond your web pages, in areas such as video results?

The hardest part of success with search engines isn't the tactical changes or techniques involved. It's simply becoming "search aware" in the first place—of understanding the importance of search and ensuring that you're not ignoring easy-to-take opportunities or establishing barriers that block your potential.

That's where this book comes in. It will help you over that hardest part: gaining search awareness. In it, Vanessa Fox illustrates the importance of search for today's marketer. She breaks down search marketing into common-sense components that won't make you feel lost in jargon or tactics.

I've written about search marketing for nearly 15 years now, and it still amazes me that more people still don't understand the incredible value it holds. Discover the importance of search in this book and how it can help you reach your customers and discover new directions to take your business. Read on about the new age in marketing—that of Google and search engines.

—DANNY SULLIVAN, EDITOR IN CHIEF,
SearchEngineLand.com

Preface

When I worked at Google, I talked to thousands of business owners seeking my help and advice. To them, Google was somewhat of a black box. They knew that organic search (the unpaid result set) was important, but they had no idea how to use search data and customer acquisition from organic search in their business processes.

We built Google Webmaster Central (www.google.com/webmasters) as a way to give business owners and Webmasters insight into how their sites were performing in Google and to help them identify problems and make improvements. During my tenure at Google and since, the business owners I talk to often fall into one of the following camps:

- Those who know search has become an important part of the customer engagement cycle but aren't sure where to start.
- Those who don't think search is that important and believe that even if it is, businesses shouldn't have to concern themselves with it. It's Google's job to sort things out.
- Those who get so caught up in optimizing their sites and ranking number one that they don't step back to look at the bigger picture: to understand how searchers behave, how to engage with them, and how to turn them into lifelong customers.

After I left Google, I wanted to take what we started with Webmaster Central and go beyond helping people pinpoint issues that might be preventing them from doing well in search. I wanted to help them fix those areas, improve their sites, and take the focus *off* of ranking and put it *on* connecting with the right audience. In short, I wanted to change the conversation about search. I wanted to help businesses understand why organic search was important to their long-term success and show them how to harness it for better customer engagement and more informed business and product strategy—and introduce them to a whole new world of customers who they may have been missing. Thus, the idea for this book was born.

If you've picked up this book, you already realize that search is becoming the primary way in which many people get information, decide what to buy, and make those purchases. And you know that as customer behavior changes, businesses remain successful by changing with them.

These days, your search strategy *is* your business strategy, whether you realize it or not, because that's how potential customers are trying to find you. Search is the new Yellow Pages, 800 number, Sunday circular, card catalog, and cash register.

But how do you build a comprehensive search strategy? And how can you take advantage of the amazing amounts of data about your potential customers that search makes available? Much as our evolution to a searching culture was a fundamental shift in behavior, fully realizing the potential of search often requires such a shift in your business. This adjustment will help you better connect with potential customers, make more informed business decisions, and remain relevant as our world continues to change. This book will get you there.

Chapter 1

How Search Has Changed Your Business

Twenty years ago, the World Wide Web as we know it today didn't exist. Ten years ago, only early technology adopters used search engines, and Google was a struggling young upstart. Now, 92 percent of online Americans use search engines (nearly 60 percent do this every day).[1] That's a lot of potential customers who are looking for you, and those lists of search queries are a lot of market research about what those customers want.

Americans conduct more than 20 billion online searches a month,[2] and worldwide, we type into a search box 131 billion times monthly. That's 29 million searches per minute.[3] (Google alone receives more than 1 billion unique visitors per month.)[4]

And what's more, we trust the search results that are returned for our queries. An Edelman study found that search engines are our number one go-to source of data (beating news sources, friends, and source media).[5] Neal Flieger, chair of Edelman's research firm StrategyOne, said of the research: "People are behaving like smart consumers when it comes to news and information, turning first to search engines to see what is available on the topic they are interested in, and then seeking out traditional media to confirm or expand on what they learn."[6]

It's safe to say that we've become a searching culture (Figure 1.1).

Just take a look at the 2011 Super Bowl to see this in action. Look at the spiking searches on Google during the game. Every single one of the top 20 are game-related (Figure 1.2). Viewers were searching for more information on commercials, performers at the half-time show, and the game itself.[7]

The @YahooSearchData Twitter feed provides daily reminders of our searching culture (Figure 1.3).

When Osama bin Laden was killed in May 2011, Yahoo! reported a nearly 100,000 percent increase in search traffic for related terms.[8]

Business leaders know that the world is changing. More customer research and transactions take place online now than ever before, and those

Figure 1.1 Google Search Volume by Language
Source: Google Data Arts Team[9]

numbers are only going to increase. Globally, the number of searches grew 46 percent in 2009,[10] and every month we continue to search more often and on more devices.

According to Jack Flanagan, comScore executive vice president, "Search is clearly becoming a more ubiquitous behavior among Internet users that

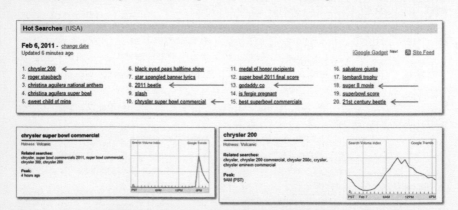

Figure 1.2 Google Search Trends, Super Bowl 2011
Source: Google Trends

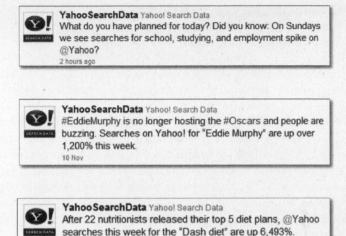

Figure 1.3 Yahoo! Search Trends
Source: Yahoo![11]

drives navigation not only directly from search engines but also within sites and across networks. If you equate the advancement of search with the ability of humans to cultivate information, then the world is rapidly becoming a more knowledgeable ecosystem." But many professionals simply aren't sure how to evolve their businesses to best take advantage of this changing landscape. This book will show you how to think about your business in a new way, better connect with your customers through search, and weave the value that search provides into all aspects of your organization.

Through organic search, you can reach potential customers at the very moment they are considering a purchase and provide them information exactly when they are looking for it. Although many businesses are attempting to connect with their potential customers through paid search (such as with Google AdWords), the opportunity to reach these customers through organic search—the results that are algorithmically generated rather than paid for—remains largely untapped.

This remains true two years after I wrote the first edition of this book. U.S. advertisers were projected to spend $14.38 billion on paid search and $12.33 billion on display advertising in 2011,[12] far outpacing search engine optimization investment.

A 2011 study found that nearly half of companies planned to spend $25,000 or less on search engine optimization in 2011 and that within that same group of companies, only 25 percent planned to spend that little on paid search.

Never before have we had access to such remarkable amounts of data about potential customers. We know what they search for (and what they don't). We know how they shop and how they buy. We can even find out where they look on a web page. Businesses spend such significant amounts of time and money on market research, focus groups, and usability studies, yet so many fail to augment this information with the abundance of free data available from those billions of searches a month.

We don't have to look further than our local newspapers to see how consumer behavior has changed. The newspaper industry spent years trying to get readers to return to their old behaviors of expecting the newspaper at their doors every morning and reading the stories as they were laid out in print. But those readers had moved on to searching online for news on topics of interest and getting that information in real time rather than a day later. Similarly, companies have to adapt and evolve with their customers instead of attempting to get their customers to return to their old ways.

■ DOESN'T GOOGLE SHOW THE MOST RELEVANT SITES TO SEARCHERS WITHOUT MY INPUT?

When writing the first edition of this book, I talked to *Wired* magazine senior writer Steven Levy (previously the senior technology editor for *Newsweek*), who had been spending a lot of time at Google researching his book *In the Plex*.[13] Levy told me he didn't believe that businesses should have to do anything "special" to their sites for Google since Google's purpose is to surface the most relevant, useful results to the top. He compared the practice of site owners trying to influence this to students having coaches for the SAT exam.

I told him I didn't see things that way at all. I see the situation as similar to a retailer who opens a store in a new city. Before leasing a building, the retailer will likely scout out the area to find the best corner. The company will do some competitive research to see where the other retailers are located, as well as some customer research to see where its target consumers shop. (Many even stand on sidewalks and count people walking by!) Retailers know that even if their stores have the most amazing merchandise at super low prices, they might not have many customers if they open their stores in an alley that's closed to traffic and they don't let anyone know they're there. John Deere probably wouldn't have many people buying riding lawn mowers from a store in Manhattan.

Companies should think of their online presence as another retail location. Organic search is the city they're in, the street they're on, the sign above their door. John Deere opens stores in towns where people have really big lawns, and they keep the doors unlocked so their customers can get in. If you don't do the same with organic search, you're missing an increasingly large percentage of your potential customers.

■ THE KEYS TO AN EFFECTIVE SEARCH STRATEGY

To incorporate search into your organization:

- Add search metrics to your data mix to better understand your audience, see industry trends, and build a better product strategy.
- Integrate offline and online marketing activities to capitalize on your offline advertising efforts and to keep from losing potential customers that your offline advertising efforts are driving to search engines.
- Develop a search acquisition strategy that fully harnesses the searching behavior of your potential customers.

To successfully execute your search strategy, you should build its importance into every aspect of the organization—not just marketing. A successful search strategy depends on information technology (IT) and engineering, product management, business development, marketing and advertising, public relations, customer support, user research, user interaction design, and any other department that thinks about the business, customers, product, or website. *Marketing in the Age of Google* will guide you toward building a successful search strategy and extending the process for execution throughout your entire organization.

This book talks about organic search—the search results that are generated algorithmically based on what the search engines think is most relevant for the query. Paid search (the ads that appear beside the organic results) is also an important piece of the search strategy puzzle, but a number of resources exist to help businesses better understand and use paid search, so in this book, we'll be talking only about it as it influences organic search.

What is your organic search strategy? If you don't have one, you're missing a key piece of your business strategy—and shutting out many potential customers who are looking for your business. If you're an executive, this book will give you a holistic view of how search fits into your overall business strategy and how to integrate it into the organization. If you're a marketer, developer, or user interaction designer or if you otherwise work on customer engagement, product development, or company awareness, this book will show you how to incorporate search into what you're already doing for an even better return.

➤ Search as the Entry Point of the Web

For many of us, the search box has become our entry point to the Web. When the Web first gained popularity, it became important for a business to have a website. As online activity became more prevalent, it became important for a business to include a domain name in advertising and other materials. Now things have shifted again, and it's vital for a business to rank well in search results both for its brand name and for queries relevant to the business.

But integrating offline and online marketing is only half the story. It's just as important to understand the needs of your customers. For years, companies have commissioned focus groups and large-scale surveys and conducted massive market research to find out what their potential customers want and how their current customers think about them. All of those activities are still valuable, but there's now an easier (and cheaper) way. Search can provide powerful data about exactly what your potential customers want and what they're thinking about you.

➤ Every Day, Millions of Potential Customers Are Telling You Exactly What They Want

Intuit sells accounting software. As of the first printing of this book, their product packaging, marketing materials, and website all referred to this software as *bookkeeping* applications. But if you take a look at what their potential customers are searching for, you'll notice that they're searching for "accounting" over "bookkeeping" software by a substantial margin. (You'll learn how to find out how your customers are searching for you in Chapter 2.) See Figures 1.4 and 1.5.

Not only was Intuit missing this audience from its search acquisition funnel, it wasn't resonating with its potential customers as well as it could have been in offline channels.

Perhaps they read this book, because as of November 2011, things have changed on the QuickBooks website. The site now talks about its "accounting" software and ranks for related queries. Based on search volume in the United States, that one wording change could be the difference between being seen by 15,000 searchers versus 250,000 searchers (Figures 1.6 and 1.7).

The National Institutes of Health (NIH) has the important mission of making accurate and useful health-related information available to the American public but limited resources with which to do so. If this group wants to help the greatest number of people first, it could start with search data. You can see in Figure 1.8 that many more people are looking for information on arthritis than on heart disease.

Figure 1.4 [Accounting Software] and [Bookkeeping Software] Search Volume
Source: Google Insights for Search

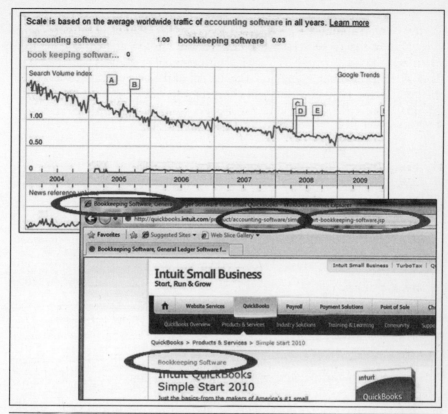

Figure 1.5 Speaking the Language of Your Customer

Source: Google Trends and Quickbooks.Intuit.com

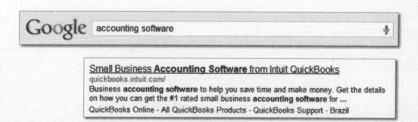

Figure 1.6 [Accounting Software] Search Results

Source: Google Search

	Keyword	Local Monthly Searches ⑦
☐	☆ accounting software	246,000
☐	☆ bookkeeping software	14,800

Figure 1.7 "Accounting Software" vs. "Bookkeeping Software" Search Volume
Source: Google AdWords Keyword Tool

Diving deeper, we can see that "rheumatoid" is the type of arthritis that people search for the most and that Ohio's population has one of the keenest interests in this topic (Figures 1.9 and 1.10).

Many factors go into prioritizing projects, but your potential audience's primary interest can be a valuable one.

Whether you run an online business, a multinational conglomerate with no online presence, or a two-person start-up out of your garage, your customers are providing you with valuable data that can help form your business strategy.

➤ *How Search Has Changed Marketing*

As defined by the Chartered Institute of Marketing, marketing consists of "identifying, anticipating, and satisfying customer requirements profitably."[14] That definition doesn't change as business moves online.

But although the core elements of marketing remain the same, it's no secret that consumer behavior is shifting. We frequently turn to online sources for things we used to get offline—from news and local directories to television shows, music, and movies. This evolution means that the expectations

Figure 1.8 [Arthritis] and [Heart Disease] Search Trends
Source: Google Trends

Search terms related to arthitis				
Top searches		⑦	**Rising searches**	
1. rheumatoid arthritis	100		1. what is arthitis	Breakout
2. arthitis pain	55		2. symptoms of arthitis	Breakout
3. arthitis symptoms	30		3. hip arthitis	Breakout
4. arthitis treatment	25		4. back arthitis	Breakout
5. arthitis knee	25		5. arthitis pain	+180%
6. arthitis foundation	25		6. arthitis treatment	+120%
7. what is arthitis	15		7. arthitis knee	+80%
8. symptoms of arthitis	15		8. arthitis foundation	+80%
9. back arthitis	15		9. arthitis symptoms	+70%
New! ⊞ Google			10. rheumatoid arthitis	+60%

Figure 1.9 [Arthritis] Search Trends

Source: Google Insights for Search

of your potential customers and their methods of interacting with you may be different than they were before. For instance, they may expect support online, whereas before they may have looked for an 800 number.

This shift also means that traditional forms of advertising don't have the reach that they used to have. If paid print newspaper circulation is down 30 percent over the past 20 years, that's 30 percent fewer people seeing your print ads.[15] If people are throwing away Yellow Pages books, then none of those people are seeing your Yellow Pages directory listing.[16]

Savvy marketers are transferring spending to online advertising—particularly paid search—but some haven't yet started to take full advantage of the vast majority of clicks that organic search produces.

Buyers Are Shifting to Searching Our buying patterns are changing along with our online behavior.[17] Nearly 12 percent of U.S.-based searches are

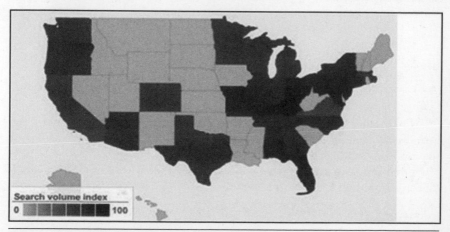

Figure 1.10 [Arthritis] Regional Search Trends

Source: Google Insights for Search

retail-focused.[18] In September 2010, Google found that nearly 90 percent of consumers research online while doing holiday shopping.[19]

Forrester Research's U.S. Online Retail Forecast, 2009 to 2014, found that U.S. online retail grew 11 percent in 2009 to reach $155 billion and forecast that online retail sales in 2014 would reach nearly $250 billion.[20] Although overall retail sales were up only 3 percent in Q4 2010, online sales were up 13.5 percent over the same period.

What better way to observe consumer shopping trends than to look at our favorite shopping day of the year: the day after Thanksgiving, known as Black Friday. According to Google, related searches were up significantly in 2011 versus 2010[21]:

- [Black Friday] and [Black Friday coupons] up 70 percent
- [Black Friday store map] up more than 450 percent
- [Black Friday store hours] up more than 200 percent
- [Thanksgiving store hours] up 400 percent
- [Thanksgiving deals] up 100 percent
- [Cyber Monday] and related searches (sales, coupons, free shipping) up 100 percent

Google also projected that 15 percent of related holiday 2011 searches would be from mobile devices.

Can Google forecast the hot new toy of the season? Maybe. Rising toy-related terms in November 2011 included:

- Lego man
- Bratz Masquerade
- Tablets for kids
- Hot Wheels Video racer
- My Keepon
- Figit Friends
- Moshi Monsters
- Nerf Vortex

The online intelligence-gathering group, Hitwise, found that in the four weeks leading to Black Friday, Uggs-related queries were three of the top 10 searches leading to shopping sites.[22]

From Bing, we can see what consumer electronics were of greatest interest throughout 2011. The top 10 were:

1. Xbox
2. Kindle
3. PlayStation

4. iPhone 5
5. iPad
6. Wii
7. iPad2
8. Nook
9. Windows Phone 7
10. Macbook Pro

So we're searching more than ever for our holiday shopping. Does that translate into purchases? That seems to be the case. U.S. online spending was up 26 percent on Black Friday in 2011 versus 2010 (for a total of $816 million spent).[23] Research company comScore also found that online research boosted in-store sales: "as the online channel increasingly influences offline shopping behavior, consumers turned to Black Friday sites on the Web to conduct research in advance of the day's events." See Figure 1.11.

The National Retail Federation predicted that although total retail sales would be up 2.8 percent in November–December 2011 versus the same period in 2010, online spending would be up more than 15 percent.[24] And comScore found that "Cyber Monday reached $1.25 billion in online spending, up 22 percent versus year ago, representing the heaviest online spending day in history and the second day on record to surpass the billion-dollar threshold."[25]

Clearly, we're now buying online. How do we get to those e-commerce sites? On Cyber Monday 2011 alone, 28 percent of online traffic to retail sites came from search.[26]

In 2007, Microsoft internal research found that 86 percent of searchers start at a major search engine when shopping and 70 percent of those product-related queries are for categories, such as [digital camera].[27]

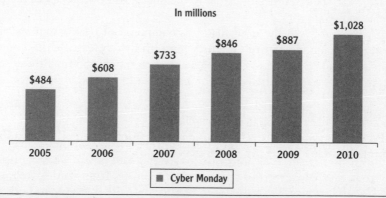

Figure 1.11   Cyber Monday Online Spending, 2005–2010
Source: comScore[28]

In part because search has become such a core way in which we navigate the Web, the home page of a site may not be the entry point for a visitor. Any page can be the entry page, which makes it increasingly difficult for marketers to craft messages that welcome visitors and compel them through the conversion funnel. We have to rethink our approach to site design and user interaction based on this new world. (We'll talk more about how to ensure every page of your site is a compelling entry in Chapter 4.)

Even those retailers who don't sell products online or who have substantial offline sales are still impacted by search. Online advertising triggers $6 to be spent offline for every dollar spent online[29] and the in-store sales boost from search is three times greater than online display advertising. Considering that those numbers were calculated for paid search, how much of a greater impact can organic search have with 85 percent of the clicks?

Sixty-three percent of search-related purchases occur offline,[30] and for some categories, this number is even higher.[31] What about local businesses? In a WebVisible/Nielsen study, 82 percent of respondents said that they've used the Internet to find local businesses; 80 percent say they've researched a product or service online before buying it locally. Yet, only 44 percent of small businesses even have a website.[32] If you have a business, you need to be visible in search engines whether you sell online or not.

Paid Search Isn't Enough As already noted, companies can connect with searchers in two primary ways: paid search and organic search.

Paid search consists of ads that advertisers can buy to display to searchers who type in particular queries. These ads are labeled "sponsored" on the search results page. These ads can be very targeted (for instance, an advertiser can show an ad that says "buy wool socks here" to a searcher who types in "where can I buy wool socks?") and the order in which the ads appear is based on a number of factors, including the amount the advertiser is willing to pay for each click, the relevance of the ad to the query, and the quality of the page linked to in the ad.

Organic search, on the other hand, is composed of results that are algorithmically generated. Search engines mine the Web, extract the content, assign value and relevance to each page, and then return and rank those pages for each query. See Figure 1.12. (You can learn more about this process in Chapter 5.)

Businesses are becoming increasingly savvy about paid search. It's a measurable advertising mechanism by which you can track exactly how much you're spending and what the return is. However, many businesses have not yet invested in organic search because they aren't sure how it works or how to measure it. But whatever the return you are getting from paid search, your organic search return will be greater. And if your site is visible in both paid and organic results, both strategies will provide an even *greater* investment.

Let's take a closer look at the numbers.

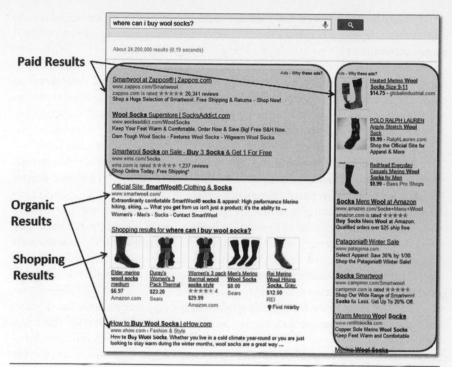

Figure 1.12 Organic Search versus Paid Search

Source: Google Search

Organic Search Performance Not only do searchers click on organic results the majority of the time, an organic listing is between two and six times more visible than a paid one. One hundred percent of searchers look at the first organic result, whereas only 50 percent look at the first paid result. As the rankings go down, the gap widens: 50 percent of searchers see the seventh organic listing, but only 10 percent of searchers see the seventh paid listing.[33] Even if you're looking for increased brand awareness rather than clicks, organic search will provide a greater return.

In May 2009, Hitwise reported that paid search engine traffic to websites was down 26 percent from the previous year, yet organic search traffic was up.[34] Research company comScore found that although 2009 U.S. search queries were up 68 percent over the previous year, paid clicks had grown only 18 percent during that same period.[35] In some cases, this was due to a reduction in paid search spending, but this was also the result of changing searcher behavior. Searchers are typing longer queries that trigger fewer paid search matches, and they are increasingly recognizing the difference between organic and paid results and have growing ad blindness. Studies have also shown that searchers trust organic listings more than paid ones and that organic results are perceived as most relevant.[36] In addition, the increasing number of videos and images in search results draws the searcher's attention away from the paid search column.

One considerable advantage of investing in organic search is that it continues to provide value over time, whereas paid search traffic disappears as soon as you stop your spend. Fifty-six percent of Google queries show no paid ads at all, so if you're counting on paid search to provide all of your visibility to searchers, you could be missing half your audience.[37]

The Additional Lift of Ranking in Both Paid and Organic Results   Numerous studies have found that when a site is visible in both paid and organic search results, both results receive more clicks than if either appeared alone. This could be because seeing a brand in both places reinforces the perception that the brand is reputable. It could be because even if we don't consciously process that we've already seen the brand, it seems familiar and, thus relevant when we see it a second time. Whatever the reason, studies have found that click-through rates, conversion rates, and revenue are all higher when both organic and paid listings appear for a search.[38]

An iCrossing study found that when a brand appears in both the organic and paid results, the searcher clicked on that brand 92 percent of the time, compared with 60 percent of clicks when the brand appeared in only one location.[39] This study found the results shown in Figure 1.13 when an organic search component was added to an existing paid search campaign.

Google research from August 2011 found that paid search triggers 89 percent incremental clicks versus organic clicks alone.[40]

A Google-sponsored Enquiro brand study, which focused on consumers in the early stages of purchasing a fuel-efficient car who hadn't yet decided on a brand, found that:

- Searchers who saw Honda in the top paid and organic result were 16 percent more likely to think of Honda as a fuel-efficient car than when the brand didn't appear in either place.

TOTAL	CLICKS	increased by 91.80%	PAGE VIEWS	increased by 43.63%
	ACTIONS	increased by 45.00%	VISITORS	increased by 40.69%
	ORDERS	increased by 44.92%	TIME ON SITE	increased by 38.91%

Figure 1.13   iCrossing Study Adding Organic Search Components to a Paid Search Campaign

Source: icrossing.com.

- Searchers were 42 percent more likely to recall Honda when the brand appeared in both kinds of results versus just the top organic listing.
- Searchers who saw Honda in both organic and paid results were 8 percent more likely to have purchase intent toward Honda and were 26 percent *less* likely to consider a Honda purchase if the brand appeared in neither spot.[41]

You Can Get Ahead of Your Competition by Focusing on Organic Search   The numbers make one thing clear: organic search is a worthwhile investment. But whereas online ad spending continues to grow—at $9.1 billion in 2007, $30 billion in 2011, and a projected $50 billion in 2015[42]—the percentage spent on paid search continues to outpace organic. Chances are, your competition isn't yet taking full advantage of what organic search can offer, meaning you can take the lead here while they're playing catch up.

Michelle Goldberg, a partner at venture capital firm Ignition Partners, stresses the importance of organic search to the companies she funds:

Understanding the differences between paid and organic search and implementing each correctly is critical to the success of an early stage company. Paid search may provide immediate volume, but only provides customers as long as the company pays for clicks. If not done right, a company can spend $1.00 to make $0.95. Organic search is a long-term and generally much better margin solution. The largest expense associated with organic search tends to be content creation, which can have long-term benefits for both search acquisition and overall customer engagement. Not only is focusing on content creation good for search, but it's also good for users and the business overall because you're creating content that consumers find valuable and that helps you build a more sustainable business over time. I make sure every startup I work with has an organic search strategy.[43]

How Search Performance Can Impact Offline Ad Campaigns   Advertising (such as TV commercials, radio advertising, print ads, and direct mail) will cause a certain number of potential customers to go into your store, call you, or type your domain name into a browser, but more often than not these days, those potential customers will search for more information. Television commercials in particular can drive search traffic, as more than half of us watch TV and surf the Internet at the same time.[44] Two-thirds of us are motivated to search due to an offline channel such as a TV ad.[45] Offline advertising can drive searches for both the ad taglines and the products themselves. For instance, Apple started airing "I'm a Mac" ads in 2006, and the search volume for the phrase has steadily gone up ever since (Figures 1.14 and 1.15).

If Apple had simply aired the commercials expecting consumers to go directly to their stores, they would have missed the entire potential customer base of searchers. But these would-be consumers have a positive experience

Figure 1.14 Apple's [I'm a Mac] Commercial Reel

Source: Apple.com

Figure 1.15 [I'm a Mac] Search Volume

Source: Google Insights for Search

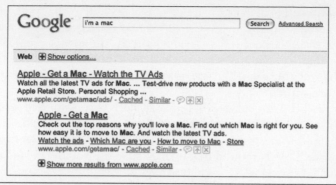

Figure 1.16 Google Search Results: [I'm a Mac]
Source: Google Search

when they search, as Apple.com is listed as the first two results for [I'm a Mac] (Figure 1.16).

However, not all companies enjoy such a successful integration of TV commercials and organic search. During the 2009 Super Bowl, Hyundai spent approximately $13.5 million on advertising by sponsoring the pregame show and running ads throughout the game. Two of its commercials centered on its new coupe (at $6 million for airing costs, plus commercial production costs). It first appeared that Hyundai understood how to integrate offline and online activities and recognized their customers' desire to interact with the company online. The ad showed the car speeding around a racetrack with exciting imagery and video and ended with a website: edityourown.com. See Figure 1.17.

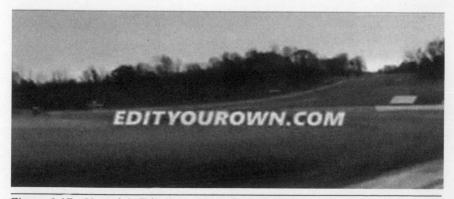

Figure 1.17 Hyundai "Edit Your Own" Commercial
Source: Personal screen capture

The site combined interactive elements and social media components and enabled visitors to create their own videos that starred the Hyundai Genesis Coupe and share them with their friends. Clearly, the ad was intended to drive visitors to the "Edit Your Own" site, and it's likely that the marketing team responsible for the campaign measured the commercial's success, in part, based on site traffic.

How well did the ad do? It probably did cause some viewers to type edityourown.com into their browser's address bar, but it also did something else. It caused viewers to search. Not long after the commercial aired, Google's Hot Trends showed that interest spiked for both [Hyundai genesis coupe] and [edit your own]. See Figure 1.18.

Did searchers find what they were looking for when they typed [edit your own] into Google? Not exactly.

Someone looking for edityourown.com would have likely been disappointed, since that domain doesn't appear anywhere in Google search results (see Figure 1.19). To Hyundai's credit, it did buy a search ad for the query, so even though it doesn't appear in the organic results, it does appear on the page. Unfortunately, since the ad shows the hyundaigenesis.com domain rather than edityourown.com, many searchers might have overlooked it and assumed it wasn't what they were looking for. And since we're an instant-gratification culture as well as a searching culture, many people likely gave up and simply went back to watching the game after their failed attempt to find the site.

It's clear from the Google Trends data that the commercial spiked interest in the campaign, but if the marketing department measured success based only on site visits, it may have considered the commercial a failure. But the failure occurred at the point of search—not due to the commercial itself. Although Hyundai appeared to understand the relationship between offline

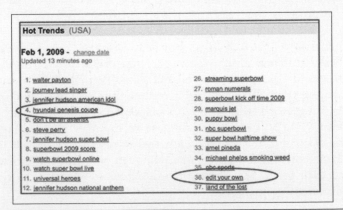

Figure 1.18 Google Search Trends, Super Bowl 2009
Source: Google Trends

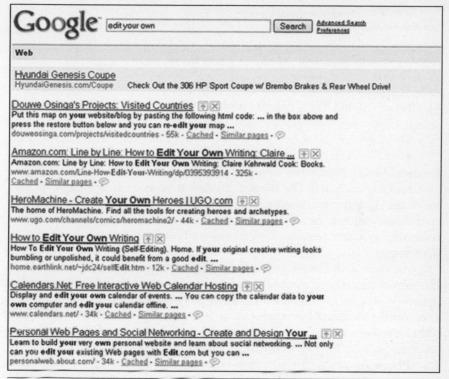

Figure 1.19   Google Search Results: [Edit Your Own]
Source: Google Search

and online media, it was missing a crucial piece—that of organic search. Harnessing the power of that relationship is a primary strategy you'll learn in this book.

Hyundai wasn't the only Super Bowl advertiser that could have benefited from a better search acquisition strategy. I watched search trends during the 2010, 2011, and 2012 games as well and found that all the top searches on game day were related to the game or commercials, and this trend continued to the day after (see Figure 1.20 for a snapshot from the morning after the Super Bowl 2011), and when I did those searches myself to build Super Bowl commercial scorecards, I found that many had results that may as well have been a locked door and a closed sign (although encouragingly, results have improved each year). See MarketingintheAgeofGoogle.com for the Super Bowl scorecards I've compiled.

Reverse Advertising: Avoiding the Advertising Death Spiral   Marketers have been bemoaning the rising problems with traditional advertising

Hot Searches (USA)			
Feb 7, 2011 - change date Updated 53 minutes ago			iGoogle Gadget New! 📶 Site Feed
1. superbowl score by quarter	6. super bowl scores by quarter	11. superbowl national anthem 2011	16. christina aguilera super bowl
2. best superbowl commercials 2011	7. danaher	12. joan rivers go daddy	17. arianna huffington
3. super bowl commercials 2011 youtube	8. pittsburgh post gazette	13. pittsburgh newspaper	18. eminem chrysler commercial
4. darth vader commercial	9. amazon eve	14. black eyed peas halftime	19. star spangled banner christina aguilera
5. christina aguilera national anthem	10. green bay press gazette	15. beckman coulter	20. half time show super bowl 2011 video

Figure 1.20 Super Bowl 2011 Day after Commercial Search Spikes

Source: Google Trends

for years. Marty Neumeier, author of *Zag: The Number One Strategy of High-Performance Brands* and *The Brand Gap*, describes the "advertising death spiral"[46] during which consumers filter out advertising because it's not relevant to their current task. In turn, advertisers get louder, causing consumers to filter more and advertisers to yell even louder. (This filter occurs online[47] as well as offline.)

Marketer Seth Godin, in his book *Permission Marketing*, refers to these traditional advertising methods of blasting a scattershot message to a large group of people (through such channels as radio and TV ads) who may or may not be interested in your product as interruption advertising.[48] But what's the alternative?

The answer: let your potential customers tell *you* what they are looking for. This way, you won't interrupt your potential audience from the task they're focusing on in order to get their attention. Instead, what you have to offer *is* crucial to their current task. Search provides results that are relevant to the activity in progress, and searchers are filtering out everything else to concentrate on that. You won't have to fight for viewers' attention and convince them they need a product (and all the while risk the advertising death spiral). Instead, you can focus on convincing this purchase-ready group that they should buy *your* product.

Danny Sullivan, one of the first search engine industry experts, calls the process of acquisition from search reverse advertising.[49] You simply find out what the members of your target audience are looking for and then meet their needs and wait for them to come to you. Someone typing [fuel efficient cars] into a Google search box is much more likely to be considering purchasing a car than someone who's sitting on the couch watching *The Oprah Winfrey Show*.

Reverse Advertising in Action To see reverse advertising in action, consider an auto manufacturer. We'll use Volvo as our example and assume that Volvo is targeting its V70 wagon to moms who don't want to drive a minivan and who are looking for safety, as well as room for two children. Volvo might opt to buy expensive TV ads that showcase these features during time slots that its target demographic is watching (such as during *Oprah*). However, only a percentage of that audience meets the target demographic (men and single women watch the show as well). And within the target demographic, only a small percentage is interested in buying a car.

Buying television ads might be a worthwhile investment, both to drive sales and raise brand awareness, but consider the additional acquisition opportunities available through the reverse advertising of organic search.

Using search data, Volvo compiles a list of what its target audience is interested in during the quest for a new car and what the audience searches for. The company adds this content to its website and uses the information in this book to ensure that that content appears for those searches. In this way, it connects with exactly the customers who are looking for the company at the exact moment those customers are focused on its product. And it ensures brand awareness by having visibility in that critical moment in the buying cycle when its competitor could have dominated.

Rather than just talking at a large group of people, hoping some of them will listen, this approach enables Volvo to be the listener and provide information to the right people at the right time.

➤ *How Search Has Changed Business*

Historically, consumer data and industry trends haven't been that easy to come by. Before launching a new product or feature, companies had to rely on expensive and time-consuming surveys and focus groups, and it often took awhile to gather enough feedback from these sources. Competitive and industry research was slow and expensive. But the abundance of search data has allowed all of that to change dramatically. We can see *exactly* what our customers want at a much larger scale than focus groups could ever provide, and competitive and industry data are just a click or two away. We can get immediate feedback about whether changes are working and see trends of consumer interest rising or falling before we invest in research and development (R&D). (We'll dive into the details of how search data can provide insight about our customers, our industry, and our competitors in Chapter 2.)

Search Data as Market Research Continuing our earlier Volvo example, search data indicates that our Volvo-buying audience is searching for "reliable" and "safe" cars. See Figure 1.21.

This audience also tends to search for [family car]. See Figure 1.22.

Based on these data, our hypothetical Volvo marketing department creates two pages of content in the V70 section of its website. One is about the V70's safety and reliability and includes crash test ratings, safety scores, and comparisons to other cars that this demographic may be considering. The other is all about how great the V70 is for kids. It provides back seat dimensions and shows photos of different passenger configurations involving car

Keywords	Advertiser Competition ⑦	▼ Local Search Volume: July ⑦	Global Monthly Search Volume ⑦
Keywords related to term(s) entered - sort by relevance ⑦			
reliable cars		33,100	22,200
reliable car		22,200	18,100
most reliable cars		18,100	12,100
safe cars		14,800	12,100

Figure 1.21   [Reliable] and [Safe] Search Volume

Source: Google AdWords Keyword Tool

seats and adult passengers. Then, rather than (or in addition to) broadcasting this content out to everyone, Volvo waits for its key demographic to find it.

Someone typing [most reliable family car] into a search box is much more likely to intend to buy a car in the near future—and a kid-friendly one at that—than someone watching a television show with the "right demographics." Volvo connects with a potential consumer who is broadcasting his or her purchasing intent and actively looking for a car just like the Volvo V70. Not only does Volvo connect with the right audience, it can actively compete in an acquisition channel that may have otherwise included only its competition.

Focusing on search doesn't mean that you should abandon your other acquisition efforts. In fact, organic search can work hand-in-hand with other marketing efforts. That commercial during *Oprah* may increase brand awareness, which in turn makes the searcher more likely to click on that Volvo result later, rather than the Toyota listing.

If You're Not among Consumers' Choices, They Can't Choose You   Consider the case of UK airline BMI, whose primary customers live in the United Kingdom and Ireland. A substantial number (including me) live in other countries and are planning trips to the United Kingdom. I was in Seattle, planning a trip to Ireland and looking for a flight from London to Dublin.

Keywords	Advertiser Competition ⑦	▼ Local Search Volume: July ⑦	Global Monthly Search Volume ⑦
Keywords related to term(s) entered - sort by relevance ⑦			
family car		135,000	110,000
car for kids		60,500	49,500
cars for kids		49,500	40,500

Figure 1.22   [Family Car] Search Volume

Source: Google AdWords Keyword Tool

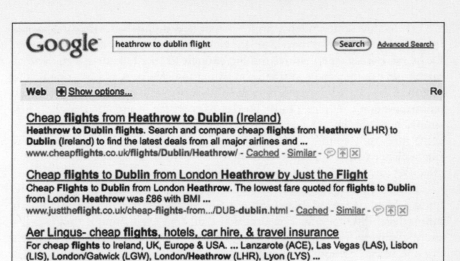

Figure 1.23 Google Search Results for [Heathrow to Dublin Flight]
Source: Google Search

Since I had flown this BMI route before, it was the most prominent brand in my mind as I started my search. I searched for [Heathrow to Dublin] and didn't see the BMI site. However, Aer Lingus appeared third in the results of my search (Figure 1.23).

Even though BMI was the brand that I recalled most vividly when I began my search, it wasn't available for consideration when I made my choice, and Aer Lingus was an easy alternative.

But what if I pressed on, determined to include BMI in my consideration set? A search for its brand name, [BMI], didn't return its site in the results either (although a fairly negative news article about them *did* appear). If potential customers can't even find you in a brand search, you are missing one of the most qualified channels of customer acquisition.

We've seen how search data can provide a wealth of market research and enable you to connect with customers early in their research cycle—at the very time that they're looking to buy your product. In the following chapters, we'll learn how to put that information in action.

➤ The Level Playing Field of Search

If you're under the impression that only big brands can compete in the game of search, you'll be pleasantly surprised to learn that smaller companies can often have the advantage. This is particularly true when potential customers are conducting nonbranded searches—that is, searches for [safe cars] rather than [Volvo]—because they evaluate choices based on the results they see. Large companies aren't always nimble enough to take full advantage of what search has to offer, and a smaller company can often beat a larger one in the rankings. Unlike TV advertising and other large-scale marketing campaigns, companies don't require a huge budget to compete in organic search. They simply need the knowledge to build an effective search strategy. In fact, a comScore study found that market segments with smaller consumer bases (for which a scattershot approach such as TV advertising wouldn't be cost-effective) can use search for significant lift to a very targeted population.[50]

For smaller organizations, organic search can provide a low-cost way to build a highly targeted audience. Avvo, a Seattle start-up that provides an online legal directory for consumers, found that even though they were a small company, they were able to quickly build a large audience through organic search by adding search engine optimization (SEO) best practices throughout their organization. Conrad Saam, in charge of marketing at Avvo at the time, noted that not only was integrating an organic search strategy into their business effective, but it complemented and enhanced their focus on quality content and an engaging user experience:

> We launched Avvo in 2007 to fill a content gap on the Web—helping consumers make informed, intelligent decisions about their legal situation. In doing that, we adhered to the most fundamental SEO principle—build a great product and fill it with content that people care about. Our primary focus was on providing consumers with something they really needed. SEO was baked into everything we did to ensure that all great content got to the people who were looking for it. We think about the search impact of everything we do—from marketing to product development, to public relations, and even customer service. In two years, we became the most popular legal directory on the Web—more popular than our huge corporate competitors with massive advertising budgets. In the end, it was much more effective to develop a robust, useful, and searchable site than to buy TV spots on CNN.[51]

Large brands can also use this knowledge to their advantage, if they can evolve their businesses to integrate search and changing customer behaviors into their product and customer acquisition strategies.

But whether you run a multinational corporation or a Napa Valley bed and breakfast, where do you start? You might be anxious about making the right move if you don't have a background in online marketing or data analysis. Well, you can relax. This book will give you everything you need to get started creating a business strategy that takes full advantage of everything that search has to offer and builds this knowledge into your organization.

Chapter 2

How to Use Search Data to Improve Your Business and Product Strategy

earchers aren't an isolated demographic from the rest of your target audience. Searchers *are* your target audience. And they're telling you exactly what will compel them to buy your products, engage with your company, and become your strongest advocates.

The largest source of this information is through the major search engines, particularly Google. Millions of people search using these search engines every day, and in aggregate, what they search for and how those searches change over time provides incredibly useful insight into their needs.

Just as valuable as the words they type are the ways they behave. Search engines know exactly what people click on after they enter a query. They know what content searchers viewed then quickly returned to the search results to look for a better answer. They can follow the entire search session to better understand intent: What did the searcher type next? What result did the searcher click on that ended the search?[1]

Research companies like Enquiro Research (now part of Mediative) augment this understanding of searcher intent with data about what searchers see as they scan the search results and what they focus on, as well as what they skip. And research into how the brain processes information as we search helps complete the picture of what searchers are really after.

Marrying *how* we search (behavior) with *why* we search (intent) and *what* we search for (query volume) is vital to understanding a business's potential audience considering that the average length of a query is three words and more than 25 percent of queries consist of only one word (Figure 2.1).[2] It's difficult to know the intent for many one-word queries, but coupled with search history, aggregate behaviors, and other data, the intent picture becomes much clearer.

Number of Words	11-Sep	8-Jan
1	26.45%	20.96%
2	23.66%	24.91%
3	19.34%	22.03%
4	13.17%	14.54%
5	7.69%	8.20%
6	4.12%	4.32%
7	2.26%	2.23%
8+	3.31%	2.81%

Figure 2.1   Query Length: September 2011 versus January 2011
Source: Hitwise

If you can track individual behavior and add this information to the rest of the data, you can get a very clear picture indeed. (You can learn more about tracking visitors on your site in Chapter 8.)

■ HOW WE USE SEARCH FOR RESEARCH: PLANNING A TRIP TO LAKE TAHOE

A Microsoft search session in February 2009 that lasted nearly four hours and included eight unique queries and 27 visited sites illustrates how searcher intent is difficult to discern from a single query and how results found in earlier queries can influence later ones (Figure 2.2).

The searcher begins the search with [family reunion Lake Tahoe]. The results generally relate to event planning, which is clearly not what the searcher is looking for, as subsequent searches are more obviously related to lodging ([large house Lake Tahoe], [large vacation home to rent in Lake Tahoe]). The searcher originally was focused on the outcome of his task—having a family reunion in Lake Tahoe—but he quickly realized that the way to reach that goal was to look for lodging that would accommodate many people (the last query in the session is [Lake Tahoe rental for large group]). At one point, he searches for [rental sleeps 30 Lake Tahoe]. If you were tracking individual visitor behavior, then when this visitor landed on your site for [Lake Tahoe rental for large group], you'd know that he's bringing 30 people for a family reunion and he'd like a large house to accommodate everyone.

This type of data may not be all that valuable for your business based on one visitor. But what if you found that you had the highest conversion rates from [Lake Tahoe large rental], that 80 percent of those conversions were from searchers who had previously searched for family reunion–related

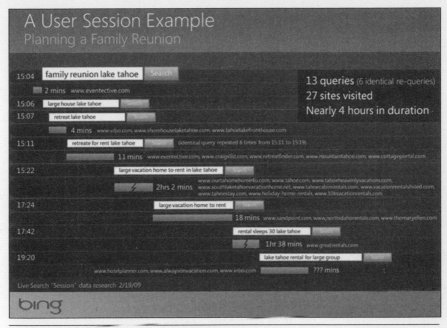

Figure 2.2 Microsoft Bing Search Session
Source: Microsoft Bing

content, and that most searchers doing that same [Lake Tahoe large rental] search who had previously searched for [college spring break] didn't convert at all?

Depending on other data you have, you might build a family reunion resources section to attract even more of the high-converting customers and you might create a page describing why the rental is great for college students on spring break (if that's an audience you'd like to convert).

Of course, testing is key to make sure it works.

■ MARKET RESEARCH: WHERE THE WILD FRONTIERS OF HUMAN NATURE MEET THE WILD POWERS OF TECHNOLOGY

In his book *Spent*, biological psychologist Geoffrey Miller talks about his experience at a 1999 conference about economic preferences. The economists in attendance were more interested in buying patterns than the psychological reasons behind them. However, the marketers in attendance *did* care, leading Miller down a road of research about marketing, at the end of which he concluded: "Marketing is not just one of the most important ideas in business.

It has become the most dominant force in human culture." He defines marketing as a "systematic attempt to fulfill human desires by producing goods and services that people will buy. It is where the wild frontiers of human nature meet the wild powers of technology." And he describes the marketing revolution of the 1950s and 1960s as a shift to understanding that a "company should produce what people desire, instead of trying to convince them to buy what the company happens to make."[3]

The discipline of market research was born and is now an $8 billion industry in the United States alone.[4]

Before the Web, it was difficult to learn about what large groups of people were interested in without conducting large-scale surveys. But today, nearly all of your potential customers are broadcasting exactly what they want through their searches. And search data may be even more honest than survey data, because people are searching for what they actually want, not telling a surveyor what they think they should want.

Miller notes that not all industries have embraced this method of creating products (such as banking, law, and medicine) and concludes that those who don't "bother using market research to shape their services to their customers' desires [will] lose market share to those that do."

The same can be said of search data. Those businesses that don't realize that we've experienced a shift in consumer behavior and that customers and customer data are now centered on search will lose market share to those that do.

Miller says that "marketing knowledge lurks as a sort of arcane magic," and the same can definitely be said of search-based consumer acquisition.

With search data, we can gain new insights into our customers, our industry, and our competitors, but many businesses think of it as a kind of arcane magic that they aren't sure how to best harness. But once you know where to get the data and how to apply it, you'll find that search data provide clear insight that makes running your business and acquiring customers easier, smoother, and more measurable.

➤ Search Acquisition Strategy: The New Product Strategy and Customer Acquisition Strategy

Effective search acquisition begins with learning more about your customers and what they're searching for. From there, you can assess your site and make sure it satisfies the needs of those searchers. Finally, you ensure that when your customers search, your site shows up in results. It stands to reason then that search acquisition strategy is really customer acquisition strategy and, at its core, product strategy.

The biggest difference between traditional market research and search-based market research is that you can gain a great deal of information about customer behavior and needs without spending a dime on focus groups, surveys, or other expensive methods. That doesn't mean you won't do some of those things to refine your strategy and confirm your conclusions or as a parallel endeavor, but an amazing amount of data is available from search and, with multivariate testing and mouse movement tracking, you can see how customers are responding in near-real time.[5]

Occupy Wall Street: A Search Data Illustration We can use search data to see a big picture view of the world, as well as to drill into specifics. In late 2011, a grassroots movement in the United States began, known as Occupy Wall Street, and as it spread beyond New York, simply Occupy. The specific issues and goals were hazy, but the name was not.

The movement name was based in part on domain name availability. Micah White and Kalle Lasn, the originators of the movement, discussed their plans over e-mail in June 2011. They knew they needed a website. White suggested OccupyWallStreet.org, AcampadaWallStreet.org, or TakeWallStreet.org. "No. 1 is best," came Lasn's response, and he registered the site on June 9.[6]

Would "acampada" or "take" have resonated as well? It's hard to know, but we do know the search response of Americans to "occupy." comScore found that "search associated with Occupy Wall Street terms ballooned almost overnight, going from nonexistent to more than 300,000 searches in just the final two weeks of September, highlighting the market demand for this content"; 1.6 million U.S. search visits were made to related websites (99 percent from clicks on organic listings).[7]

With Google Insights for Search (described more later in this chapter), we can see the rise in interest and even the potential news-related triggers for each spike (Figure 2.3).

We can also see where in the United States search-related interest is the highest (Figure 2.4).

Figure 2.3 Google [occupy] Search Trends
Source: Google Insights for Search

Figure 2.4 Google [occupy] Regional Search Trends
Source: Google Insights for Search

Digging in a bit more, we can see exactly what people are looking for. Certainly, people are looking for information on particular regional movements, such as [occupy boston] and [occupy Oakland], but they are also looking for information on what the movement is and what the demands are.

Let's dive in a bit further using the Google AdWords Keyword Tool (also described further later in this chapter). First let's look at broad match. Remember that broad match aggregates all of the searches that contain a particular phrase. So, for instance, the number you see for "what is occupy" would include the queries [what is occupy], [what is the occupy movement], and [where is the best place to find what occupy is].

In Figure 2.6, we can see that queries related to "what is occupy" has fairly high volume and that more people are searching for Boston specifics than Seattle ones. We can also see, not surprisingly, that there is some worldwide interest in the more general terms ("what is occupy") but not as much in the regional ones. One interesting note is that when most Americans search for

Search terms				
Top searches		?	**Rising searches**	
1. occupy wall	100		1. oakland	Breakout
2. occupy wall street	100		2. oakland occupy	Breakout
3. wall street	95		3. occupy boston	Breakout
4. oakland	10		4. occupy demands	Breakout
5. occupy wallstreet	10		5. occupy movement	Breakout
6. oakland occupy	10		6. occupy news	Breakout
7. wallstreet	10		7. occupy protest	Breakout
8. what is occupy	10		8. occupy wallstreet	Breakout
9. occupy movement	5		9. portland occupy	Breakout
10. occupy protest	5		10. wallstreet	Breakout

Figure 2.5 Google [occupy] Related Searches
Source: Google Insights for Search

Keyword	Global Monthly Searches ⑦	Local Monthly Searches ⑦
☆ what is occupy	1,500,000	1,000,000
☆ occupy wall street	673,000	550,000
☆ ows	450,000	135,000
☆ boston occupy	27,100	27,100
☆ occupy demands	22,200	22,200
☆ occupy movement	18,100	14,800
☆ oakland occupy	14,800	12,100
☆ occupy protest	14,800	12,100
☆ occupy seattle	9,900	9,900
☆ occupy dc	9,900	8,100
☆ zucotti park	3,600	2,900

Figure 2.6 [occupy] Related Searches and Volumes

Source: Google AdWords Keyword Tool

the region that started it all, they search for [occupy wall street], but a much higher proportion of those outside the United States search for [ows].

This is likely an example of how the news media refers to events triggering how people search for them.

Now we have details about how people are searching for things broadly. How do volumes stack up for specific queries? For that, we turn to "exact match." These numbers show us how many searches were done for these exact queries. [occupy wall street] has by far the most interest, both in the United States and globally (Figure 2.7).

Keyword	Global Monthly Searches ⑦	Local Monthly Searches ⑦
☆ [occupy wall street]	450,000	301,000
☆ [ows]	22,200	9,900
☆ [occupy seattle]	6,600	6,600
☆ [occupy dc]	5,400	5,400
☆ [occupy movement]	6,600	4,400
☆ [zucotti park]	1,900	1,900
☆ [oakland occupy]	1,600	1,300
☆ [occupy protest]	1,300	880
☆ [what is the occupy movement]	720	590
☆ [what is occupy]	720	480
☆ [occupy demands]	260	260
☆ [boston occupy]	210	170

Figure 2.7 [occupy] Search Volume for Specific Queries

Source: Google AdWords Keyword Tool

what is the occupy movement

what is the occupy movement

what is the occupy movement **all about**

what is the occupy movement **protesting**

what is the occupy movement **trying to accomplish**

Figure 2.8 Google Suggested Searches for [occupy]
Source: Google Search

We can dive further into what people are looking for using Google Suggest (Figures 2.8 and 2.9).

How well does the website that started it all do at engaging those searchers and putting the movement's message in front of them? Let's start with the easy one: [occupy wall street] (Figure 2.10).

As one would hope, the website chosen and registered on June 9, 2011, shows up first and second. The words in the title tag show how they've chosen to present their message: "NYC Protest for World Revolution." That becomes the first impression that searchers see when looking for information about what the movement is. Could it be more descriptive? Only the founders can say for sure if that's how they want to present their cause. But this is a great lesson for anyone: What do you want that first impression to be? How can you best present your message succinctly in a way that resonates with searchers?

Certainly, the title tag of the second result could be more descriptive and less repetitive. With 550,000 searches for this single term in one month, they could use the search results display to their best advantage.

Now let's check out the description under the title. As we'll learn in Chapter 5, search engines often use what's in the meta description element

occupy demands

occupy demands

occupy demand **list**

occupy demands **group**

occupy demands **working group**

Figure 2.9 Google Suggested Searches for [occupy]
Source: Google Search

occupy wall street

About 105,000,000 results (0.23 seconds)

Occupy Wall Street | NYC Protest for World Revolution
occupywallst.org/ [+1]
1 day ago – News and resources for protesters attending the mass demonstration on
Wall Street against financial greed and corruption.
Nine Arrested & Released Without ... - Why? | OccupyWallSt.org - About - Forum

About Us | OccupyWallSt.org - **Occupy Wall Street**
occupywallst.org/about/ [+1]
OccupyWallSt.org is the unofficial de facto online resource for the growing occupation
movement happening on **Wall Street** and around the world. We're an ...

Figure 2.10   Google Search Results for [occupy wall street]
Source: Google Search

in the HTML source code of a page to determine what to display here. Nearly all content management systems these days have a place for you to easily type in what you'd like this to be.

In this case, the occupywallstreet.org home page does in fact use the meta description tag to provide a clear message about the site:

<meta name="description" content="News and resources for protesters attending the mass demonstration on Wall Street against financial greed and corruption"/>

And that is in turn what Google is using to display as the description for the site in search results.

For this query, I'd say the site gets a 4 out of 5. They could better use the title tag of the About page to showcase their message, but otherwise, things look great for them.

What about a specific region, like [occupy boston]?

As you can see from Figure 2.11, although the regional site also appears first (after the News onebox), the site owners aren't using the site's title or description to their best advantage to get their message in front of searchers. The title is simply "Occupy Boston" and the description is "Information about the events planned. And a link to their LiveStream Channel with live streaming Internet TV and archive of previous videos." There's no mention at all of what the movement is about, much less inclusion of engaging phrases like "financial greed and corruption."

occupy boston

About 129,000,000 results (0.20 seconds)

<u>News for **occupy boston**</u>

WHDH-TV

<u>Judge bars Framingham woman from Occupy Boston after alleged ...</u>
Boston.com - 22 hours ago
By Jaime Lutz, Globe Correspondent A Boston Municipal Court judge
has barred a young Framingham woman from all **Occupy Boston**
activities in the city after ...

27 related articles

<u>What's behind those **Occupy** hand signals</u>
The Boston Globe - 2 related articles

<u>Mayor: **Occupy** LA must leave City Hall camp Monday</u>
Boston.com - 1500 related articles

Occupy Boston
www.occupyboston.org/ +1
5 hours ago -- Information about the events planned. And a link to their LiveStream
Channel with live streaming Internet TV and archive of previous videos.

Figure 2.11   Google Search Results for [occupy boston]
Source: Google Search

In this case, the home page also has a meta description tag, but unfortunately, it's too short for Google to use:

> *<meta name="description" content="We Are The 99 percent. Stand Up!*
> *Fight Back!"/>*

This means that Google is instead pulling the longer description from the
Open Directory Project (Figure 2.12).

Now let's look at [what is the occupy movement] and [occupy demands].
The official site doesn't appear first for [what is the occupy movement]
(Figure 2.13).

Wikipedia comes in and first and second, which is probably an okay
result for a movement that prides itself on being open and leaderless. But
for those who do want to rank well for key searches, we can learn a bit from
these results. Due to how the movement is structured, many sites exist. In
addition to occupywallstreet.com, occupyboston.com, and other regional
sites, we can see at least two others in these set of search results: occupyto-
gether.org and adbusters.org/campaigns/occupywallstreet (adbusters.org is
the site run by Micah White and Kalle Lasn where the ideas for the movement came from).

d|m|o|z open directory project

In partnership with
Aol Search.

home | feedback

Search: **occupy boston**

Restricting Search to Category: **Society: Activism: We Are The 99 Percent**

Open Directory Categories (1-1 of 1)

1. Society: Activism: We Are The 99 Percent (180)

Open Directory Sites (1-20 of 180)

1. BU Occupy Boston - Facebook page to talk about the actions on Boston University. [USA - Boston, MA]
   -- https://www.facebook.com/groups/BUoccupiesboston   Society: Activism: We Are The 99 Percent ()

2. Occupy Boston - Official LiveStream Channel for #occupyboston and #bostonGA. With live streaming Internet TV and archive of previous videos. [USA - Boston, MA]
   -- http://www.livestream.com/occupyboston   Society: Activism: We Are The 99 Percent ()

3. Occupy Boston - Information about the events planned And a link to their LiveStream Channel with live streaming Internet TV and archive of previous videos. [USA - Boston, MA]
   -- http://occupyboston.com/   Society: Activism: We Are The 99 Percent ()

Figure 2.12   Open Directory Project Listing for Occupy Boston
Source: Open Directory Project

Links, sharing, and other types of engagement are split among all of these sites, so value signals that search engines see are diluted. In Chapter 7, you can learn more about why this is one of the reasons why microsites generally are a bad idea.

Another key is knowing what people are searching for. In this case, the data are clear that a lot of people are searching for variations on "what is the occupy movement." Always find out what the top searches are related to your brand, product, organization, or cause and then create a page that specifically answers those questions. In this case, none of the movement sites include the phrase "what is the occupy movement."

We can see just how useful it can be to address questions specifically with another common query: [occupy demands] (Figure 2.14).

In this case, a page exists on the occupywallstreet.org site titled "Occupy Demands," and as you might expect, it ranks very well for the query.

In Chapter 4, we'll talk more about engaging searchers once they land on the page, and here we see an example where the site could improve. Once you click the search result, you see what's shown in Figure 2.15.

Again, in this case, we're looking at a leaderless movement, and this page is simply a forum post of an anonymous poster. But we can still learn from this

what is the occupy movement

About 113,000,000 results (0.21 seconds)

Occupy movement - Wikipedia, the free encyclopedia
en.wikipedia.org/wiki/Occupy_movement +1
The **Occupy movement** is an international protest movement which is primarily
directed against economic and social inequality. The first Occupy protests to be ...

Occupy Wall Street - Wikipedia, the free encyclopedia
en.wikipedia.org/wiki/Occupy_Wall_Street +1
For the wider movement, see **Occupy movement**. .... The report was released just as
concerns of the Occupy Wall Street movement were beginning to enter the ...

Occupy Together | Home
www.occupytogether.org/ +1
3 days ago – Liberty Plaza (Zuccotti Park), home of **Occupy** Wall Street for the past two
months and birthplace of the 99% **movement** that has spread across ...

News for what is the occupy movement

No, the Crackdown Against **Occupy** Wall Street is Not the Work of ...
Forbes - 1 hour ago
Much to the dismay of those of us who value civil liberties and the right
to peaceful dissent, the nascent **Occupy** Wall Street **movement** has
been met with ...
421 related articles

Why, Why Occupy?
Berkeley Daily Planet - 65 related articles

Occupy movements nationwide celebrate Thanksgiving
Wall Street Journal - 1510 related articles

Occupy Wall Street | NYC Protest for World Revolution
occupywallst.org/ +1
1 day ago – The **Occupy movement** is born of the simple belief that humanity could
meet our common needs if not for the predation and greed of the very ...

[PDF] What is the #Occupy movement?
rosswolfe.files.wordpress.com/.../what-is-the-occupy-movement_-1.p... +1
File Format: PDF/Adobe Acrobat - Quick View
What is the #Occupy movement? A series of roundtable discussions hosted by The
Platypus Affiliated Society. First roundtable discussion,. Friday 7pm | October ...

Occupy movements nationwide celebrate holiday - Yahoo! News
news.yahoo.com/occupy-movements-nationwide-celebrate-holiday-... +1
2 days ago – From Yahoo! News: Most Americans spent Thanksgiving snug inside
homes with families and football. Others used the holiday to give thanks ...

Occupy Wall Street | September 17th | #OCCUPYWALLSTREET ...
www.adbusters.org/campaigns/occupywallstreet +1
- Block all www.adbusters.org results
#OCCUPYWALLSTREET is a leaderless people powered **movement** for democracy
that began in America on September 17 with an encampment in the ...

Figure 2.13   Google Search Results for [what is the occupy movement]
Source: Google Search

> **occupy demands**

About 24,600,000 results (0.24 seconds)

Occupy Wall Street - Wikipedia, the free encyclopedia
en.wikipedia.org/wiki/Occupy_Wall_Street [+1]
Occupy Wall Street (OWS) is an ongoing series of demonstrations initiated by the ...
Adbusters' website said that from their "one simple **demand**, a presidential ...

Forum Post: Occupy Demands - Pass it along - Post on Facebook ...
occupywallst.org/.../occupy-demands-pass-it-along-post-on-facebook... [+1]
Nov 18, 2011 – **Occupy Demands** 1: Campaign Finance Reform: Campaigns will be
100% funded by the $3 Presidential Campaign Fund. This will no longer ...

Figure 2.14   Google Search Results for [occupy demands]
Source: Google Search

example. Certainly if you are relying on user-generated content (see Chapter 9 for more on this), make sure that the content is laid out in an engaging way. And if you are creating the content yourself, remember that the user interface can be as important as the content itself in keeping visitors on the site.

Building a Better Digital Camera   Consider a new digital camera manufacturer, BetterCamera. They are looking to build the right set of features into their inaugural product. But what do people care about most in a camera? The product development team at BetterCamera can gain some insight into what that might be by looking at search logs.

First, how big is the digital camera market? According to Google, there were more than 20 million camera-related searches in October 2011.[8] And that number doesn't include all of the variations of related searches such as searches for specific digital camera brand names.

According to Google AdWords, the top searched-for digital camera features are:

- SLR
- Waterproof
- Lenses
- Underwater
- Size
- Pixels

OccupyWallStreet

The revolution continues worldwide!

News   LiveStream   #HowToOccupy   Forum   Chat   User Map   NYCGA   About   Don

Forum Post: Occupy Demands - Pass it along - Post on Facebook

Posted 1 week ago on Nov. 18, 2011, 11:21 a.m. EST by neilson2
This content is user submitted and not an official statement

Occupy Demands 1: Campaign Finance Reform: Campaigns will be 100% funded by the $3 Presidential Campaign Fund. This will no longer be optional on returns and $3 will be taken from everyone in lieu of having the choice to pay that $3 in taxes. No more dinner events where people pay thousands of dollars per plate of food to donate. This will take the candidates out of the pockets of those more fortunate and put it back in the hands of the American people. 2A: 3 Term Limit for Congress: This needs to be done to keep fresh ideas flowing, as well as to prevent a pack mentality and life-long political enemies that evolve and begin to erode the political process. This is most evident over the past few years where almost no bills of any importance can pass through congress without the opposing side attaching the names of the most disliked members of congress with the bill as a way to prevent it from passing. Term one for all current members would start in the 2012 election cycle. 2B: Terms served determines percentage of benefits for Congress. This is self-explanatory, but as with any job, the longer you work the more benefits you generally received. We propose members of Congress who serve three full terms receive full benefits. 75% for two term members and 50% for a single term. 3A: No more bonuses for Management in pseudo government business such as Fanny Mae and Freddie Mac. Any agency that would cause the American tax payer to be held liable for its failure should not be permitted to pay bonuses to executives for taking risks to boost their numbers. 3B: Break-up any company that is deemed to be "too large to fail". Any private business entity has the risk of failing in a capitalistic system, but when they become so large that they would take down the entire economy if they fail, they have to be split. If there is no risk of going under and failing due to the belief they will be bailed out, then they can do unsafe things to reap rewards in the good times without having to worry about the consequences in bad. 4: No more trading of commodity futures by investors. This has been written off as non-consequential, but the fact remains, when people can change markets without the intention of actually purchasing that commodity it raises the prices of food, heating and other fuels for everyone. Commodity investing should not be allowed unless the person making the purchase is deemed to be able to take the delivery they purchase.

These are our demands – We will be heard

Anonymous

Figure 2.15   "Occupy Demands" Page of occupywallstreet.org

Source: occupywallstreet.org

BetterCamera hasn't had breakthroughs with its lens technology that would rival the competition, and its megapixel and size specs are comparable to other brands. The company decides to explore the idea of building an underwater (and thus waterproof) camera.

Keywords	Advertiser Competition ⑦	Local Search Volume: August ⑦
Keywords related to term(s) entered - <u>sort by relevance</u> ⑦		
waterproof digital camera		550,000
underwater digital camera		135,000
canon waterproof digital camera		90,500
waterproof digital cameras		60,500
olympus waterproof digital camera		74,000
underwater digital cameras		33,100
underwater digital camera housing		18,100
canon underwater digital camera		9,900
canon underwater digital cameras		9,900
nikon underwater digital camera		3,600
olympus underwater digital camera		4,400

Figure 2.16   [Underwater Camera] Search Volume

Source: Google AdWords Keyword Tool

The BetterCamera team uses search data for a bit of competitive research and finds that the top searched-for brands for waterproof and digital cameras are:

- Olympus
- Canon
- Fuji
- Nikon

This is an area that the team feels it can compete in because only a small number of searchers are looking for specific brands. Most are looking simply for variations of [waterproof digital cameras] and [underwater digital cameras]. See Figure 2.16.

Could BetterCamera gain insight into the audience for waterproof and underwater cameras and what features are most important to them? The first thing the product team notices is that, not surprisingly, search interest spikes in the summer. Overall interest appears to be declining, though, but the team decides that although overall consumers may have less demand for digital cameras due to better cameras on mobile phones, it may be a while before phones are waterproof. So they decide the market is still healthy enough to press on. See Figure 2.17.

Searchers in Hawaii and Florida appear most interested in underwater cameras, but third-place Alaska is unexpected (Figure 2.18). The market research team will have to look more closely into that. Are these searches driven primarily by Alaskans planning vacations to tropical destinations?

Web Search Interest: underwater digital camera
United States, 2004 - present
Categories: Photo & Video (50-75%), Shopping (0-10%), Computers & Electronics (0-10%)
⚠ An improvement to our geographical assignment was applied retroactively from 1/1/2011. Learn more

Figure 2.17 [Underwater Digital Camera] Search Trends
Source: Google Insights for Search

Looking at specific searches, the BetterCamera team finds that those in the market for an underwater digital camera are particularly interested in disposable versions, waterproof housings, and inexpensive options. Perhaps the company should consider offering low-cost alternatives to expensive waterproof digital cameras for those potential customers who need to take pictures underwater only during short vacations and, therefore, aren't looking to invest in high-cost solutions. But quality is still important to this audience (after all, why take underwater pictures at all if they aren't going to turn out?), so the product team at BetterCamera looks into designing a waterproof housing that will enable the two-week-a-year scuba divers to turn their existing high-quality digital cameras into underwater versions.

Regional interest	
1. Hawaii	100
2. Florida	32
3. Alaska	27
4. California	20
5. Colorado	19
6. New Jersey	18
7. Washington	18
8. Oregon	17
9. Texas	17
10. Arizona	16

Figure 2.18 [Underwater Digital Cameras] Regional Search Trends
Source: Google Insights for Search

Keywords	Advertiser Competition ⑦	Local Search Volume: August ⑦
Keywords related to term(s) entered - <u>sort by relevance</u> ⑦		
waterproof digital camera		550,000
underwater digital camera		135,000
canon waterproof digital camera		90,500
waterproof digital cameras		60,500
olympus waterproof digital camera		74,000
underwater digital cameras		33,100
underwater digital camera housing		18,100
canon underwater digital camera		9,900
underwater housing for digital camera		6,600
waterproof digital camera housing		12,100
nikon underwater digital camera		3,600
olympus underwater digital camera		4,400

Figure 2.19   [Underwater Digital Camera] Search Trends

Source: Google Insights for Search

Some of this potential audience clearly knows that buying a waterproof housing is an option based on the high volume of existing searches, so a consumer base already exists. In addition, the BetterCamera team brainstorms ways of marketing to the audience segment looking for inexpensive and disposable underwater digital cameras. After all, the number of monthly Google searches for waterproof housings is approximately 40,000, whereas the number of Google searches for waterproof digital cameras is around 600,000. So if the team went after only those already looking for waterproof housings, it would be neglecting a substantial target market. See Figure 2.19.

■ SEARCH DATA: A POWERFUL SOURCE OF MARKET RESEARCH

With all the searching your potential customers are doing, you can gain a great deal of information about exactly what they're looking for.

And we get more than just a list of queries from search data. We can find out what searchers looked for next, where they were searching from, and what they were searching for most.

➤ Using Keyword Research for Market Insights

As you saw with BetterCamera, you can use keyword research to determine the keywords with the highest query volumes, which have the most competition and which are most likely to attract searchers to your site and turn them into customers.

➤ *How Keyword Research Is Valuable*

- You gain insight into what searches have the highest volume (and can bring the most traffic).
- You get data on the competitive landscape of each query category.
- You learn the language of the customer, so you can better engage them (in clicking on the search result, staying on the page, and converting).
- You can better prioritize features and content additions based on expected traffic lifts.

➤ *Predicting Future Trends*

But how reliable are search data in predicting future trends and influencing business decisions? The Google research team has spent a great deal of time considering this. As the team noted in its blog:

> *Having predictable trends for a search query or for a group of queries could have interesting ramifications. One could forecast the trends into the future, and use it as a "best guess" for various business decisions such as budget planning, marketing campaigns, and resource allocations. One could identify deviation from such forecasting and identify new factors that are influencing the search volume. We were therefore interested in the following questions:*
>
> - *How many search queries have trends that are predictable?*
>
> - *Are some categories more predictable than others? How is the distribution of predictable trends between the various categories?*
>
> - *How predictable are the trends of aggregated search queries for different categories? Which categories are more predictable and which are less so?*[9]

From this investigation, the team published a paper that describes how its research found that, among other things:[10]

- More than half of the most popular Google search queries are predictable in a 12-month forecast. Categories such as health, food and drink, and travel have the highest percentage of predictable queries.
- The rest are not predictable (which makes sense, as Google can't predict who will be the next Britney Spears or Twitter). Entertainment, for instance, has a low percentage of predictable queries.
- Eighty-eight percent of the aggregated category search trends of more than 600 categories in Insights for Search, one of Google's free keyword research tools, are predictable.[11]

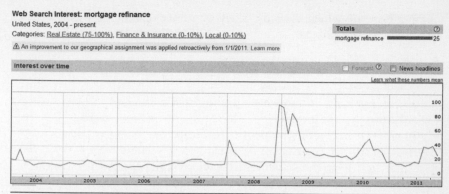

Figure 2.20 [Mortgage Refinance] Search Trends

Source: Google Insights for Search

Based on this research, Google launched the forecasting feature for Google Insights, which predicts future search volume for those queries in which it has some degree of confidence. (You'll see this feature in action later in this chapter.)

In its paper *Predicting the Present with Google Trends*, the team found that "Google Trends data *can* help improve forecasts of the current level of activity for a number of different economic time series, including automobile sales, home sales, and travel behavior."[12]

Look, for instance at the search trends for [mortgage refinance] shown in Figure 2.20.

Interest spiked sharply in late 2008 and began to decline in the latter half of 2009. It's had two smaller spikes since, which do seem to mirror market trends.

This data can also provide competitive research, diving into the top searches shows that [Wells Fargo] is the dominant searched-for bank (Figure 2.21). And the data can provide product strategy insights as well. If we

Search terms					
Top searches			**Rising searches**		
1. refinance rates		100	1. refinance my mortgage	+140%
2. refinance mortgage rates		100	2. should i refinance	+130%
3. mortgage rates		100	3. wells fargo mortgage	+120%
4. refinance home		45	4. wells fargo refinance	+100%
5. home mortgage refinance		45	5. refinance mortgage rates	+90%
6. home mortgage		45	6. refinance rates	+80%
7. refinance calculator		35	7. mortgage rates	+80%
8. mortgage refinance calculator		35	8. how to refinance	+80%
9. mortgage calculator		35	9. mortgage rates current	+70%
10. refinance loan		30	10. refinance fha mortgage	+60%

Figure 2.21 [Mortgage Refinance] 2009 Top Search Terms

Source: Google Insights for Search

Search terms		
Top searches ⑦	**Rising searches**	
1. refinance rates ———————— 100	1. wells fargo mortgage	+300%
2. mortgage refinance rates ———————— 100	2. refinance my mortgage	+250%
3. mortgage rates ———————— 100	3. wells fargo refinance	+190%
4. mortgage calculator refinance ——— 50	4. how to refinance	+160%
5. refinance calculator ——— 50	5. mortgage rates	+140%
6. mortgage calculator —— 45	6. mortgage refinance rates	+140%
7. refinance home mortgage —— 45	7. refinance rates	+140%
8. home mortgage —— 45	8. refinance a mortgage	+130%
9. refinance home —— 45	9. mortgage calculator refinance	+90%
10. refinance mortgage loan — 30	10. home mortgage rates	+80%

Figure 2.22 [Mortgage Refinance] 2011 Top Search Terms

Source: Google Insights for Search

want to attract searchers to our mortgage products, we'd be wise to provide a mortgage calculator. (Both of these trends were apparent when I was writing the first edition of this book in 2009 and remain true as I write the second edition in late 2011. See Figure 2.22.)

Google says it expects this forecasting data to help businesses make decisions about budget planning, marketing campaigns, and resource allocations. If tools powered by such high volumes of customer data exist for free to help you gain insight into your market planning, marketing campaigns, and resource allocations, don't you want to take advantage of them?

➤ Search Data as Economic Indicator

A September 2009 *Washington Post* story described Google chief economist Hal Varian's efforts to lobby government agencies to use Google search tools to better understand "customer sentiment, corporate health, and social interests." Varian said he was confident of the national economic recovery—not because of government data, but because of search data. He noted that in March 2009, the number of Google searches about unemployment benefits and centers began to drop (corresponding to the decline of new jobless claims): "As a contemporaneous predictor, predicting the present through search queries has been a pretty good predictor of initial (jobless) claims."[13]

He also noted an increase in home and real estate agent searches, which he believed indicated a strengthening housing market. He compared this with rising interest earlier in the year for the government's "cash for clunkers" program that he said the government could have used to forecast budgetary needs for the program. (The government underestimated demand and initially didn't allocate the budget necessary to keep up.)

Government agencies might be slow to embrace innovation, but you can be nimble and adopt Varian's advice as it applies to your business. Search data

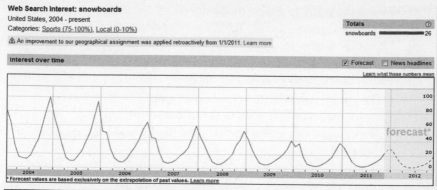

Figure 2.23 [Snowboards] Search Trends

Source: Google Insights for Search

can provide a powerful point of triangulation for other corporate data, market research, and industry trends and can predict potential industry changes early. By paying attention to how your customers are searching, you can get a jump on the competition, who might not realize such data exist.

➤ Seasonality and Prediction

Google research has found that many queries are seasonal and can therefore be fairly reliably predicted. (Those who searched for skiing conditions last winter are likely to search for them this winter as well.)

You can see how the forecasting works with the query [snowboards] in Figure 2.23.

If you have a seasonal business, search data can help you pinpoint just when demand is likely to peak. Even if you don't think your business is impacted by seasonality, this trend data can help you be sure.

■ USING SEARCH DATA FOR BETTER BUSINESS STRATEGY AND STRONGER CUSTOMER ENGAGEMENT

The following example formulates a business strategy for a hypothetical bed and breakfast (B&B) in Sonoma County, California. (We take a closer look at some of the tools available for conducting this research throughout this chapter and you can find a comprehensive list of resources at MarketingintheAgeof Google.com. See Chapter 4 for more details on the strategy for our B&B.)

➤ Business Goals

Before you dive into search data, you should clearly define your business goals. For the B&B, we'll answer the questions as follows:

- What is the primary goal of the business?
  ⇒ To book guests into the B&B.
- What does success look like?
  ⇒ 70 percent occupancy at 90 percent of list prices.
- What is the primary goal of the website?
  ⇒ To attract potential guests to book rooms.
- What are the secondary goals of the website?
  ⇒ To engage with guests so that they have a positive experience and return.
  ⇒ To reduce manual overhead of providing maps, directions, nearby wineries, restaurants, and so on, by having all of the information available on the website.
- Who is the primary audience of the business?
  ⇒ Those interested in B&Bs who want to tour wineries in Sonoma and who can afford to pay list prices.

The answers to these questions provide us with a foundation: Who is interested in winery tours in Sonoma and like to stay in B&Bs? Where do they live? What do they like? What are they looking for in a B&B?

Knowing this information can help us build a compelling website that makes the audience want to book a room, as well as help us craft the B&B itself so that it meets the needs of the guests. Web strategy and business strategy intertwine. The customers are the same. Their needs are the same. What compels them is the same. What you as a business owner want them to do is the same.

➤ General Trends

How is the B&B business in wine country doing these days? For that, we can check Google Insights for Search[14] (Figure 2.24).

The first thing we see is that the interest in B&Bs is down slightly, but we also find that many more people are searching for [bed and breakfast] than [b&b].

We also find that people are searching for both Sonoma and Napa and that, whereas searches for Sonoma spike at the end of each year, Napa searches stay fairly constant (Figure 2.25).

The searches for [wine country] have similar spikes (Figure 2.26).

We'll have to keep those spikes in mind when we start planning promotions. (Digging further, it seems that the spikes are due to searchers looking to buy Christmas gifts.)

Where should we target those promotions? We can see that, not surprisingly, Californians have the most interest, followed by those in other nearby

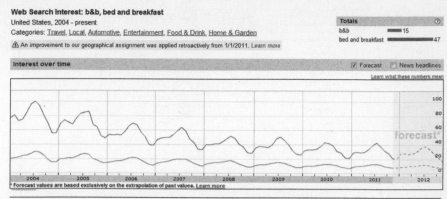

Figure 2.24 [B&B] and [Bed and Breakfast] Search Trends

Source: Google Insights for Search

Figure 2.25 [Sonoma] and [Napa] Search Trends

Source: Google Insights for Search

Figure 2.26 [Wine Country] Regional Search Trends

Source: Google Insights for Search

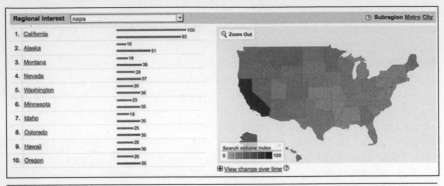

Figure 2.27 [Napa] Regional Search Trends
Source: Google Insights for Search

states. But both Minnesota and Maine show higher-than-expected interest for their distances.

Interest is highest in the United States, but there's substantial interest from Canada, as well as other countries (see Figure 2.27).

Diving into the top search terms and rising searches, we see that people seem to be interested in:

- Wine country maps
- Visitor information
- Airport information
- Weather
- Wine
- Hotels
- Wine country packages, vacations, and gift baskets

This gives us a starting point for considering how to position our B&B.

We know we want to include visitor information on our site (such as maps, airport details, and weather), but we may also want to consider providing vacation packages and even creating gift baskets that can be ordered online. Since gift baskets aren't our core competency, however, we'll hold that idea for when we're ready to expand.

► *Diving Into Keyword Research*

Before we get started, a few words about numbers. Although most keyword tools list numbers, you shouldn't think of them as exact counts. Rather, you should think of them as a way to compare terms on a relative scale. Google clusters and approximates its numbers, and many of the other tools use sampling. So, for instance, if Google lists [Napa Valley] at 823,000 queries,

[Napa hotels] at 246,000 queries, and [wine country inn] at 14,800 queries, you can conclude that more searches were done for [Napa Valley] and that [wine country inn] had substantially fewer queries. But you can't conclude that Google saw exactly 14,800 searches for [wine country inn].

Another thing to keep in mind is that you'll see a lot of references to "keywords" but what this really means is "queries." A "keyword" might actually consist of several words.

Many free and fee-based keyword research tools exist. The search engine tools are generally based on paid search data and are often presented as relative rather than as absolute. Third-party tools tend to be based on data from Internet service providers, toolbars, or consumer panels. (See the end of this chapter and marketingintheageofgoogle.com for a list of tools.)

We now have an initial seed list of words for our B&B based on our business goals, target audience, and trends information. Based on this seed list, we can build an expanded list with volume information.

➤ *Determining Keywords to Use*

We've already gotten started with this for our B&B. But there are lots of ways to develop seed lists, including:

- Industry trends
- Existing targets
- Analytics data (which we'll discuss more in Chapter 8)
- Site search logs
- Google Webmaster Tools data
- Competitor primary keywords (we'll talk about competitive research later in this chapter)
- Related sites, social media sites in related topics, and other written publications to find out what the audience is interested in
- Data from all of the departments in your organization that deal with customer needs (including product research, customer support, marketing, and public relations)—what data can be shared?

We'll start with the Google AdWords Keyword Tool[15] (which you don't need an AdWords account to use). Enter your initial seed list of words. You'll get back a list of queries with search volumes based on "broad match." Broad match means that the listed word(s) appeared somewhere in the query. You can switch this list to "exact match," which lists only exact queries.

For instance, we see that the local (United States) search volume for [Napa Valley] in one month in 2011 was 550,000 (Figure 2.28). But this doesn't mean that 550,000 searches were for [Napa Valley] specifically. This number aggregates all queries that included the words "Napa" and "Valley."

Keyword	Competition	Global Monthly Searches ⑦	Local Monthly Searches ⑦
☆ sonoma	Low	2,740,000	2,240,000
☆ napa valley	Medium	673,000	550,000
☆ wine country	Medium	246,000	246,000

Figure 2.28   [Napa Valley]–Related Search Queries

Source: Google AdWords Keyword Tool

For instance, [Napa Valley lodging] and [Napa Valley wineries] would both be counted in this number.

In addition to showing local (based on the chosen country and language, which you can change) and global search volumes, this tool also generates advertiser competition information.

An easy way to work with these lists is to export them to Excel, sort them by volume, filter out the queries that don't align with your business goals and target audience, and then categorize them. Once you have a general sense of what you're looking for, you can take a look at exact matches.

We can do this with our B&B data.

As we categorize the queries, patterns start to emerge. Not surprisingly, these searchers are interested in regional activities such as wine tours, trains, restaurants, and spas. They are looking for B&Bs that are historic, luxurious, and romantic. We may decide to partner with a local spa and offer lodging and spa packages. And we may want to decorate at least one of our rooms in romantic tones and offer a romance package, complete with wine train tour.

We also can see smaller details about how people search. They are much more likely to use the abbreviation "CA" than to spell out "California." And they're much more likely to search for "bed and breakfast" than for "bed & breakfast" or "B&B." These may seem like small points, but when you consider that major search engines are still, at their core, text based—matching up queries to pages—you realize that how you word content can make a big difference. Using the language of your customer can help you engage with them better as well.

Use of language becomes even more important with companies selling products that may inadvertently lapse into corporate speak and alienate their potential customers. (We'll talk more about using the language of your customers in Chapter 4.)

Now we have a general sense of how we should position our B&B and how we should talk about it. What else can the data tell us?

We can get a list of questions that people are asking from the Word-tracker Keyword Questions Tool.[16] From this, we see that the most asked questions about Napa Valley include:

• Where to go in Napa Valley
• Where to stay in Napa Valley

- What vineyards do you recommend Napa Valley
- When do they harvest grapes in Napa Valley
- Where is the Napa Valley
- What vineyards should you go to in Napa Valley
- Where is the Napa Valley in California
- Where is Napa Valley
- Where is Napa Valley vs San Francisco
- Where is a visitor guide for Napa Valley
- What to do in California Napa Valley
- What is the best winery in Napa Valley
- When is harvest time in the wine country Napa Valley
- What to wear in Napa Valley
- When is the best time to visit Napa Valley
- What airport do you fly into for the Napa Valley
- Where to taste Napa Valley cult wines
- What is closest city to Napa Valley
- How far is Napa Valley from San Diego
- When to go to Napa Valley
- What to do in the Napa Valley

We can learn at least a couple of things from this list. We see that people are looking for:

- Where to stay in Napa Valley
- Location and direction information about Napa Valley
- The best time to visit Napa Valley
- Things to do in Napa Valley

We also see how people craft their queries. We may want to include copy on our site such as "Looking for where to stay in Napa Valley?" Be sure to use this data to add useful content to the site that matches what your potential customers are looking for; don't just include text that matches keyword strings.

➤ Meeting Your Business Goals

Now we have a list of ideas about how to position and expand our business offerings and have gained insight into our target audience. Next, we want to focus on those areas that will bring us the highest rate of conversion.

These data are easier to obtain if your site is already running. You can use your analytics data and paid search data to find out what is attracting the most attention and what topics attract visitors who are most likely to convert.

Pinpointing conversion is tricky though, since it's based not only on attracting qualified visitors who are searching for the right things but also on how well the content is positioned on the page and how effective the call to action is. We'll talk more about those components of the funnel in Chapter 4. For now, just know that the numbers you see in your Web analytics program and paid search reports may not tell the whole story.

► Using Web Analytics Data

You can categorize Web analytics data in much the same way as keyword research data. Export the information into Excel, categorize by topic, and then discern patterns. We'll talk more about using Web analytics data in Chapter 8, but for now, we'll just look at the data that helps us understand how our audience is converting.

For instance, if you use Google Analytics, you can generate information about search queries that brought visitors to your site by looking at unpaid search traffic.

We'll cluster all of the branded searches (that is, searches for our brand name or domain name) together and exclude them, as those searching specifically for us should convert at a higher rate. And we'll exclude queries that clearly aren't targeted for our business. These will be fairly easy to recognize, as they'll have little relevance to your core business. For instance, untargeted queries for our B&B may include [where to buy Napa Valley brand clothing in Rhode Island], [Napa Auto Parts], and [San Diego B&B].

We may find good engagement from people searching for wine-related information but poor engagement from those searching more generally for things to do. From this, we can decide to either concentrate on adding wine-related information or evaluating the section of the site that focuses on things to do to ensure it is compelling and has a strong call to action.

By default, Web analytics data generally capture only things like visits, time on site, number of pages visited, and bounce rate (the percentage of visitors who abandoned the site immediately). For better insight, you'll want to have your analytics team add conversion tracking. With conversion tracking, you specify what constitutes a conversion (in the case of our B&B, this may be completing an online reservation form or sending a message via the contact form) and can then track this across search queries.

► Using Paid Search Data

If you run paid search campaigns, you can use the collected data for better insight into your potential customers as well. And if you don't run paid search campaigns, you might consider running a small one just to gather data on how potential customers react to the ads and resulting landing pages before investing a lot of resources building out that content.

Your paid search data should look something like that shown in Figure 2.29 and include information such as average ad position, number of

Keyword	Average Pos	Impressions	Clicks	CTR	Conversion Rate %	Average CPC	CPA
sonoma bed and breakfast	1.4	396,797	13,415	3.38%	10.53%	$1.08	$10.25
sonoma inn	1.3	371,257	12,213	3.29%	9.14%	$0.94	$10.32
sonoma lodging	1.2	74,532	5,759	7.73%	9.15%	$0.83	$9.07
sonoma hotels	1.5	25,695	1,433	5.58%	12.07%	$0.62	$5.13
napa valley b b	1.8	10,112	793	7.84%	11.48%	$0.90	$7.88
sonoma chamber of commerce	1.3	14,988	752	5.02%	9.44%	$0.60	$6.31
sonoma resorts	1.4	103,643	923	0.89%	7.80%	$0.46	$5.94

Figure 2.29   Using Paid Search Data for Search Insights

Source: Personal screen capture

impressions, number of clicks, resulting click-through rate (CTR), number of conversions, and conversion rate.

So, for instance, you may run two ads that result in the AdWords comparison as shown in Figure 2.30.

From this, you can see that 36 percent of searchers who saw your "Napa Valley B&B" ad clicked through to the site, and nearly 3 percent of those visitors booked a room (or filled out a request for information form or performed any other action you've set up as a conversion event). On the other hand, only 12 percent of those who saw your "wine country lodging" ad clicked through to the site, but once there, nearly 4.5 percent of those visitors converted. Which is the better audience? We can discern the following:

- More people are likely searching for the phrase "Napa Valley B&B" than for "wine country lodging" since that ad has considerably more impressions.
- A higher percentage of searchers are clicking on the Napa Valley ad, but a higher percentage of wine country searchers are converting. What does each ad look like? Is the Napa Valley ad substantially more compelling?
- Since the wine country searchers are converting at a higher rate, they are worth seeking out. What related terms are they searching for? ("wine country B&B"? "wine country inns"?)
- The Napa Valley searchers are converting at a lower rate. Is this because, as a group, they aren't quite as qualified, or is it because the

	A	B	C	D	E	F	G
1	Query	Ad Position	Impressions	Clicks	CTR	Conversions	Conversion
2	Napa Valley B&B	2	5,253	1,880	36%	56	2.98%
3	Wine country lodging	1	3,617	450	12%	20	4.44%

Figure 2.30   Using AdWords to Compare Searcher Behavior

Source: Google AdWords Keyword Tool

page is geared toward the wine country group? Does the page talk about wine country lodging but not about Napa Valley B&Bs? It may be a good idea to implement A/B testing to try out different versions of the page that cause the Napa Valley group to convert at a higher rate, while not driving down the conversion rate of the wine country group.

- As a data source for organic search keyword research, it's likely worth catering to both of these groups and you can likely modify the pages in a way that benefits both paid and organic search traffic and conversions.

You can also use other business data to formulate a more complete picture. What do offline sales look like? Direct mail? E-mail campaigns? What press releases picked up the most interest?

► *Competitive Research*

We've already seen some competitive research with the data available from the Google AdWords Keyword Tool. Let's take a closer look. In the tool, competitive information shows up as high, medium, or low, and when you export the information, it shows up as a number between 0 and 1. Since these data are based on the competition for paid search terms, it may not correlate exactly with organic search, but it can provide a pretty good gauge to start from.

For instance, consider the four queries shown in Figure 2.31, which have about the same query volume each month.

We can see that about the same number of people search for each of these per month, but [winery Napa] has much lower competition than the others. If we ran a Northern California winery and were wondering how best to craft our website messaging, we may want to go with the terms with lower competition, as it may be easier to rank for those terms.

We can use Google Trends for Websites for insight into particular competitors. You not only can compare traffic for various websites over time but also can see other sites visited and what those visitors searched for (Figure 2.32).

Query	Volume	Competition
napa wineries	74,123	0.73
sonoma hotels	73,831	0.93
sonoma wine	74,213	0.80
winery napa	74,021	0.46

Figure 2.31 Query Competition

Source: Google AdWords Keyword Tool

Figure 2.32 Using Google Trends to Compare Websites

Source: Google Trends

Other types of competitive research are available. We'll look at a few in the sections that follow. A more comprehensive list of tools is available at the end of this chapter and at marketingintheageofgoogle.com.

➤ *Site Comparison and Traffic Tools*

A number of tools exist that compare sites and provide traffic estimates for them. Although these tools provide adequate comparisons and good insight into relative changes over time, don't put too much faith in the absolute numbers. Because of the different data collection methods and estimation processes, the exact numbers are, at best, wildly inaccurate.

Compete[17] provides competitive data about sites and paid versions provide the top keywords that are sending searchers to a particular site (Figure 2.33).

SpyFu[18] provides organic and paid search data about any website (Figure 2.34).

Alexa[19] gathers data from its toolbar users and makes available trends data, comparative information, and keyword data, among other things (Figures 2.35 and 2.36). From Figure 2.36, we can see the search queries that drove the most traffic to the site, as well as the percentage of site traffic coming from search engines. In the case of bedandbreakfast.com, nearly 25 percent of traffic came from search engines over the previous 30 days.

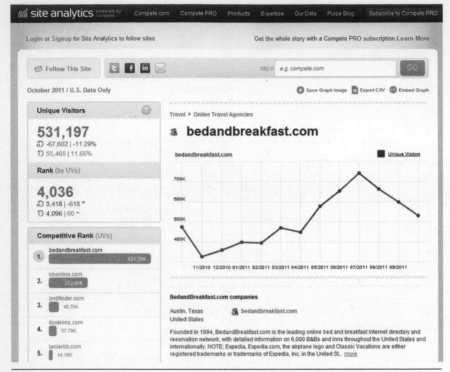

Figure 2.33 Compete as Comparison and Traffic Tool

Source: Compete.com

Digging further, we can see what countries visitors were from as well as substantial additional demographic information (Figure 2.37).

Hitwise[20] data come from partnerships with Internet service providers that log the sites their users visit and what they search for. Hitwise products are paid services that include competitive analysis, keyword research, clickstream reporting, and demographic information. It also provides free industry reports (Figures 2.38 and 2.39).

ComScore[21] provides panel-based research, and like Hitwise, it produces industry reports and offers fee-based services. Its products include comScore Marketer, which provides search market share, audience, and analytics analysis, and comScore qSearch, which reports on searcher behavior and activity across the Web (not just at major search engines) (Figure 2.40).

Nielsen NetRatings also provides panel research—an extension of its television panel research—and provides both free and paid reports on searcher behavior and keyword volumes.

Figure 2.34 SpyFu as Comparison and Traffic Tool

Source: Spyfu.com

Google Ad Planner provides competitive research (intended for advertisers looking to place banner ads on those sites) as well (Figure 2.41).

You can also simply look at competitors' websites. What terms do they use on their pages? Do their sites cover additional topics? What sites link to them?

➤ *Using Search Results for Competitive Intelligence*

A wealth of data is available from simply looking at the search results. When you search for the queries you're targeting, you can see exactly what sites the search engines think are the most relevant for those queries and how they stack up. You don't know, of course, what the conversion data is like for those sites, but you can click over and see what the searcher workflow experience is like. (We'll be discussing the searcher workflow experience more in Chapter 4.) Look, for instance, at the search results for [accounting software] shown in Figure 2.42.

Figure 2.35 Alexa as Comparison and Traffic Tool

Source: Alexa.com

The top three brands Google lists in the results are QuickBooks, Quicken, and Peachtree. Those are the primary brands you'll be competing with in search and in brand mindshare among searchers.

Looking at those top three pages that rank organically, we can see that the QuickBooks page has a compelling value proposition and clear call to action, although some potential customers might not be initially ready to sign up right away and would be more effectively engaged with a larger "learn more" link (Figure 2.43).

Interestingly, Quicken, which is made by the same company as Quick-Books (Intuit) makes its software seem complicated, with potentially too

| Traffic Stats | Search Analytics | Audience | Contact Info | Reviews | Related Links | Clickstream |

Search Traffic

The percentage of site visits from search engines.

Period	Percent of Site Traffic
Last 30 days	23.6%
Last 7 days	21.2%
Yesterday	28.9%

Top Queries from Search Traffic

The top queries driving traffic to bedandbreakfast.com from search engines. Updated monthly.

	Query	Percent of Search Traffic
1	bed and breakfast	4.45%
2	b&b sicily	1.11%
3	chambres d'hotes	0.64%
4	bedandbreakfast.com	0.56%
5	bed & breakfast	0.48%
6	bed and breakfast london	0.36%
7	b&b	0.28%
8	bnb	0.26%
9	bed and breakfast boston	0.22%
10	b & b	0.21%

Keyword Research Tool - Find More Keywords   Sponsored Links

Identify which keywords are searched for, which keywords drive the most traffic and what the PPC bids are using Trellian's KeywordDiscovery.com keyword tool.

Search Traffic on the Rise and Decline

The top queries from search engines driving relatively more/less traffic to bedandbreakfast.com in the current month than the previous month. Updated monthly.

	Search Query	1 Month Increase		Search Query	1 Month Decline
1	chambres d'hotes	0.64%	1	bed and breakfast	1.87%
2	b&b sicily	0.27%	2	bedandbreakfast.com	0.45%
3	cape cod bed and breakfast	0.13%	3	b&b	0.39%
4	b & b	0.12%	4	vancouver bed and breakfast	0.35%
5	bed and breakfast jaipur	0.11%	5	b and b	0.27%
6	b&b london	0.10%	6	bed and breakfasts	0.17%
7	bed and breakfast boston	0.09%	7	key west bed and breakfast	0.12%
8	b&b malaga	0.08%	8	bed breakfast	0.06%
9	bed and breakfast york	0.08%	9	bnb	0.06%
10	bed and breakfast lincoln	0.08%	10	bed and breakfast deals	0.06%

Figure 2.36   Search Terms Driving Traffic for bedandbreakfast.com

Source: Alexa.com

many choices (Figure 2.44). Because this product is for a home consumer audience, it probably should be even easier and friendlier than the Quick-Books home page.

Peachtree does a better job with inviting visitors to learn more and not requiring the visitor to make a product choice right away (Figure 2.45).

When I click on the related search [top accounting software], I see that the results primarily focus on the comparison of articles rather than brands,

Visitors by Country for Bedandbreakfast.com

Country	Percent of Visitors
United States	45.4%
Italy	7.3%
India	6.3%
Philippines	3.3%
France	3.2%
United Kingdom	3.1%
China	2.7%
Canada	2.4%
Germany	2.2%
Pakistan	2.2%

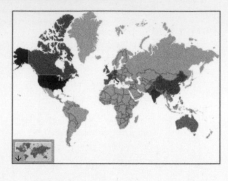

Figure 2.37   Traffic Sources for bedandbreakfast.com

Source: Alexa.com

which means ranking a brand site for that query would likely be difficult. (The same is true of the [accounting software lists] and [types of accounting software] and related searches at the bottom of the page.) However, the related searches [simple accounting software], [bookkeeping software], and [personal accounting software] all bring up brand results, so those are good initial targets.

Top 10 Retail Fast Mover Terms

The following report shows **search terms** for the custom category **'Top 500 Retail sites'**, ranked by **largest increase** for the **week** ending **11/26/2011**, compared with the **week** ending **11/19/2011**. (Filters applied)

Rank	Search Term	Volume	Change
1.	lcd televisions	0.03%	New
2.	jenny mccarthy	0.02%	New
3.	cyber monday sales	0.01%	New
4.	2011 lowes black friday ...	0.01%	New
5.	online black friday deals	0.01%	New
6.	2011 jc penney black friday	0.01%	New
7.	macy black friday 2011 ad	0.01%	New
8.	calphalon convection oven	0.01%	New
9.	black friday 2011 best bu...	0.01%	New
10.	radio shack black friday ...	0.01%	New

Figure 2.38   Top 10 Retail Fast Moving Search Terms, November 2011

Source: Hitwise.com

Top 10 Overall Search Terms

The following report shows **search terms** for the industry '**All Categories**', ranked by **Search Clicks** for the **4 weeks** ending **11/26/2011**.

Rank	Search Term	Search Clicks
1.	facebook	3.72%
2.	youtube	1.19%
3.	craigslist	0.59%
4.	facebook.com	0.48%
5.	facebook login	0.43%
6.	ebay	0.40%
7.	yahoo	0.39%
8.	www.facebook.com	0.29%
9.	walmart	0.24%
10.	amazon	0.18%

Figure 2.39   Top 10 Overall Search Terms, November 2011

Source: Hitwise.com

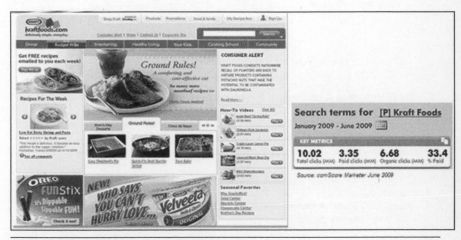

Figure 2.40   Kraftfoods.com comScore Data

Source: ComScore.com

Sites also visited

Site	Affinity ⑦
iloveinns.com	1357.0x
bnbfinder.com	1121.6x
lanierbb.com	1120.8x
bbonline.com	927.3x
secure.rezovation.com	843.0x
rezovation.com	843.0x
convoyant.com	766.1x
webervations.com	633.4x
secure.webervations.com	633.2x
resnexus.com	575.7x

Audience Interests

Interest	Affinity ⑦
Vineyards & Wine Tourism	43.9x
Vermont	43.9x
California Central Coast	24.7x
Hotels & Accommodations	15.4x
Timeshares & Vacation Properties	15.4x
Sightseeing Tours	15.4x
New England	14.0x
Boston Metro	14.0x
Maine	14.0x
Hospitality Industry	12.7x

Keywords searched for

Keyword	Affinity ⑦
bed breakfast	633.2x
tripadvisor	36.2x
trip advisor	33.0x
hotels	22.5x
priceline	20.5x
kayak	18.6x
travelocity	16.9x
orbitz	15.4x
booking	12.7x
southwest airlines	12.7x

Worldwide Top Subdomains

Subdomain	Worldwide UV (u) ⑦
secure.bedandbreakfast.com	19K

Figure 2.41   Google Ad Planner Search Data

Source: Google Ad Planner

Small Business **Accounting Software** from Intuit QuickBooks

quickbooks.intuit.com/ +1

Business **accounting software** to help you save time and make money. Get the details
on how you can get the #1 rated small business **accounting software** for ...

QuickBooks Online - QuickBooks Products - QuickBooks Support - QuickBooks Pro

Quicken - Personal Finance **Software**, Money Management, Budget ...

quicken.intuit.com/ +1

America's #1 Personal Finance **Software** ... View your **accounts** in one place ... credit
card, loan, investments, and retirement **accounts** in one place: no more ...

Sage Peachtree **Accounting Software** Program Solutions

www.peachtree.com/ +1

Sage Peachtree is a network-ready **accounting software** system for small businesses
under 50 employees. Save time and money with Sage Peachtree.

Figure 2.42   Google Search Results for [Accounting Software]

Source: Google Search

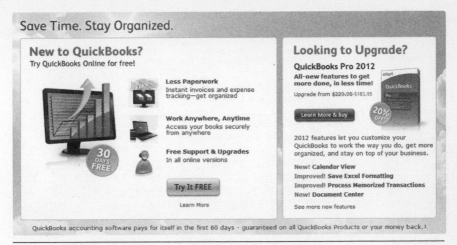

Figure 2.43   QuickBook's Compelling Value Proposition

Source: Intuit

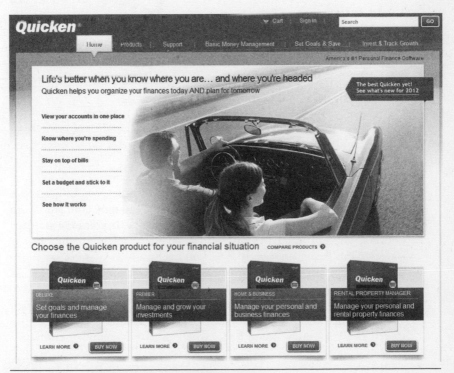

Figure 2.44   Quicken's Confusing Home Page

Source: Intuit

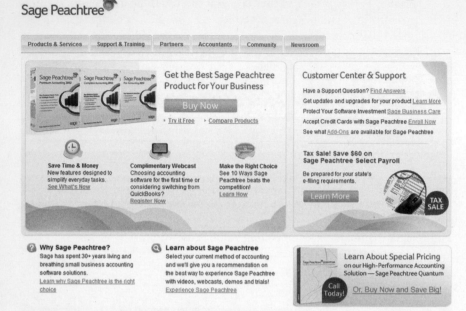

Figure 2.45 Peachtree Focuses on Price

Source: Peachtree

■ A BETTER STRATEGY FOR INCREASED CUSTOMERS AND A MORE SUCCESSFUL BUSINESS

Once you've got a sense of the types of things your target audience is interested in the most and how competitive those markets are, you can consider the impact on your business in a number of ways:

- *Product strategy:* Are you providing the types of things your audience is looking for? Are you investing resources in areas that your audience isn't interested in at the expense of areas that it is? If you identify gaps between your product offering and what you find your audience is interested in based on search data, you may want to spend a bit more time asking your customers, setting up focus groups, or analyzing spending patterns.
- *Business strategy:* Is your industry in decline or a state of growth? Are you using the best revenue model for your business? Or are you trying to sell everyone new home loans when they're looking to refinance their mortgages?
- *Search acquisition strategy:* What audience and interests lead to the highest conversion rates? What audience is large enough without overwhelming competition? What search terms should you target, and what kind of experience should you make available on the site? This

process is very similar to the ways you can use these data when building your product and business strategies.

You already know how to use data effectively to improve your product and business strategies, but what about your organic search strategy? The key is to understand the search acquisition workflow: focus on the searchers, what they are looking for, how you can meet their needs, and how you can compel them to meet your business goals.

We'll learn more about developing a search acquisition strategy in the next few chapters.

Chapter 2 Checklist: Using Search Data

Identify your business goals.

- ❑ What's the primary goal of the business?
- ❑ How will you measure success?
- ❑ What is the primary goal of the website?
- ❑ Who is your target audience? What are they trying to accomplish?
- ❑ What are the general industry trends based on external search data?

  Use Google Trends to see search volume trends for relevant queries across regions.

- ❑ What core topics are the primary audience most interested in?

  Use the Google AdWords Keyword Tool to determine highest-interest topics.
  Use Web analytics data and other internal data in conjunction with external search data.
  Use Web analytics data to determine how most visitors are finding the site.
  Use Web analytics referral data to determine the pages that bring in the most traffic through links.

- ❑ Of the high-interest topics, which intersect with business goals?

  Use Web analytics data, paid search data, business goals, and conversion data from other departments to isolate a subset of topics that attract the most qualified potential customers.

- ❑ Which topics align with brand messaging, product plans, and overall strategy?

(continued)

(*continued*)

❏ Do any of these topics indicate that product plans and business goals should be revisited?

❏ What is the competitive landscape?

Use tools such as Google Trends for websites, Compete, and Hitwise to better understand the competition.
Use data for audience analysis.

❏ Which audience needs are not being met that your business can capitalize on?

❏ Now that you've identified a subset of topics to focus on, who is this audience and what is it really looking for?

CHAPTER 2 SAMPLE RESOURCES: SEARCH DATA

- Google Trends www.google.com/trends
- Google Trends for Websites trends.google.com/websites
- Google Insights for Search www.google.com/insights/search
- Google Ad Planner www.google.com/adplanner
- Google AdWords Keyword Tool adwords.google.com/select/KeywordToolExternal
- Google Suggest www.google.com
- Google Webmaster Tools www.google.com/webmasters
- Wordtracker www.wordtracker.com
- Wordtracker Keyword Questions freekeywords.wordtracker.com/keyword-questions
- Soovle www.soovle.com
- SpyFu www.spyfu.com
- Compete compete.com
- Alexa www.alexa.com
- Hitwise www.hitwise.com
- comScore www.comscore.com/Products_Services/Search_Marketing
- Quantcast www.quantcast.com

Chapter 3

How We Search

A successful search acquisition strategy begins with understanding the searcher. Searchers themselves provide very little that indicates their intent. Search queries are an average of three words long, and more than 25 percent are only a single word.[1]

Fortunately, we have a great deal of data beyond the queries themselves to help us derive potential intent. Search engines track searcher behavior, and by looking at what searchers click on and what they search for next, search engines can learn a surprising amount about what someone might mean by those one to three words.

We can see much of what the search engines have learned just by looking at what content search engines rank highly for a particular query.

As we've learned, search engines also make a wide variety of data available that can provide detailed insight into the intent and motivation of potential customers.

■ QUERY TYPES

One way search engines derive intent is by classifying queries into intention categories. Each search engine group queries slightly differently, but for our purposes, a good classification system is:

- *Navigational:* With this type of query, the searcher is looking for something specific. These are often one-word queries that have a high likelihood of a single meaning. Many, but not all, navigational queries are branded. Some examples are [Volvo], [amazon.com], and [Twitter Vanessa Fox]. Approximately 18 percent of search queries are navigational.[2]
- *Commercial (also called transactional):* These searches are likely purchase-related, and the search engines tend to favor results that enable the searcher to buy something, such as e-commerce sites. Some examples of this type of search include [buy shoes online] and [book vacation rental in Greece].

- *Informational (also called research):* This query tends to be more generic and noncommercial. Search engines tend to favor results that are not commercial in nature. Examples include "when was Abraham Lincoln born" and "highest mountain in the world."
- *Prepurchase research:* For our purposes, it's useful to consider this subset of informational queries in which the searcher is doing research with a high likelihood of a later purchase. Some examples of this type of search include "digital camera reviews" and "what cars get the best gas mileage." This category of searchers is useful to seek out because it's an audience that is not yet ready to purchase but will be soon and is currently gathering data to make decisions about what to buy. You want to provide information to these searchers so that they later include you in their list of purchase choices.
- *Action:* This type of query signals that the searcher wants to do something, such as download an application or watch a video. I performed an action query not long ago when riding in the car with my five-year-old niece. Results for [funny cat videos] on a mobile phone browser can provide hours of entertainment. This type of search can be considered a subset of informational queries.

As noted, search engines determine intent in part based on past search behavior. Search engines see millions of searches a day, and over a period of years, these data can be very valuable in determining likely intent.

For instance, if 1 million people a day search for [Britney Spears] and 80 percent of those searchers clicked on a search result that linked to a video or did a second search for [Britney Spears video] (called query refinement), then the search engine looking at these data might conclude that generally, searchers looking for Britney Spears are actually looking for Britney Spears videos. To provide the most useful results for those searchers, the search engine might start surfacing videos in the search results even though the query alone didn't indicate that desire.

How is this useful to you? If you run a Britney Spears site, you can increase your coverage by adding videos so that your site has the opportunity to rank not only for the web page but for videos as well.

■ DETERMINING INTENT

Most searches are short because of what economist and psychologist Herbert Simon called bounded rationality.[3] We exert the smallest effort (short queries) to get an adequate result. We exert more effort (query refinement) only if the initial work didn't get us what we needed.

Google's quality guidelines give an example of how difficult it can be to determine intent from a single-word query:

Someone searching for [calendar] could be looking to find and print a calendar for the current month. Or they could be looking for a calendar of holidays. Or they could be looking for an online calendar to use for appointments.

Google breaks the query interpretation into three categories:

- Dominant interpretation
- Common interpretations
- Minor interpretations

Some of the factors that Google uses to determine intent include:

- *Current events:* The searcher likely wants the latest of something (such as latest sports scores versus historical ones).
- *Location:* If the query is regional in nature but doesn't include a location, the searcher likely is interested in their current location (such as local pizza restaurants versus national ones).
- *Previous behavior:* Google uses both overall searcher behavior in aggregate and individual searcher behavior to predict current intent.

Intent factors heavily into how search results are generated globally and in personalized results (discussed in Chapter 5).

The easiest way to find out what search engines have learned about searcher intent is to conduct searches and evaluate the results. Take the query [iPad2], for instance. The results include not only the official Apple site but also video results, news results, and shopping results (see Figures 3.1 and 3.2).

These results are a clear indication that many searching for [iPad2] went on to view videos, news, and e-commerce sites. The suggested related searches (Figure 3.3) tell us that many did subsequent searches for reviews, specs, covers, news, and availability.

■ QUERY REFINEMENTS

Query refinements are the queries searchers type in after doing an initial search. They might do these refinements right away (without clicking on results) or after visiting a few pages and then returning to the search engine. Searchers often enter refinements when the initial search doesn't provide satisfactory results, but the results do provide clues on what to search for.[4]

For instance, if someone does a search for a high school name and gets a set of results with that high school name but not the correct one, the searcher might notice that the results that appear have geographic information and add that to the query. [South High School] might be refined to [South High School Bakersfield CA].

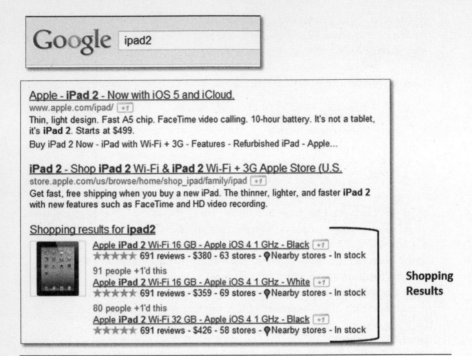

Figure 3.1 Google Shopping Listed in Search Results for [iPad2]

Source: Google Search

Why do searchers refine their queries? An August 2009 Hitwise study about Canadian searchers found that searches were successful only 70 percent of the time and the rest of the time searchers had to "re-search to find relevant results."[5]

In this particular study, Hitwise found that the lack of relevance might stem from the international nature of the searches. Since the searches were conducted in North America in English, search engines seemed to weigh U.S. sites more heavily. So, for instance, a search for a particular retail store in Canada might produce results for U.S. store locations.

A Penn State researcher found that 22 percent of queries are refined. At the beginning of a search, searchers narrow their queries, and then as the search progresses, searchers reformulate queries (often based on what results appear).

A Microsoft Bing internal study found that searchers refine their queries, bounce back to the search results, or abandon the search 50 percent of the time. The breakdown of that 50 percent is shown in Figure 3.4.

Microsoft also found that searchers repeated 24 percent of their queries during a session. Forty-one percent of searchers change their search term (or search engine) if they don't find what they're looking for on the first page of results, and 88 percent do so after three pages.[6]

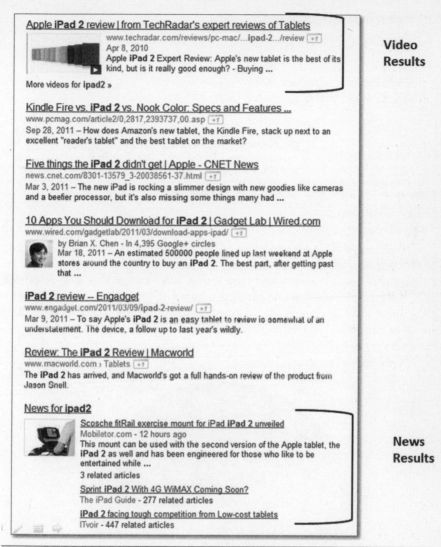

Figure 3.2 Google Video and News Listed in Search Results for [iPad2]

Source: Google Search

During information retrieval, searchers often change focus to different aspects of their tasks.[7] This change may cause searchers to refine their queries to broader or narrower concepts, from topical to nontopical searches, and to unexpected shifts.

The search engines try to help searchers narrow in on what they're looking for and to provide refinement suggestions in a number of ways.

Searches related to **ipad2**

apple ipad2	ipad2 **availability**
ipad2 **review**	ipad2 **news**
ipad2 **specs**	**verizon** ipad2
ipad2 **cover**	**buy** ipad2

Goooooooooogle ▶

1 2 3 4 5 6 7 8 9 10   **Next**

Figure 3.3 Google Related Searches for [iPad2]

Source: Google Search

It can be valuable to make note of what refinements the engines suggest, both because it sheds light on what searchers are likely looking for (since refinements tend to be based on past search behavior) and because searchers will often choose the refinement in the initial search. It may be difficult to rank for the initial term due to a lot of competition, but you might be able to more easily rank for the longer term.

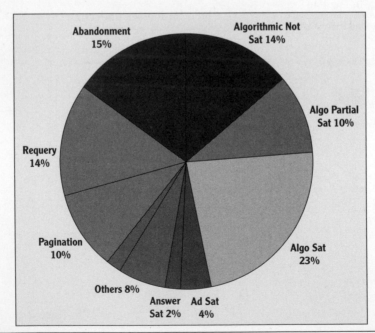

Figure 3.4 Microsoft Bing Internal Study Results

Source: Microsoft Bing

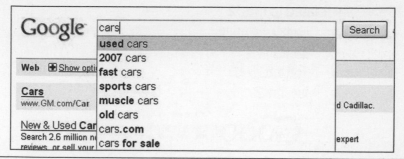

Figure 3.5 Google Search Suggest for [Cars]

Source: Google

➤ *Google Search Suggest*

Google provides refinement suggestions as the searcher is typing. For a company that sells used cars online, it may be helpful to know that when someone searches for [cars], Google suggests sports cars, old cars, used cars, and cars for sale. The company may have included information on its site about used cars, but perhaps it didn't think about mentioning "old" cars (Figure 3.5).

➤ *Google Related Searches*

Google's related searches can also help businesses understand their audience and ensure they can be found for relevant searches. Again, with [cars], we see that Google is suggesting [old cars] as a follow-up search, so chances are good that a lot of people looking to buy a used car will click on the old cars link; this means you want to make sure that your used car site ranks highly for that search (Figure 3.6).

➤ *Yahoo! Search Suggestions*

Yahoo! provides a similar set of suggestions in its search box (Figure 3.7).

➤ *Yahoo! Related Searches*

Yahoo!'s related search feature is similar to Google's and provides trending searches as well (Figure 3.8).

Searches related to: **cars**

electric cars	sports cars	old cars	disney cars
cars pixar	car pictures	autotrader	car games

Figure 3.6 Google Related Searches for [Cars]

Source: Google Search

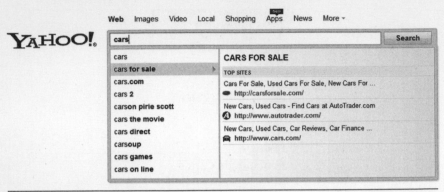

Figure 3.7 Yahoo! Search Suggestions for [Cars]
Source: Yahoo!

➤ *Bing Related Searches*

Bing can provide yet more insight into what searchers are really looking for (Figure 3.9).

■ USING DEMOGRAPHIC DATA

Microsoft Advertising Intelligence (an Excel add-in)[8] provides demographic information about searchers based on the search patterns of MSN users. For

TRENDING SEARCHES

cars for sale philippines

mecum **cars for sale**

RELATED SEARCHES

used **cars**

autotrader

carmax

carmax used **cars**

autotrader used **cars**

Figure 3.8 Yahoo! Trending and Related Searches for [Cars]
Source: Yahoo!

Web

RELATED SEARCHES
Used Car
New Cars
Hot Cars
Ford muscle Car
Hertz Rental Car
Most Expensive Cars
Cars Rental
Car Pictures

Figure 3.9 Bing Related Searches for [Used Cars]

Source: Microsoft Bing

instance, when looking at shoe searches, we see that 75 percent of searches for [Payless shoes] are from women, whereas men and women search for [running shoes] in nearly equal numbers (with the 25 to 35 age group searching the most, accounting for more than 28 percent of searches).

If we combine search volume and gender data, we can generate a shoe-related top 10 keyword list for both men and women (Figures 3.10 and 3.11). By volume, the top three shoe-related terms men search for are [running shoes], [Jordan shoes], and [Nike shoes]; the top three shoe-related terms women search for are [Payless shoes], [running shoes], and [DSW shoes].

This information could be highly useful to Nike. Their site currently isn't on the first page of Google search results for [running shoes] (Figure 3.12).

Women Top 10 (Weighted by Volume)		
Keyword	% Female	W
payless shoes	74.26%	
running shoes	48.25%	
dsw shoes	74.77%	
nike shoes	52.94%	
jordan shoes	45.14%	
bakers shoes	77.38%	
aldo shoes	75.66%	

Figure 3.10 Demographic Information: Searching for Women's Shoes

Source: Microsoft adCenter

Men Top 10 (Weighted by Volume)		
Keyword	% Male	W
running shoes	51.75%	
jordan shoes	54.86%	
nike shoes	47.06%	
payless shoes	25.74%	
dc shoes	51.84%	

Figure 3.11 Demographic Information: Searching for Men's Shoes

Source: Microsoft adCenter

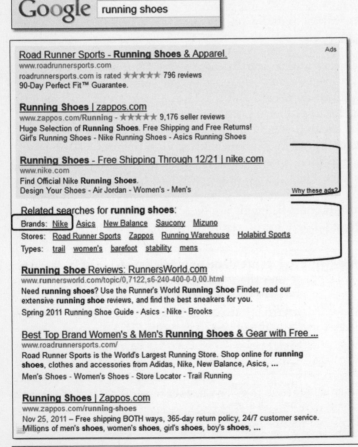

Google running shoes

Ads

Road Runner Sports - **Running Shoes** & Apparel.
www.roadrunnersports.com
roadrunnersports.com is rated ★★★★★ 796 reviews
90-Day Perfect Fit™ Guarantee.

Running Shoes | zappos.com
www.zappos.com/Running - ★★★★★ 9,176 seller reviews
Huge Selection of **Running Shoes**. Free Shipping and Free Returns!
Girl's Running Shoes - Nike Running Shoes - Asics Running Shoes

Running Shoes - Free Shipping Through 12/21 | nike.com
www.nike.com
Find Official Nike **Running Shoes**.
Design Your Shoes - Air Jordan - Women's - Men's   Why these ads?

Nike AdWords Ad

Related searches for **running shoes**:
Brands: Nike Asics New Balance Saucony Mizuno
Stores: Road Runner Sports Zappos Running Warehouse Holabird Sports
Types: trail women's barefoot stability mens

Nike Related Brand Search

Running Shoe Reviews: RunnersWorld.com
www.runnersworld.com/topic/0,7122,s6-240-400-0-0,00.html
Need **running shoes**? Use the Runner's World **Running Shoe** Finder, read our
extensive **running shoe** reviews, and find the best sneakers for you.
Spring 2011 Running Shoe Guide - Asics - Nike - Brooks

Best Top Brand Women's & Men's **Running Shoes** & Gear with Free ...
www.roadrunnersports.com/
Road Runner Sports is the World's Largest Running Store. Shop online for **running
shoes**, clothes and accessories from Adidas, Nike, New Balance, Asics, ...
Men's Shoes - Women's Shoes - Store Locator - Trail Running

Running Shoes | Zappos.com
www.zappos.com/running-shoes
Nov 25, 2011 – Free shipping BOTH ways, 365-day return policy, 24/7 customer service.
Millions of men's **shoes**, women's **shoes**, girl's **shoes**, boy's **shoes**, ...

Figure 3.12 Google Search Results for [Running Shoes]

Source: Google Search

This was the case when I was writing the first edition of this book in 2009 and remains true now at the close of 2011 (even though the top related brand search for [running shoes] is [nike] and they are buying AdWords for the search phrase).

The top results are www.runnersworld.com, www.roadrunnersports.com, and www.zappos.com/running-shoes. Their competitors Saucony, Brooks, and New Balance all rank on the first page.

In November 2011, 1 million searches were done in the United States that contained the phrase [running shoes].[9] Nike would probably like to be seen by those searchers.

What could Nike do with this information? It could prioritize this category of searches, take a look at what technical issues may be preventing its site from being fully crawled and indexed (see Chapter 7), and make sure that it uses the same language as its customers in the text of their web pages. All of the pages that rank of the first page of results for the query [running shoes] use that term in the title tag of those pages, whereas Nike has "Nike – Home" as the title tag of their website's home page. Something as simple as changing "home" to "running shoes" could make all the difference in being seen by 1 million potential customers. Again, Chapter 7 talks more about these technical details.

Many of the competitive research tools described in the previous chapter provide demographic information as well (although on a site basis rather than a keyword basis). For instance, Google Ad Planner provides much of this information (Figure 3.13), as does Alexa (Figure 3.14).

Google Correlate[10] enables you to correlate search trends with any data source.[11] Figure 3.15 shows search terms correlated with the [cheap flights] search query. Figure 3.16 shows that the highest correlated term with higher-income states is the query [team captain]. State-based income data is just one example of how you can use demographic and other data to learn more about how we search.

If searches for your product are done primarily by one gender, consider how they process language and shop differently. Researchers from Northwestern University and the University of Haifa found that the areas of the brain associated with language work harder in girls than in boys. So, perhaps copy aimed at men should be succinct and to the point.

In *Why We Buy: The Science of Shopping*, Paco Underhill noted that fewer men look for price tags.[12] And some research has found that men are more likely than women to make impulse purchases online. You can incorporate these data into other audience analysis and market research that you have, and you may then decide that your product pages aimed at women should have highly visible prices and ensure information that answers questions is easily available.[13]

Studies have also shown that online, women are more engaged with images and men are less patient. This means that men are more likely to

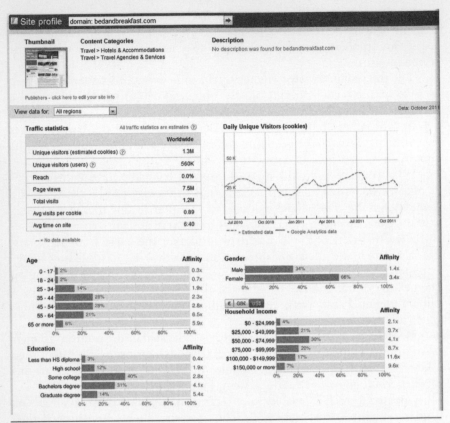

Figure 3.13 Google Ad Planner Demographic Data

Source: Google Ad Planner

abandon your home page if it starts loading a Flash module. Men are also more impatient with poor navigational structure.

A study that focused on differences in how men and women search found that "on average, men make decisions quicker, spend less time on sites, are more likely to have preestablished 'favored' vendor sites that they use in the search process and show less resistance to sponsored listings. Women tended to be more deliberate in reading search results, spend more time with their searches, and spend more time on sites before making decisions."[14]

Consider the age of your target audience as well. If you cater to an older audience, make sure that when they click the search results to your site, the type is larger and clear and easy to read.

➤ How Searchers Interact with Results

Gord Hotchkiss, previously chief executive officer (CEO) of Enquiro Research and now senior vice president of Mediative (which acquired

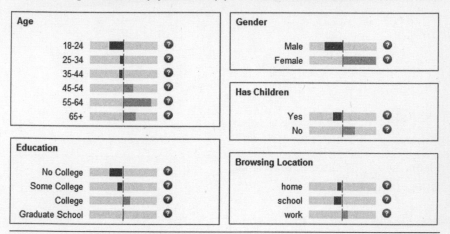

Figure 3.14   Alexa Demographic Data

Source: Alexa.com

Enquiro Research), has given us fascinating insight into the way searchers view and click on results.

He describes how our brains use cognitive shortcuts when performing mental tasks. As we learn a behavior, we internalize it and perform that behavior on autopilot so that our brains are free to concentrate on other tasks. Up to 45 percent of our daily actions are done by habit, without conscious thought.[15] Our brains take similar shortcuts when scanning the search results

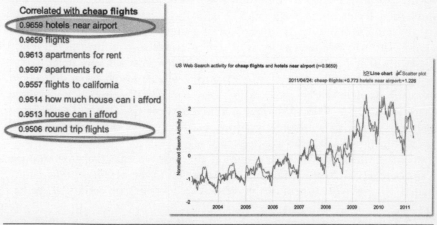

Figure 3.15   Search Terms Correlated with [Cheap Flights]

Source: Google Correlate

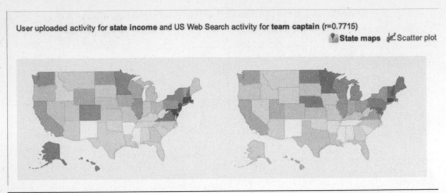

Figure 3.16 State Income Correlation

Source: Google Correlate

page. We don't initially read the text on the page; we look for matches in the shape of the characters in the query. Hotchkiss notes:

> *In cognitive psychology, this is called the "pop out" effect. We can recognize shapes much faster than we can read words. The shapes of our query literally "pop out" from the page as a first step toward matching relevance. The effect is enhanced by query (or hit) bolding. This matching game is done at the sub-cortical level.*[16]

How Working Memory Plays into Evaluating Search Results Multiple tracking studies have shown that we scan the page in an F-shaped pattern: we start in the upper left and then move down the left margin (Figure 3.17). In a 2011 such study,[17] User Centric found that not only did between 70 percent and 80 percent of searchers ignore paid search ads (while all of them looked at the organic results), but nearly everyone scanned results the same way: by skimming the left side of the results.

Because of the capacity of our working memory, we break the page into chunks of three to four results. This corresponds to cognitive psychologist George Miller's rule of "7 ± 2," which posits that our working memory can hold around seven chunks of information.[18] We can hold more digits than words in our working memory, which may partially explain how we evaluate search results. A 2008 study at the University of California, Davis found that our working memory only allows us to consider three to four things at one time.[19]

Rather than evaluate all results on the page at once, we first evaluate a single three- to four-item chunk and move on to the next if we don't find a match. Roughly 50 percent of the time, searchers click on results in the first chunk.

This is one reason why a number one ranking is less important than people think. If you rank in the top three to four results and have the most

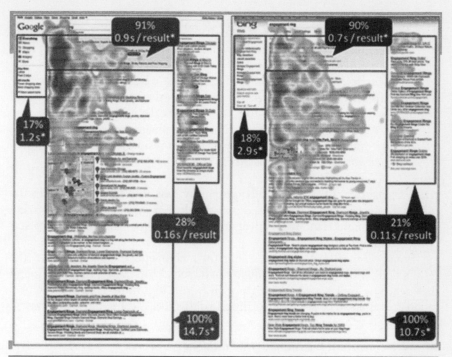

Figure 3.17 Eye-Tracking Heat Map of Search Results

Source: User Centric

compelling title and description, you may win the click over the sites ranking above you.

Why don't we feel compelled to review the results in all of the chunks before making a decision? It likely has to do, once again, with bounded rationality. If we reach an adequate solution within the first chunk, we have no reason to continue our evaluation.

All of this chunking and scanning takes place in milliseconds. Once we see a positive pattern match in a result, our eyes rest on that result long enough to read the words. When we see words that reinforce that this result is relevant for the query (we may recognize the brand) or see a description that includes the positive attributes we were looking for but didn't include in the query (such as a regional location or price attribute), we may click.

One Enquiro Research study involved finding out if searchers with different intents (commercial versus information gathering) scanned results differently. They showed both groups the same set of algorithmic and sponsored results. They found that both groups scanned the results in nearly the same way. The difference happened at the click. In the commercial-intent group, half of the searchers clicked the algorithmic results and half clicked the paid search results. In the information-gathering group, everyone clicked the algorithmic results. This happened even though both groups looked at the algorithmic and paid search results in exactly the same way and for the same amount of time.[20]

Our search autopilot switches off only once we are ready to click on a result. The entire interaction generally takes less than 10 seconds. We spend less than two seconds evaluating each result before the click.

So if we scan results a chunk at a time and evaluate each cluster of results, what are we evaluating? What is displayed in that result can make a big difference in whether that listing gets a click.

What Compels a Click? We subconsciously look for relevancy clues in the title and snippet once we've paused on a result. For instance, if we're looking for a car, we might respond positively to words like "fuel efficient" and "5 star crash rating."

Some businesses don't like seeing their competition rank highly in the results along with them. But this might not be such a bad thing. One study found that when a well-known competitor was missing from results, searchers found the results to be less trustworthy and didn't feel as comfortable clicking.[21]

➤ *How Important Is a Number One Ranking?*

As we discovered earlier, if your search result is more compelling than those around it, searchers very well may click on it if it's within the cluster they're evaluating, even if it isn't ranked highest. But ranking well does make a difference. Of searchers, 62 percent click a result on the first page of results and 90 percent click within the first three pages.[22] Data leaked from AOL shows that first-page rankings are even more important, as 90 percent of clicks within that data set were on the first page of results.[23]

You can see more specifically how your site performs by looking at Google Webmaster Tools data, which display where your site ranks for top queries and what the click-through rate is for each. As you can see with the example in Figure 3.18 for searchengineland.com, although the site is ranked in the first position for each of the listed queries, the click-through rate varies from 21 percent to 70 percent.

Breakdown of the Search Results Page According to a study by Bernard J. Jansen at Penn State University, 60 percent of searchers rely primarily on the title of the result when evaluating whether to click.[24]

And as we saw earlier in the eye-tracking heat maps, searchers don't even evaluate the entire title—they look primarily at the left half of it. The description displayed under the title and the URL also factor into what a searcher clicks on. Search engines bold words in all three places that match the query, which can draw a searcher's attention.

Query	Impressions	Change	Clicks	Change	CTR	Change ↓	Avg. position
cool things to search on google	170	↑ ∞	50	↑ ∞	29%	↑ 30	1.0
google tv player	170	↑ 962%	35	↑ ∞	21%	↑ 20	1.0
google 2.0	60	↓ -33%	30		50%	↑ 20	1.0
google scooby doo	50		35	↑ 17%	70%	↑ 10	1.0
cool things in google earth	110	↑ 817%	70	↑ ∞	64%	↑ 60	1.0

Figure 3.18   Varied Click-Through Rate for a Number One Ranking

Source: Google Webmaster Tools, SearchEngineLand.com

In the search results for the query [rheumatoid arthritis], searchers may focus in the second and third result, since the first part of those titles match the query (Figure 3.19).

Many businesses don't think about optimizing the description listed under the title of their search results, but that is your one opportunity to provide a compelling marketing message and entice potential customers to click. We'll take a closer look at these descriptions in Chapter 6.

Even worse than not optimizing the title and description of your listing is not providing them at all. For instance, see the search results display of some high-profile brands that have spent considerable ad dollars on offline campaigns that have spurred search volume.

With the Sprint listing in Figure 3.20, for instance, no description appears and the title is less than helpful.

And in Figure 3.21, the text that compels searchers to click is from an Atlas tracking code.

Verizon doesn't do much better (Figure 3.22).

Patient Education - **Rheumatoid Arthritis**
www.rheumatology.org › ... › DISEASES AND CONDITIONS
While **rheumatoid arthritis** (RA) has long been feared as one of the most disabling types of arthritis, the outlook has dramatically improved for many newly ...

Rheumatoid Arthritis
labtestsonline.org/understanding/conditions/rheumatoid/
Oct 13, 2011 – Overview of **rheumatoid arthritis**, a chronic autoimmune disorder that usually affects the joints, and related laboratory tests.

Rheumatoid Arthritis - Your Orthopaedic Connection - AAOS
orthoinfo.aaos.org/topic.cfm?topic=A00211
Aching joints are common in arthritis. In **rheumatoid arthritis**, the joint lining swells, invades surrounding tissues, and produces chemical substances that attack ...

CDC - Arthritis - Basics - Definition - **Rheumatoid Arthritis**
www.cdc.gov/**arthritis**/basics/**rheumatoid**.htm
Sep 1, 2011 – **Rheumatoid arthritis** (RA) causes premature mortality, disability and compromised quality of life in the industrialized and developing world (1). ...

Figure 3.19   Analyzing Search Snippets

Source: Google Search

Sprint | NFL ⬆⊠
www.sprintenterprise.com/NFL/ - 4k - Cached - Similar pages - 💬

Figure 3.20 Poor Search Results Display
Source: Google Search

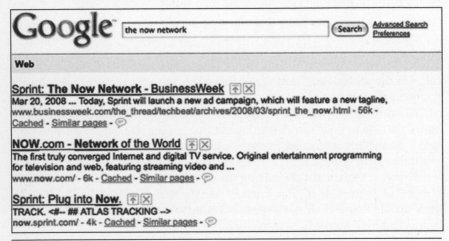

Figure 3.21 Broken Code Impacting Search Results Display
Source: Google Search

Enhancing Your Results We can see that descriptive, compelling search results can help motivate a click, and you can take further advantage of how the search engines are evolving the way these results are displayed.

Google in particular has rolled out a number of enhancements called "rich snippets," and Google and Bing launched a joint project called schema .org[25] to provide standards for marking up content to be used in enhanced search results.

In Figure 3.23, you can see two examples of enhanced display in Google's search results. The first result uses markup called "rel=author" to include the author's name, photo, and Google+ details. The second result includes short links to popular articles and the number of times that page has been "+1'd."

Verizon
Residential
www22.verizon.com/wireless · Cached page

Figure 3.22 Even Large Brands Can Have Poor Search Results Descriptions
Source: Google Search

Yahoo Deletes 75000 **Associated Content ...** - **Search Engine Land**
searchengineland.com/yahoo-deletes-75000-associated-cont...
 by Matt McGee - In 11,833 Google+ circles
1 day ago – **Yahoo** is cleaning up **Associated Content** by deleting some of the
articles, moving the keepers to **Yahoo's** domain and giving the site a new ...

Search Engine Land: Must Read News About Search Marketing ...
searchengineland.com/
2 days ago – **Search Engine Land** is a must read hub for news and information about
... **Yahoo** is cleaning up **Associated Content** by deleting some of the ...
Google: Bing Is Cheating, Copying ... - What Is SEO? - News - What is SEM?
2,962 people +1'd this

Figure 3.23   Google's Enhanced Results
Source: Google Search

The details of these programs go beyond the scope of this book, but refer to Chapter 7 for suggestions about how you can ensure your Web developers are taking full advantage of these initiatives and see marketingintheageof google.com for additional resources.

How important is it to take advantage of enhancing your results with descriptive titles, rich snippets, breadcrumbs, and other details?

When Yahoo! operated its own search engine (it now uses Bing's), it had a program called SearchMonkey that enabled Web developers to include additional details such as photos, links, ratings, and store hours to the listing.

Amit Kumar, of Yahoo!'s SearchMonkey, stated, "Our tests uncovered that users found these [SearchMonkey] apps useful; in fact, in some cases, we saw a lift in click-through rate of as high as 15 percent."[26]

■ HOW SEARCHERS EVALUATE THE PAGE THEY'VE CLICKED ON

We can judge a site visually in as little as 50 milliseconds.[27] And when performing a task, we focus on that and become blind to anything else. Even if visitors to a site look directly at something, they may not see it at all if it doesn't obviously apply to their task.

This behavior correlates well with customer behavior in a store. In *Why We Buy*, Paco Underhill describes how shoppers enter stores. They don't stop at the front door and look around. They walk in and scan as they go. Much of what they see during this transition is lost on them.[28]

Even in physical stores, shoppers scan words quickly. "Putting a sign that requires 12 seconds to read in a place where customers spend four seconds is just slightly more effective than putting it in your garage," says Underhill.

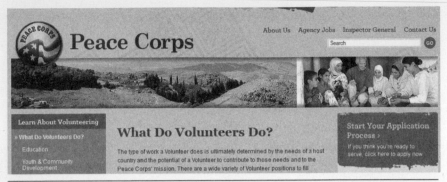

Figure 3.24 Peace Corps Website Visitor Experience
Source: Peacecorps.gov

Product placement can help maximize sales both in stores and on your site. The salsa will sell better next to the chips than next to the mustard.

A vital part of search acquisition success is knowing what page the searcher lands on and how easily the searcher can scan the page and recognize that it answers his or her query.[29]

Consider the query [what do Peace Corps volunteers do]. It leads searchers to a page that clearly answers the searcher's question. The context and purpose of the page are clear on even a quick scan (Figure 3.24).

► From Page to Conversion

Once the searcher lands on your page and confirms the content will satisfy the search, make sure the page will also fulfill the business need and not simply lead to a dead end. In the next chapter, we'll dive into the details of developing searcher personas, which include pinpointing company goals and ensuring that those are presented as clear calls to action on the page. In the case of the Peace Corps example in Figure 3.24, we can see that the page has a clear and obvious call to action with the Start Your Application Process link.

In contrast, consider the PEAK6 recruiting page shown in Figure 3.25. It not only doesn't provide a clear heading to anchor the visitor about the context of the page, but the primary business purpose for creating the page at all (gathering job applicants) is hidden in a tiny link at the bottom of the page that is easily overlooked.

An effective way to intersect searcher interest and business needs—and thereby identify key audience segments—is by building searcher personas (see Chapter 4). You can then map out a compelling conversion path for these personas by way of searcher conversion workflows. You can use these workflows to determine key points of collaboration between departments of your organization.

Figure 3.25 PEΛK6's Call to Action Is Unclear

Source: PEAK6.com

CHAPTER 3 RESOURCES: HOW WE SEARCH

- Google Search (results, related searches, and search suggest) www.google.com
- Bing Search (results and related searches) www.bing.com
- Yahoo Search (related searches) search.yahoo.com
- Microsoft Advertising Intelligence advertising.microsoft .com/small-business/adcenter-downloads/ microsoft-advertising-intelligence
- Google Ad Planner www.google.com/adplanner
- Alexa www.alexa.com
- Google Correlate www.google.com/trends/correlate

Chapter 4

Building Searcher Personas

Opening the Door to the Crowd of Customers You've Been Keeping Out

By now you have learned how to use search data to improve your overall product and business strategies and seen the value of developing a search acquisition strategy. Next, we'll put these pieces together by using what you've learned about your business and potential customers to create searcher personas and search acquisition workflows that harness the power of search data for opening a whole new channel of acquisition.

Your customers are already looking for what you have to offer, but they often aren't searching specifically for your brand. If your site doesn't appear for their nonbranded searches, you could very well fall off their consideration list.

If you're doing offline advertising and not ensuring your brand shows up for the subsequent search traffic that advertising triggers, you may as well be running TV commercials but keeping the store locked up with no way for customers to get in.

Remember those old Mervyn's super sale ads in which the crowds of customers stood outside the closed store chanting, "Open, open, open"? That's exactly what's happening when you don't ensure organic search is a fundamental part of your customer acquisition strategy. Your audience is standing at the door, and you're not letting them in.

■ SEARCH ACQUISITION STRATEGY PROCESS

As you probably realize by now, a successful search acquisition strategy involves more than just someone at the company with the job title of search engine optimizer (see Chapter 6 for more details about search engine

O] and how it ties into a successful search strategy). A suc-
olves:

- ...suring all business and product goals are aligned and using search data as a key part of market research.
- Identifying a target audience that is most likely to turn into customers.
- Determining the queries that fit your business needs and are conducted by your target audience in significant volumes.
- Building content that not only ranks well for those queries but also provides a user experience that helps searchers complete their tasks and engages them more deeply with your business.
- Offering a call to action that compels the searcher deeper into the conversion funnel.
- Understanding what metrics provide actionable insights into the effectiveness of the strategy.

This process involves the following steps:

- Identify your business goals:
  ⇒ What is the business's purpose?
  ⇒ What is the website's purpose?
- Assess the market opportunity:
  ⇒ Based on keyword research, what searches are relevant to your business?
  ⇒ What's the overall volume?
- Assess the conversion potential:
  ⇒ What queries will drive conversion (based on your business goals)?
  ⇒ Who is the target audience?
  ⇒ What's the competitive landscape?
- Create a tactical plan.
- Develop searcher personas.
- Develop search conversion workflows:
  ⇒ Build a content strategy based on the searcher personas and search conversion workflows.
- Execute the technical implementation (see Chapter 7).
- Monitor progress.
- Identify actionable metrics (see Chapter 8).
- Create rollout and adjustment strategies.

Identify Your Business Goals It's important to have a clear sense of your business goals in mind as you embark on developing a search strategy (because they provide context for using the search data you collect), identifying your target audience segments, and building a conversion workflow that supports those overall goals.

In a 2011 Econsultancy/SEMPO survey of U.S. companies and search marketing agencies,[1] the most common primary stated objective from companies for SEO was driving website traffic (beating out generating leads and selling products). But driving traffic is not a business goal. You want to drive the right traffic to the right pages and convert those visitors into customers.

Consider both your primary and secondary business goals. For instance, in the case of the Napa Valley B&B, the primary business goal is to keep the rooms fully booked, but it's also important to book those rooms at a profitable price, to engage with guests so they have a good experience and return often (and tell their friends), and to make as much information available to them as possible in advance to reduce manual overhead (such as providing directions, recommendations, and assistance with booking wine tours).

It's also important to set concrete goals for the website. It's not enough to say that the goal of the website is to give your business an online presence. That's not a goal that you can measure, nor is it something that can align all of the departments in the organization toward a common purpose. For our B&B, website goals might include the following:

- Generate leads for offline bookings.
- Enable online bookings.
- Provide answers to frequently asked questions from guests.

We can measure these goals using data points such as:

- Increase the number of offline bookings by 10 percent over six months.
- Book 10 bookings online per month.
- Reduce number of phone calls asking for directions by 50 percent.

A great first step in the goal-articulation process is to step way back and remember what your company is all about at the most basic level. Start your goal discussions by remembering why your company exists: What are you trying to do? Who are you trying to do it for?

Based on your goals, you can build searcher personas that identify the key queries and target audiences that will help you reach them.

Assess the Market Opportunity   We've seen in Chapter 2 how to dive into search data to discover who your customers are, what they're looking for, what the overall industry trends are, and what the competitive landscape looks like.

You can use this data to construct an initial set of target searches.

For every category of content on the site now and for every type of new content you plan to introduce, answer these questions. You should have most of the answers based on the research we've just done.

- What are my business goals (and conversion goals)?
- Who in the target audience is most likely to convert?
- What is this target audience searching for?
- What searches are most likely to lead to conversions?
- What content best meets audience needs for those identified searches?
- What information will compel those visitors to convert?

Evaluate Site Pages for Alignment with Content Strategy Another way of using this information is evaluating the pages currently on the site and any proposed pages. Ask the following questions:

- What are you trying to accomplish with each page?
- Who are you trying to attract?
- What is that audience searching for?
- Will this page satisfy that search?
- What's the call to action?
- Will this page compel the audience to convert?

Assess the Conversion Potential Based on your business goals, searcher data, and competitive landscape, you can refine the initial list of target searches to subsets that are most likely to convert and that are reasonable areas for your business to initially compete in. For example, [cheap Viagra] searches have high value and volume, but you'll face strong competition if you choose that as your initial market. On the other hand, [pictures of cute bunnies] may have fairly low competition, but there's not much money to be made in bunny photography.

Create a Tactical Plan Now we've made it to the core of the work. You've identified a core set of searches and have a good understanding of audience and competitive landscape. You know what actions you'd like those searchers to take once they reach your site. The next step is to develop searcher personas and search conversion workflows that will help you build a content strategy. The rest of this chapter dives into searcher personas and search conversion workflows.

Monitor Progress Search strategy is an iterative process. One of the most powerful aspects of search as an acquisition channel is that you are provided with near real-time feedback about what's working and what's not. (In Chapter 8, I describe how to measure success and monitor actionable metrics for adjustments after launch.)

Creating Searcher Personas A *persona* is a highly detailed description of an individual who embodies key goals and behaviors of an important group of target customers. Typically, a project team will create a set of prioritized personas and use them to drive decisions throughout a design process. Product design personas are built to embody the "differences that make a difference" between the goals and needs of various intended users of a product or service; searcher personas should capture the "differences that make a difference" in the ways target customers search for (and find) the things you are offering.[2]

Product design personas help organizations build products, sites, and services that make sense once the customer or user starts using them; in the case of a website, for example, design personas help teams craft the paths visitors take once they arrive. Searcher personas will help you get the visitors to the site in the first place. In effect, they help you begin the user experience design well before the potential customer reaches your site or store and, indeed, before that customer may even have your brand in mind.

Searcher personas also provide snapshots of your potential customers at different phases of the buying cycle. Since searcher personas can describe both a particular searcher demographic (moms who are looking for safe cars that can fit two children and two adults) as well as a potential customer in a particular part of the purchase cycle (preretirement couples who are researching the best places to live once they retire versus those same couples once they have retired and are ready to move), they are flexible constructs that you can modify to best meet your needs.

Note that searcher personas aren't different from product design personas; they're simply descriptions of those same personas earlier in the process of interacting with your brand and products.

When developing searcher personas, you generally classify and identify search query categories from the list of queries you've built. For instance, O'Reilly, which produces technical books and conferences, might begin with the following query categories:

- *Navigational/branded queries:* These include variations of the domain and brand, such as [oreilly], [oreilly.com], and [oreilly website]. These queries may also include existing book series names such as [head first].
- *Code queries:* These are searches for information about coding-related topics. The searcher may be looking for anything that answers the question or may be specifically looking for a book, conference, or forum/blog. In this case, O'Reilly will want to investigate if it makes sense to set up a separate conversion path for books, conferences, and forums or if it would serve these searchers better to have a topic landing page ("All About AJAX") that links to the various components available for that topic (such as conference, books, forums, and latest blog posts). Queries along these lines include [Blackberry hacks], [C# design patterns], [C# cookbook], [iPhone development].
- *Book-specific queries:* These could include writing-related queries such as [book writing] and [how to write a book].

- *Author searches:* Searches for author names can likely be aggregated into one persona type. It may make sense to build out author pages with bio information, links to related sites, books written, and upcoming speaking events.

Next, perform query category analysis. Aggregate the list of queries for each category, and then determine the market opportunity, search volume, competition, and conversion potential. This information will vary for each category and is useful information for later success metrics. For each query category, assess the following:

- What are the related keywords for the category?
- What are the highest-volume keywords for each category?
- Does the site rank for any of these terms now? If so, which pages?
- What is the intent of these searchers?
- What are the current ranking, bounce rate, number of pages viewed, and other conversion event metrics?
- What's the competitive analysis for the category?

Tamara Adlin, author of *The Persona Lifecycle: Keeping People in Mind throughout Product Design*

To identify the audiences for your query categories, try completing an "I want/I need" exercise that's used in an ad hoc persona creation process I developed with John Pruitt. Gather your team in a room and hand out sticky notes. Ask everyone to spend a few minutes writing a person + situation on each sticky note. For example, the O'Reilly team might create sticky notes like these:

> Coder looking for a code snippet
>
> Professor trying to find the best book to use for his upcoming class
>
> *Wired* reader who remembers an author name from an article she read
>
> Marketer who heard something about a "polar bear book"
>
> Student who needs bibliographic details to include in a paper
>
> Aspiring author wondering who might print his book idea
>
> etc.

After everyone has written as many pairings on stickies as they can think of (typically, each person in the room will come up with at least 20), have everyone cluster the stickies on a large sheet of paper.

To do the clustering, use a different color sticky note and create "I want . . ." or "I need . . ." category labels. In the O'Reilly example, the team might come up with:

Category: "I need an answer to a question I have right now."

Stickies—Coder looking for a code snippet; student who needs bibliographic details to include in a paper

Category: "I want to find a book I heard about."

Wired reader who remembers an author name from an article she read

Category: "I'm interested in learning about publishing."

Aspiring author wondering who might print his book idea

etc.

The category labels you come up with can form the foundation for your searcher personas and can be a good way to do the query classification.

Once you have begun to categorize your audience into searcher personas, you can define the audience for each query category by answering the following questions:

- What do you know about this category of searchers?
- What does success look like for them?
- How can you help them accomplish their tasks?
- What conversion goal applies to them, and what is the likelihood of conversion?
- What stage of the buying cycle are they in? Are they researching? Intending to purchase?
- How can you compel them to conversion?
- What is the lifetime value of this searcher? (This last question is a stretch that most companies haven't quite figured out, so if you haven't gotten there yet, don't worry! Just know that it's useful data to compile once you're able to.)

You may end up with something like Figure 4.1.

Creating Searcher Conversion Workflows Once you've created searcher personas for each query category (and audience type, if applicable), you can turn that information into an optimal searcher conversion workflow. When writing

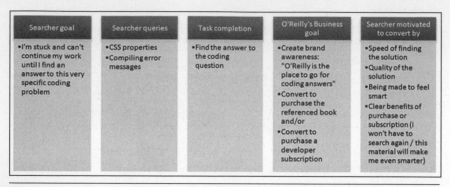

Searcher goal	Searcher queries	Task completion	O'Reilly's Business goal	Searcher motivated to convert by
•I'm stuck and can't continue my work until I find an answer to this very specific coding problem	•CSS properties •Compiling error messages	•Find the answer to the coding question	•Create brand awareness: "O'Reilly is the place to go for coding answers" •Convert to purchase the referenced book and/or •Convert to purchase a developer subscription	•Speed of finding the solution •Quality of the solution •Being made to feel smart •Clear benefits of purchase or subscription (I won't have to search again / this material will make me even smarter)

Figure 4.1   Creating a Searcher Persona

the first edition of this book, I came up with the illustration in Figure 4.2 to visualize the process from query to search engine results page (SERP) to conversion.

Since then, I've continued working on ways to integrate search into all other elements of product strategy and user interaction. Figure 4.3 is an illustration that takes this more holistic approach into account.

For your search acquisition strategy to be effective, all phases of this workflow must be in place.

- *Who your audience is:* You need to understand your customers and what they're searching for (identified in the searcher persona definitions). You can use search data, such as described in the earlier chapters, to better understand your customers, as well as incorporate all other market research and what your audiences are talking about on social media

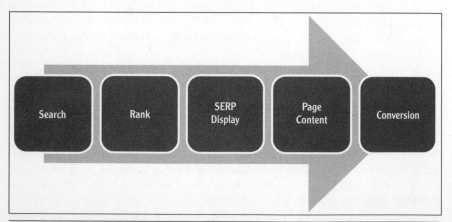

Figure 4.2   Searcher Persona Workflow

Figure 4.3 Integrated Persona Workflow

sites (see Chapter 9) to better know what your customers need and what problems they are trying to solve.

- *Where your audience is:* Your site has to rank well for the queries your target audience is searching for (see Chapter 5), but you should also make sure you are engaging those audiences where they are, whether that's via search engines, social media sites, or someplace else. Each organization's customers are different, and you shouldn't, for instance, invest all of your time on Facebook just because Facebook has a lot of users. Are *your* customers using Facebook to seek what you offer?
- *What your audience wants:* The key is to solve your customers' problems. From a search perspective:
  - The *search results display* must compel searchers to click through to your site.
  - The *page content* that the searcher clicks to should be quickly identifiable as relevant to the searcher's task.
  - The page should *propel the visitor to conversion* with an effective call to action.

Once you've outlined searcher conversion workflows for each searcher persona, you can create a content strategy that takes full advantage of the search opportunity. (You'll learn how best to build this strategy in Chapter 6.)

➤ What Queries to Target

When options brokerage PEAK6 decided to branch out and provide educational information about the stock market to novice investors, they created a virtual trading space that enabled visitors to practice investing with no real money at stake.

Knowing that to learn about the stock market and to invest can be daunting to some (and—sorry brokers!—boring to others), they built WeSeed.com, educational content around topics that got people excited and related those topics to the stock market:

- Excited about that new Apple iPhone? Learn how the release impacted Apple stock.
- Psyched for the next Britney Spears tour? How has it impacted the stock of Sony Corporation, which owns her record label.

Sounds great, right? And it is. But they weren't gaining much traction in customer sign-ups. Looking at their Web analytics, it was clear that few visitors were coming from search, even though investment advice is likely a hot search topic.

Two of the areas we looked at were:

- How well were the visitors they *were* getting converting to customers?
- Was there a different product strategy that would attract more visitors?

We discovered some interesting data in the logs. Most visitors were searching for variations of "virtual stock market" and "stock market game." Although this is exactly what We Seed offers, that's not obvious from the pages those searchers were landing on.

Another large subset of searchers was looking for information on teaching their kids to invest, with queries such as [investing for kids] and [stocks for children]. We Seed hadn't considered creating a product that helped teach kids to invest.

We Seed already provided a section for educators, but it was aimed at those teaching at the university level. We considered adding a subsection to the site focused on elementary school teachers—giving them advice, sample games, and educational material they could provide to their students.

We also looked into creating a stock market game that parents could play with their children. Expanding into this product had several advantages. The parents would control the user accounts, so although the kids would be playing, they wouldn't need accounts of their own. We Seed could take advantage of the visitor traffic they were already getting from search and acquire more traffic, which would in turn add activity to the site. And the parents would be introduced to We Seed and the PEAK6 suite of products, which might motivate some of them to sign up for We Seed or PEAK6 accounts.

Determining value to the business is key. A site could build out a number of content and product areas based on search volumes and analytics data. And that would likely add substantial search traffic to the site. But the point behind acquiring search traffic is to convert those visitors to customers. Would building out a section for kids result in conversion?

The process to determine the answer is the same as for any business. Will adding a pool result in the gym seeing more memberships? Will fixing that leaky roof get the house sold quicker?[3]

When I ask business owners what their site goals are, they tell me things like, "I want to increase my site traffic by 50 percent" and "I want to rank number one for this particular keyword." But neither of those is a site goal. Those are both steps that can lead to the goal, but neither is the reason behind the site.

In the case of We Seed, conversion goals are hard to pin down. The site doesn't generate revenue—it doesn't sell anything, display ads, or sell memberships. The site simply produces educational content.

Since the site was already getting search traffic for queries related to [investing for kids] without having a targeted product for those visitors (as it ranks on the first page for those queries), odds are that we could vastly increase that traffic fairly easily by focusing on that product strategy.

We also determined that parents who were interested enough in the stock market to want to play an online stock game with their kids that teaches kids investing were a good audience that aligned with the site's goals: increasing awareness of the PEAK6 brand and positioning it as an authoritative thought leader on investment-related advice by providing educational content.

Looking at the competitive landscape, there's room for a better product choice. The top-ranking site on Google is called "Investing for Kids," but its content doesn't seem to be targeted to kids, and it appears to be abandoned. It appears to be ranking because the site contains a lot of content and the title of the site matches the query. The next few sites are article-based sites, also mostly abandoned. There don't seem to be any sites that provide easy-to-use educational content for parents and kids with a game component. Related queries such as "educational games kids investing" list articles from 2001.

By using Google AdWords Keyword Tool, we found that the top three related search queries were:

- Stocks for kids
- Kids stock market
- For kids stock market

None of these queries had significant competition, so the market seemed a good bet for expansion. Looking more closely at the search data, we can begin to paint a more detailed picture of the persona we're targeting. Some searchers want to explain the stock market to kids. Another set of searchers is looking to buy stock *for* their kids, so we decided to exclude it from our targeting. Later, we could expand into educational content around that topic to reach additional searchers.

Next, we did searches for the identified queries to see what the search results would tell us about this audience. Many of the related searches at the bottom of the search results page are about *teaching* kids about the stock market.

WeSeed.com now has data about a potential new target audience, just from looking at search data and their Web analytics. So should they drop their current strategy and redirect their business efforts toward kids? Not so fast.

Remember, this research also uncovered a key segment of their existing business strategy that they weren't taking advantage of during searches for virtual
stock markets and stock market games. Those searchers are a great audience
for the existing content on WeSeed.com and are likely highly qualified. We
Seed chose to start there and will consider new audiences once they've
reached this group who are already searching for exactly what they offer.

But you can see how looking at search data can help you uncover new
potential avenues of connecting with an audience and directions your product
strategy could go.

➤ Ensuring Each Page Has a Clear and Valuable Call to Action

Every business wants to achieve its goals and doesn't want to invest substantial
resources on acquiring an audience to whom it doesn't even offer the chance
to convert. But you might be surprised at how easily it can be to overlook the
last step in the search conversion workflow—the conversion itself.

Take a look at the website for Kasbah Tamadot ("Sir Richard Branson's
Moroccan Resort") in Figure 4.4. Presumably, the resort's primary business
goal for the website is new bookings, but the page showcasing the rooms has
no strong call to action encouraging visitors to make a reservation. In fact, it's
difficult for the visitor to know where to click to do so.

Consider the reviews page for the Turtle Nest Inn in the Cayman Islands.
Although the page shown in Figure 4.5 ranks number one for several related
queries, it may not be doing the inn much good, as the page not only includes
no way to make a reservation but has no navigation at all. Visitors can't get to
the home page or any other page of the site.

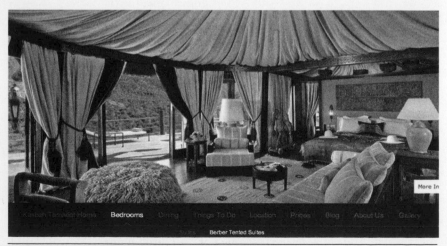

Figure 4.4   Kasbah Tamadot Lack of Call to Action
Source: www.kasbahtamadot.virgin.com

- *"We had a lovely stay at the Inn. It is cozy & intimate. Diving at the East End was great. Our hosts were very sweet and helpful." J.B.&G.B., Chatham, New Jersey, USA (August 31, 2000)*

- *"Dear Marleine & Alain: Thank you for creating such a wonderful place. We spent 8 days here for our 16th Anniversary and everything was perfect. The Caribbean Night dinner on Tuesday was fantastic. Marleine, you are an excellent chef! We hope to return someday with our children to share your place with them. We will highly recommend the TNI to everyone we know! Thanks!" E.B.&A.B., Souderton, Pennsylvania, USA (August 29, 2000)*

- *"Thanks for one of the most relaxing vacations ever. The hospitality & tranquility are unsurpassed." B.R.&K.R., Damascus, Maryland, USA (August 28, 2000)*

- *"Wow! If only we had known how wonderful this place would be, we would have made longer reservations. As honeymooners, we were looking for peace & tranquility and we found it here at the Inn." Bronx, New York, USA (August 27, 2000)*

> Since opening, Turtle Nest Inn has had the honour of welcoming residents of Argentina, Austria, Belgium, Bermuda, Brazil, Canada, Cayman Islands, Costa Rica, England, France, Germany, Italy, Jamaica, Scotland, Singapore, South Africa, Spain, Wales and the United States.

- *"Dear M and A: This is our third stay at the TNI and it is always delightful. Thanks for a great dinner on Friday night and another hospitable and relaxing stay. With best wishes!" B.L.&L.L., Baltimore, Maryland, USA (August 27, 2000)*

Figure 4.5   Turtle Nest Inn Page as the Entry Page of the Site

Source: www.turtlenestinn.com/inns-travel-G0800.htm

➤ Harnessing the Long Tail

One benefit of categorizing queries is that it helps you harness the long tail of search. The concept of the "long tail" was popularized by Chris Anderson's book by the same name.[4] The idea as it applies to search acquisition is that up to 80 percent of visitors might come from low-volume queries. For instance, in the case of O'Reilly, the site may get 100 visitors a day from the query [oreilly], and only two visitors a day from the query [conference about Java-Script for e-commerce websites]. However, the site may also get two visitors a day from [JavaScript conference for implementing product lists on the Web] and three visitors a day from [how to use JavaScript to build product pages]. In aggregate, the site may get 1,000 visits a day from conference-related queries, 1,500 visits a day from JavaScript-related queries, and 1,200 visits a day from e-commerce-related queries. So whereas individually, the two visits may seem insignificant, in aggregate, the visits from the low-volume query categories far outweigh the traffic from the highest-volume individual search.

Although the resource investment for monitoring each individual query and providing content for it isn't reasonable, monitoring and building content for categories of queries is a manageable and worthwhile investment.

➤ The Hotel without a Sign: Branded Search and the Importance of Title Tags

I stayed in a small town in Ireland recently, and some friends and I drove through the main street, looking for a hotel we had decided to check out. (The town was too small for individual addresses. Instead, every business simply listed its name and the name of the town.) At one end of the village, we saw a large sign with a huge arrow pointing toward the direction of the hotel.

Aha. We had come to the beginning of the search funnel. We had a need (to get hotel rooms), and we knew the answer to that need (the specific hotel). That huge arrow was the beginning of our search.

But that's where things started to go off course. We drove down a small windy road with several forks, but no more signs for the hotel. We pressed ahead toward the water, thinking surely the hotel would be in that direction. The road ended at a parking lot for a large building that appeared abandoned. It vaguely resembled a hotel. The only sign was a small one over the door that read "hotel entrance" (Figure 4.6.).

Was this in fact the hotel we were looking for? Whether it was or not, it was going to be our hotel for the night. Even though we were on a branded search (a search for a particular brand), the path wasn't clear. Had we seen another hotel on the way, we likely would have just stopped there, since we didn't have much confidence that we were going the right way. And we were resigned to staying at this hotel whether it was the right one or not. But apparently the hotel assumed everyone would just know where and who they were.

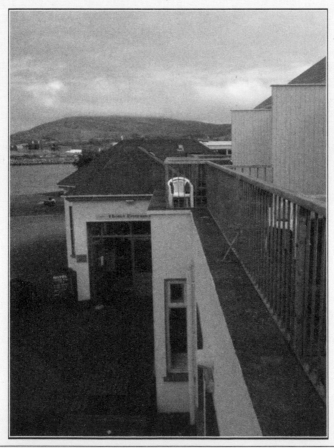

Figure 4.6   Is This the Hotel We Were Looking For?

Top 5 Paid and Organic Search Terms among All U.S. Websites				
Rank	Paid Terms	Clicks	Organic Terms	Clicks
1	ebay	0.12%	myspace	0.78%
2	ebay.com	0.02%	craigslist	0.42%
3	home depot	0.02%	myspace.com	0.29%
4	map quest	0.01%	youtube	0.26%
5	people search	0.01%	ebay	0.23%
Note - data is based on the percentage of paid and organic clicks generated by all search terms within all industry Categories for a four-week period ending Aug. 30, 2008 based off of the Hitwise sample of U.S. Internet users.				
Source: Hitwise				

Figure 4.7 Top Search Terms

Source: Hitwise.com[6]

Can your site be found for searches for your brand? In a recent study, 55 percent of business-to-business buyers said that they would navigate to a site they already knew through search. You can see this trend in the top search terms.[5] All are branded (Figure 4.7). And many of the top retail terms for November 2011 (the beginning of the holiday shopping season) are branded as well (Figure 4.8).

Top 10 Retail Fast Mover Terms

The following report shows **search terms** for the custom category **'Top 500 Retail sites'**, ranked by **largest increase** for the **week** ending **11/26/2011**, compared with the **week** ending **11/19/2011**. (Filters applied)

Rank	Search Term	Volume	Change
1.	lcd televisions	0.03%	New
2.	jenny mccarthy	0.02%	New
3.	cyber monday sales	0.01%	New
4.	2011 lowes black friday …	0.01%	New
5.	online black friday deals	0.01%	New
6.	2011 jc penney black friday	0.01%	New
7.	macy black friday 2011 ad	0.01%	New
8.	calphalon convection oven	0.01%	New
9.	black friday 2011 best bu…	0.01%	New
10.	radio shack black friday …	0.01%	New

Figure 4.8 Top 10 Retail Fast-Mover Terms

Source: Hitwise.com

Enquiro Research has found that if a brand the searcher hadn't previously considered shows up in results, it is added to a consideration set 40 percent of the time.[7] And a brand not listed may be dropped from a consideration set. So, appearing in results is important even if the searcher doesn't click. In fact, Enquiro Research found a 16 percent lift in brand awareness when the brand appeared in both the top organic and top paid positions (versus appearing in neither). When searchers were asked if they remembered seeing brands in the search results, fewer than 30 percent did if the brand was only in a paid search ad, but nearly 60 percent did when the brand appeared on top of both paid and organic results. The study also found that appearance in the organic results only versus the paid results causes only more brand lift.

And the positive brand perception doesn't stop at just recall. A 2006 iProspect and JupiterResearch study found that 36 percent of those surveyed felt that "seeing a company listed among the top results on a search engine makes me think that the company is a top one within its field."

Organic search should have a clear place in your brand awareness strategy. Visibility for your brand name, domain name, and primary tagline in organic searches should be a key requirement for any website initiative or advertising campaign. A quick search for [just do it] on the major search engines illustrates how this can easily go wrong even for large brands with a long-standing tagline (Figure 4.9).[8]

Review the result of the top 10 organic search results for your brand. If negative items exist, can you add positive content to the Web (for example, through social media, video and images, blog posts, interviews or articles on other sites, conference appearances, or media mentions) that could have the opportunity of outranking that negative content? Google calls this "proactively publishing information."[9]

Ensure any project that you do with an outside agency has organic search visibility as a project goal.

Track customer acquisition from branded organic search separately from other types of organic search and, if possible, track how the volume is influenced by other branding initiatives (such as display advertising).

You've Been Warned. Search: 2012 Sony Pictures built a marketing campaign around the movie *2012* that centered on search. Billboards cropped up sporting the cryptic message: "You've been warned. Search: 2012." The Search: 2012 tagline also was incorporated into other campaign elements, such as the movie trailer (Figure 4.10).

At least in some cases, the campaign worked. A screenshot of the search results for [*2012*] on Flickr includes the description, "Spotted a billboard off the 405 South in Gardena hyping the movie with this headline above ["You've been warned. Search: 2012"]. So of course I had to see what the fuss was all about." (Figure 4.11)[10]

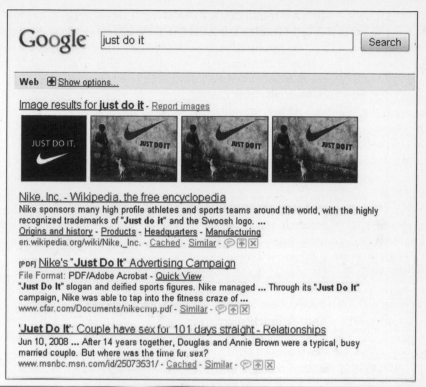

Figure 4.9   Google Search Results for [Just Do It]

Source: Google Search

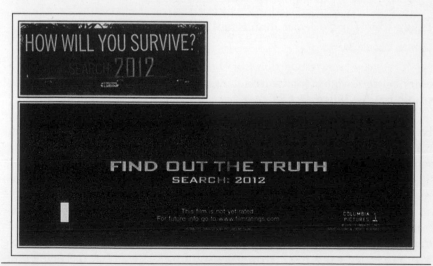

Figure 4.10   *2012* the Movie Search Campaign

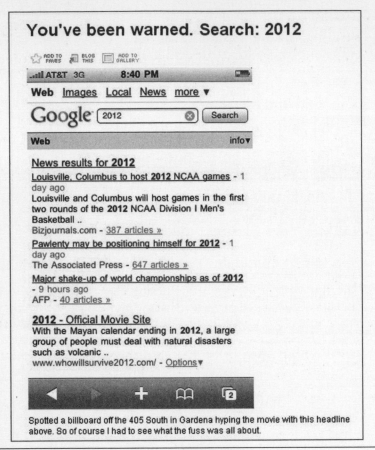

Figure 4.11 Google Search Results for [2012]

Source: Google Search

Google Insights for Search confirmed that the campaigns triggered search interest (Figure 4.12).

Sony Pictures could have further used Google Insights for Search to see how well the campaign did at a regional level by comparing search volume across cities to the billboard, television advertising, and other investments regionally (Figure 4.13).

Unlike Hyundai, which, as we saw earlier, didn't appear in organic search results at all for the tagline they were promoting, the *2012* movie site appeared number one on Google during the promotion. Sony Pictures clearly was more focused on understanding how to be visible in organic search. However, including only the search term and not a website address in marketing material seems like a risky advertising strategy. Organic search results positions can't be guaranteed and are always fluctuating. And Sony Pictures added

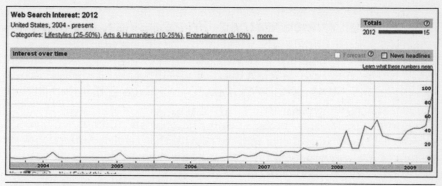

Figure 4.12   [2012] Search Trends
Source: Google Insights for Search

to the risk by creating an all-Flash site, which, as we'll learn in Chapter 7, can be problematic.

Google does a much better job at indexing Flash than Microsoft Bing, which could have contributed to the fact that the movie site did not rank number one on Bing. Sony Pictures further created search issues by maintaining several identical sites. Google and Yahoo! listed whowillsurvive2012.com (which, from a branding perspective, is likely the site Sony Pictures is looking to promote). Microsoft, however, listed sonypictures.com/movies/2012, which was simply a duplicate site. Why is this such a problem? Beyond the branding confusion, promoting two identical sites means that the links from other sites will be split between both of them (and in fact, as of this writing, both sites had approximately the same number of links). As a result, whowillsurvive2012.com had half the link value it otherwise would, and the site may never have achieved the rankings it otherwise would. (See Chapter 5 for more information on how external links impact rankings.)

Regional interest		ⓘ Subregion Metro City
1. Richardson	100	
2. Los Angeles	96	
3. Milpitas	95	
4. Sterling	90	
5. New York	89	
6. Irvine	84	
7. Miami	84	
8. Houston	93	
9. Phoenix	83	
10. Orlando	82	

Figure 4.13   [2012] Regional Search Trends
Source: Google Insights for Search

Sony Pictures had additional obstacles since it chose to promote a search term that was already well covered online. The movie was about a real theory, which is the potential end of the world in 2012 as evidenced by the end of the Mayan calendar. Numerous websites exist about this theory. Sony Pictures risked having those who searched based on seeing billboards clicking to survive2012.com or december212012.com and never realizing that the billboard was meant to promote a movie.

Fortunately for Sony Pictures, both Microsoft and Yahoo! had blended search elements that used data feeds to provide movie-related information at the top of any search page that appears to be for a movie.

Should advertising campaigns integrate organic search at all? Absolutely. Throughout this book, we've discussed how potential customers often turn to search first, so integrating it from the beginning meets your customers where they are. Keep the following in mind when incorporating organic search into an advertising campaign:

- Ensure someone on the team (whether that person is in-house or with the ad agency you're working with) fully understands the complexities of organic search, including content development, technical Web infrastructure, and external links.
- Assess the competitive landscape. If possible, drive search interest in a tagline that's not already well covered by unrelated sites.
- Unless it negatively impacts the campaign, include a website address and not simply a search term.
- When creating a plan for technical implementation, involve the organic search expert at every stage of the process and ensure you are accounting for all likely queries, including company name, product name, tagline, and website address.
- Have your organic search expert help design solutions for common issues, including:
  ⇒ Microsites that don't launch until the campaign starts, and, therefore, aren't available for search engine indexing in time for the initial searches
  ⇒ All-Flash sites that don't provide unique URLs and textual content for the search engines to index
  ⇒ Duplicate content that can slow down indexing and dilute link value (and subsequently, ranking)
  ⇒ Sites that redirect, preventing the promoted website address from ever being indexed

Now that we've identified whom to target through organic search and how to target them, let's learn a little more about how search engines work and how to build websites that searchers can easily find.

CHAPTER 4 CHECKLIST 1: BUILDING SEARCHER PERSONAS

❑ Refer to the business and website goals identified in Chapter 2.

❑ Gather the relevant keywords gathered in Chapter 2.

❑ Cluster keywords into categories based on topic and searcher intent.

❑ For each category, answer:

    ❑ What are these searchers trying to accomplish?

    ❑ What will help them accomplish this?

    ❑ What will compel them to conversion?

❑ For each category, identify the web page that satisfies the audience need.

❑ How does that web page display in search results (what is the title and description that will appear)?

❑ Does this page provide context about what the site is about?

❑ What on the page compels the visitor to conversion?

❑ What is the call to action?

CHAPTER 4 CHECKLIST 2: EVALUATING EXISTING WEB PAGES FOR STRATEGY ALIGNMENT

❑ What are you trying to accomplish with this page?

❑ What audience are you trying to attract?

❑ What is that audience searching for?

❑ Will this page best satisfy that search?

❑ Does this page provide context about what the site is about?

❑ What on the page compels the visitor to conversion?

❑ What is the call to action?

Chapter 5

How Search Engines Work

We've seen how searchers behave and how they interact with search results. We've decided what queries we want our sites to be found for. How do search engines compile these lists?

■ THE EVOLUTION OF SEARCH ENGINES

In the emerging days of the Web, directories were built to help users navigate to various websites. Generally, these directories were created by hand— people categorized websites so that users could browse to what they wanted. As the Web got larger, this effort became more difficult. Web spiders that "crawled" websites were created. Web spiders, also known as robots, are computer programs that follow links from known web pages to other web pages. These robots access those pages, download the contents of those pages (into a storage mechanism generically referred to as an "index"), and add the links found on those pages to their list for later crawling.

Although Web crawlers enabled the early search engines to have a larger list of sites than the manual method of collecting sites, they couldn't perform the other manual tasks of figuring out what the pages were about and ranking them in order of which ones were best. These search engines started working on computer programs that would help them do these things as well. For instance, computer programs could catalog all the words on a page to help figure out what those pages were about.

■ THE INTRODUCTION OF PAGERANK

Google's PageRank algorithm in 1998 was a big step forward in automatically cataloging and ranking websites.[1] This algorithm used data from the links on the Web to determine what pages were about and which pages were more popular and useful. Links were like votes for a site, and the text from those links was used for cataloging them.

For instance, consider two web pages. One is at the address www.my usedcars.com, and the other is at the address www.yourusedcars.com. Both contain text about cars and have the title "Used Cars." Five websites link to www.myusedcars.com. Three use the text "site about used cars," and two use the text "lots of used Fords" in the links. Ten sites link to www.yourusedcars .com. Five use the text "site about used cars," and the other five use the text "lots of used Hondas" in the links (Figure 5.1).

Google's PageRank algorithm would use the information from the links to determine that both sites were about used cars. But when someone searched for "used cars," Google might show www.yourusedcars.com first because it had twice as many links to it (10 versus 5). In addition, when someone searched for "used Fords," Google might show www.myusedcars.com, and when someone searched for "used Hondas, "Google might show www .yourusedcars.com.

Although Google patented the specific PageRank algorithm, this general method of categorizing sites became the standard for search engines and the basis of how search engine technology has evolved.

Although people still refer to PageRank as a major factor in ranking well in search engines, this reference is now simply shorthand for the hundreds of signals that search engines use to compile a list of the most relevant results

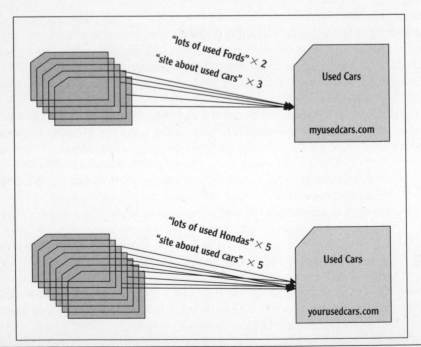

Figure 5.1   Anchor Text and Links Help Search Engines Understand Pages

possible for a query. We'll take a closer look at some of these signals throughout this chapter.

■ THE CURRENT STATE OF SEARCH ENGINES

As the Web has evolved, a vast number of search engines have launched. They
generally fall into one of the following categories:

- *Human-edited directories:* These are either constructed entirely by hand
  (as Yahoo! was originally) or constructed via a Web crawl or site owner
  submission and categorized and ranked by hand. Examples include the
  Open Directory Project (dmoz.org), About.com, and, more recently,
  Mahalo.com.
- *Automated search engines:* These are built algorithmically via Web
  crawlers and cataloged and ranked algorithmically as well. Since these
  types of search engines (such as Google) are the kind used by most
  searchers today, performing well in these is what this book focuses on.
- *Meta search engines (aggregators):* These search engines generally use
  results from other search engines and present them in a different way
  either by presenting the results from multiple other engines together
  (such as dogpile.com) or with a different visual look.

■ HOW SEARCH ENGINES WORK

The major search engines that account for most market share today are the
automated type: Google, Yahoo!, and Microsoft Bing[2] (although Yahoo! now
uses Bing's search index).[3]

Google and Bing, as well as other smaller search engines in the United
States that exist and operate their own technology, and search engines
throughout the world, have similar overall infrastructure as follows:

- Web crawlers crawl the Web. These crawlers follow links to discover
  the pages on the Web.
- Extraction processes gather information from those pages (such as textual content, metadata, and links).
- Indices stores the content from web pages. Content is generally stored
  using word-based keys, similar to the index in a book. When you look
  up a word in the index of a book, you learn the page number that word
  is on. Similarly, with a search engine index, the search engine can look
  up a word that someone is searching for and find out all the web pages
  associated with that word.
- Results are scored to determine what pages are the most relevant for
  each search. When someone does a search (called a query) and the

search engine checks the index for all the web pages associated with that search, the search engine needs a way to rank those web pages in an order that is useful for the searcher. Search engines use a number of factors in scoring, and these factors are adjusted all of the time based on new algorithms, tests, and other criteria. Search engines keep the details of these scoring factors secret. Once the search engine compiles and ranks the pages that are relevant for the query, it displays them in a list referred to as organic results. The ranking process happens at the time of the query.

■ THE DIFFERENCE BETWEEN ORGANIC AND PAID RESULTS

Search engines primarily make money via advertising, called paid search ads. These ads are also called pay per click (PPC) ads, because advertisers generally pay a certain amount each time a searcher clicks on them. For instance, Google's advertising program is called AdWords. The way the system works is that when someone does a search, the search engine shows two lists of results: organic and paid (Figure 5.2).

The organic results are based on the crawling, indexing, and results scoring infrastructure, and search engines strive to have the most comprehensive, relevant results they can to provide an optimal user experience. Most search engines (such as Google) don't accept payment for placement in the organic

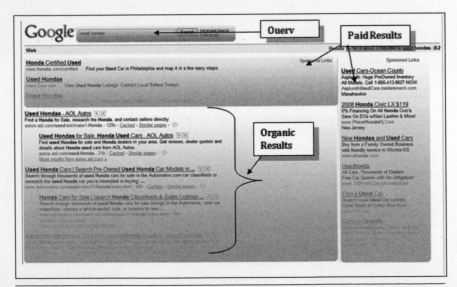

Figure 5.2   Google's Search Results Page

results and make no guarantees about whether a site is indexed and where that site will rank. The paid search ads appear next to the organic results, and although engines also attempt to show relevant, useful results in their ads, companies pay for them. Paid search ads are the primary source of income for search engines.

■ HOW SEARCH ENGINES RANK RESULTS

As Google noted in mid-2009:

> *Ranking is hard, much harder than most people realize. One reason for this is that languages are inherently ambiguous, and documents do not follow any set of rules. There are really no standards for how to convey information, so we need to be able to understand all web pages, written by anyone, for any reason. And that's just half of the problem. We also need to understand the queries people pose, which are on average fewer than three words, and map them to our understanding of all documents. Not to mention that different people have different needs. And we have to do all of that in a few milliseconds. . . . By some estimates, more than one thousand programmer/ scientist years have gone directly into their [search engines'] development, and the rate of innovation has not slowed down.*
> *The life span of a Google query normally lasts less than half a second, yet involves a number of different steps that must be completed before results can be delivered to a person seeking information.*[4]

Search engines use a number of factors to determine how to rank content. At a high level, search engines associate each set of content with a set of keywords they determine that content is about. When a searcher performs a query, the search engine retrieves all of the pages that are associated with that query, orders them according to relevance and usefulness (based on things like the number of relevant external links pointing to those pages, the anchor text of those external links, and calculations about intent—for instance, the search engine will try to show more e-commerce sites if the searcher intends to purchase something), and then ensures the resulting set of pages has sufficient diversity (doesn't include duplicates or doesn't consist of only sites of a single type).

■ HOW SEARCH ENGINES ARE USING DATA ABOUT SEARCHER INTENT

Over time, as search engines have gotten more confident about understanding intent, they've become more aggressive about displaying what they think the searchers want. Overall, this is a good thing because they're providing what searchers are looking for even more quickly, without requiring searchers to make extra choices. Most searchers aren't power users and just want to type the words into a search box and get back the results they're looking for with as little work as possible (remember bounded rationality?).

■ SEARCH ENGINE SUGGESTIONS AND PROMPTS

As noted earlier in the section on query refinements, search engines incorporate many methods for integrating browser navigation into the search experience to enable searchers to drill into what they're really searching for. These search prompts are typically based on past searcher behavior.

In 2010, Google launched Google Instant,[5] which not only predicts what searchers likely want as they type but shows the results of the predicted query before a searcher finishes typing it! Google says this saves time for the searcher, not only because the prediction is often correct, but also because when searchers see the predicted results, they can more quickly realize what types of refinements are necessary. Google described it this way:

> *Google Instant is search-before-you-type. Instant takes what you have typed already, predicts the most likely completion and streams results in real-time for those predictions—yielding a smarter and faster search that is interactive, predictive, and powerful.*
>
> *Our testing has shown that Google Instant saves the average searcher two to five seconds per search. That may not seem like a lot at first, but it adds up. With Google Instant, we estimate that we'll save our users 11 hours with each passing second!*

You can see this in Figure 5.3. The searcher has only typed "a," but Google has filled in the rest of the word ("amazon") in gray and has displayed

Figure 5.3   Google Instant Results

Source: Google Search

corresponding search results. As the searcher types additional letters, the predictions and search results change accordingly.

Paying attention to what the search engines suggest for topics important to your business can both give you insight into what your potential customers are really looking for and help you understand how your company should be represented in search results.

■ PERSONALIZATION

Search engines customize results based on individual searcher behavior. They continue to ramp up their efforts over time to understand not only searcher intent in aggregate but also intent for specific searchers.

Search engines need to provide relevant results to searchers (so that they'll keep coming back to that search engine and be an audience for its advertising); and because searchers provide few clues about what they're really looking for, we've seen that search engines use aggregate knowledge to discern meaning. But searchers are individuals, not the sum of their aggregated searches, so extrapolating the intent of one search based on the actions of all the searches that came before can rarely provide results as relevant as those tailored to the individual searcher.

Over the years, search engines have tried various customization options to enable searchers to take an active role in improving their results—everything from sliders to adjust ranking factors, filtering specific types of files, date ranges, and type of content.

But even though all of these could indeed improve results, for the most part, searchers have overwhelmingly ignored them. One reason for this goes back, again, to the idea of bounded rationality.

Usability expert Jakob Nielsen describes this tendency as follows:

> *The basic information foraging theory, which is, I think, the one theory that basically explains why the Web is the way it is, says that people want to expend minimal effort to gain their benefits. And this is an evolutionary point that has come about because the people, or the creatures who don't exert themselves, are the ones most likely to survive when there are bad times or a crisis of some kind. So people are inherently lazy and don't want to exert themselves. Picking from a set of choices is one of the least effortful interaction styles which is why this point and click interaction in general seems to work very well . . . [w]hereas tweaking sliders, operating pull down menus and all that stuff—that is just more work.*[6]

So the search engines have begun inferring customizations for searchers, rather than requiring them to explicitly set them. Search engines use a number of methods for personalizing search results. For instance, the engines may take into account what sites you've clicked on before and the ones you never click on, no matter how highly they're ranked. Google also takes the previous search into account. If you search for [Hawaii vacations] and then search for [flights], Google may show you flight information for Hawaii, even though the word "Hawaii" wasn't in the second search. If you have the Google Toolbar installed, Google will even track the sites you visit independently of those you reached from Google and will use those to shape your search results.[7]

These efforts continue to advance. Marissa Mayer, Google's vice president of search products and experience, noted when personalized search results initially launched:

> *The actual implementation of personalized search is that as many as two pages of content, that are personalized to you, could be lifted onto the first page and I believe they never displace the first result, because that's a level of relevance that we feel comfortable with. So right now, at least eight of the results on your first page will be generic, vanilla Google results for that query and only up to two of them will be results from the personalized algorithm. I think the other thing to remember is, even when personalization happens and lifts those two results onto the page, for most users it happens one out of every five times.*
>
> *I think that overall, we really feel that personalized search is something that holds a lot of promise, and we're not exactly sure of the signals that will yield the best results. We know that search history, your clicks and your searches together provide a really rich set of signals, but it's possible that some of the other data that Google gathers could also be useful. It's a matter of understanding how.[8]*

Frequent Google spokesperson Matt Cutts has also intimated that personalization is likely to increase:

> *The idea of a monolithic set of search results for a generic term will probably start to fade away, and you already see people expect that if I do a search and somebody else does the search, they can get slightly different answers. I expect that over time people will expect that more and more.[9]*

In December 2009, Google expanded how they personalize results, causing search expert Danny Sullivan to comment, "The days of 'normal' search results that everyone sees are now over. Personalized results are the 'new normal,' and the change is going to shift the search world and society in general in unpredictable ways."[10] With this change, Google is now personalizing everyone's results, not just the ones of those searchers who are logged in. If the searcher isn't logged in, Google uses the search history from that computer to personalize results. Why is this such a radical shift in the search world?

Because there's no longer a base set of results. Now, more than ever, rankings reports don't have much meaning.

Google says they won't skew things so much that searching narrows our view of the online world. Google product manager Johanna Wright explained, "We want diversity of results. This is something we talk about a lot internally and believe in. We want there to be a variety of sources and opinions in the Google results. We want them in personalized search to be skewed to the user, but we don't want that to mean the rest of the Web is unavailable to them."

■ ANATOMY OF A SEARCH ENGINE RESULT

In Chapter 4, we looked at how the search results are displayed and how important it is to ensure your site has a compelling listing. Let's look a little more closely.

A search engine results page (SERP) typically contains 10 Web results for a query. Each search result contains the following three elements (Figure 5.4).

1. *Title:* This is generally the same as the title of the page. (See Chapter 7 for more details on influencing this.)

2. *Snippet:* This is the snippet beneath the title. This is your main opportunity to provide a marketing message to searchers to entice them to click through to your site. (See Chapter 7 for more details on influencing this.)

3. *URL:* The page address. Any keywords from the query are bolded.

Search results can include a number of other components as well (Figure 5.5), such as:

- Navigational links to sections within the site
- The date the page was published
- Links to forum content
- Rating and review information

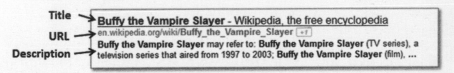

Figure 5.4   A Typical Search Result

Source: Google Search

Star Rating

> Amazon.com: **Marketing in the Age of Google**: Your Online Strategy...
> www.amazon.com/Marketing-Age-Google-Strategy.../0470537191 [+1]
> ★★★★★ 25 reviews - $16.78 - In stock
> Review. 'Her passion shines through when explaining how smaller firms can gain huge benefits...this book is a winner.' (Growing Business, September 2010). ...

Content Link

Sitelinks

> **Vanessa Fox** - Wikipedia, the free encyclopedia
> en.wikipedia.org/wiki/Vanessa_Fox [+1]
> Jump to Events: Events. **Vanessa Fox** is a frequent speaker at conferences worldwide, including Search Engine Strategies, Search Marketing Expo, Web ...
> Career - Events - Books and Writing - References

Author Photo & Details

> **Yes, Virginia, There Is An iPhone 5**
> daggle.com/virginia-iphone-5-2715 [+1]
> by Danny Sullivan - In 111,405 Google+ circles
> Oct 4, 2011 – **Yes**, Virginia, there is an iPhone **5**. It exists as certainly as the love and generosity and devotion that Apple has for the world exists. You know ...

Video Playlist

> FOX Broadcasting Company - **Glee** TV Show - **Glee** TV Series - **Glee**...
> www.fox.com/glee/ [+1]
> **Glee** TV Show - Enter the world of FOX's **Glee** TV series and learn more about characters, episodes, and cast.
> ► 2:59 Directing With Adam Shankman   Apr 15, 2010
> ► 1:21 Who Are You?   Nov 1, 2011

Breadcrumb

Publish Date

> **Proust Was a Neuroscientist** by **Jonah Lehrer**: review - Telegraph
> www.telegraph.co.uk › Culture › Books › Book Reviews [+1]
> Mar 1, 2011 – Helen Brown admires **Proust Was A Neuroscientist** by **Jonah Lehrer**, a dazzling marriage of science and literature.

Figure 5.5   Optional Search Results Display Elements

Source: Google Search

- Breadcrumbs from the page in place of the URL
- A photo of the author of the content on the page

With Google's launch of "Search Plus Your World," which integrates Google+, results have changed even more. See Chapter 9 for details.

■ THE EVOLUTION OF ORGANIC SEARCH RESULTS: BEYOND WEB PAGES

Originally, search engines indexed text on web pages and matched text-based searches to that content. As the Web evolved, search engines began looking at ways to catalog the new types of content on web pages, such as video and images. They created "vertical" indices that enabled searchers to look specifically for images, for instance. However, search engines found that few searchers noticed these vertical indices and that most searchers looked for everything from the main search page.

In 2007, Google introduced universal search, a new way of compiling results that blended content from all of their indices, including textual web content, images, videos, news, and product listings.[11] The other major search engines soon implemented their own versions of "blended search" and today, it's common to see all of these things appearing together in search results (Figure 5.6).

This blending provides opportunity for site owners. Now, in addition to listing your textual content, you can showcase your multimedia content as well.

Figure 5.6   Google Multimedia Search Results

Source: Google Search

When searchers see blended results, they view the page in a slightly different way than when the results are text only. Look at this eye-tracking heat map from Enquiro Research (Figure 5.7).

Most searchers looked at the image; in fact, more looked to the results below the image (D) than to those above it (B).

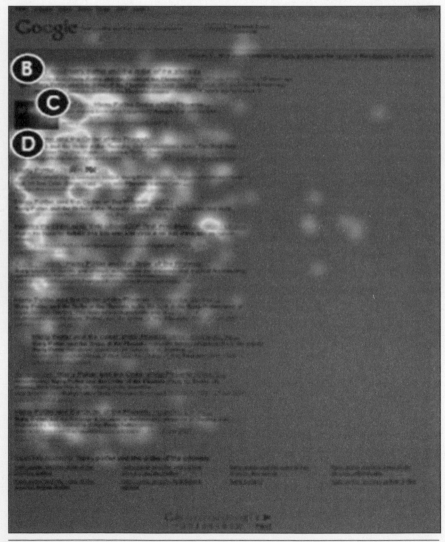

Figure 5.7   Eye-Tracking Heat Map: Multimedia Results

Source: Enquiro Research

how high is the space needle

About 3,080,000 results (0.20 seconds)

Space Needle - Wikipedia, the free encyclopedia
en.wikipedia.org/wiki/Space_Needle +1
The **Space Needle** is 605 feet (184 m) **high** at its highest point and 138 feet (42 m)
wide at its widest point and weighs 9550 tons. When it was completed it was ...
Architecture - History - Suicides - In culture

Figure 5.8 Google Answers Questions in Search Results
Source: Google

The appearance of nontextual content in the search results continues to rise. Marissa Mayer of Google noted:

I think there's a ton of challenges, because in my view, search is in its infancy, and we're just getting started. I think the most pressing, immediate need as far as the search interface is to break the paradigm of the expectation of "You give us a keyword, and we give you 10 URLs."
We need to look at results pages that aren't just 10 standard URLs that are laid out in a very linear format. Sometimes the best answer is a video, sometimes the best answer will be a photo, and sometimes the best answer will be a set of extracted facts. If I type in general demographic statistics about China, it'd be great if I got a set of facts that had been parsed off of and even aggregated and cross-validated across a result set.[12]

And, in fact, Google has begun providing more answers in their search results, in a way very similar to what Mayer described. In January 2010, Google began using its Google Squared service to extract facts from web pages and display them in the search results.[13] For instance, with the query [how high is the space needle], Google no longer simply lists the pages that might contain this information but surfaces the answer in the search results, shown in Figure 5.8.

The next section of this chapter discusses content beyond web pages that has become standard in search results. As you can see in Figure 5.9, Google's latest advances have been voice search capabilities and search by image capabilities (both discussed in Chapter 10).[14]

■ BLENDED SEARCH: IMAGES

One common type of blended result is images. To see the value of blended image search results in action, let's take a look at a trip I took to Bologna while

Figure 5.9   Advances in Google Search

Source: Google Search

I was writing the first edition of this book. I had heard that I should visit the church of San Luca, but I knew nothing about it. So, I logged on to Google and typed in [San Luca Bologna], hoping to find a description and perhaps a map. But Google (likely based on the clicks of millions who had come before me) knew my intent even better than I did and showed me not only descriptive details and a map but also images (Figure 5.10).

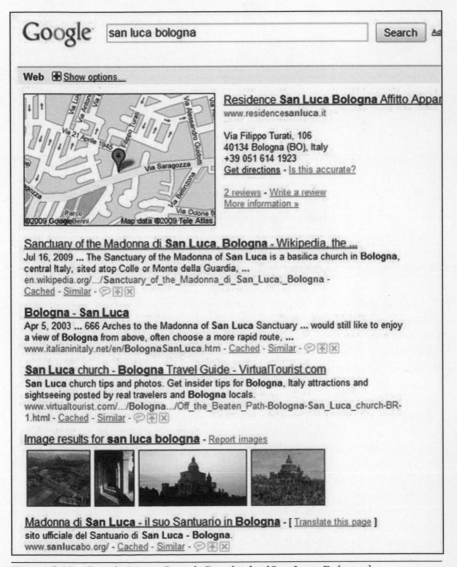

Figure 5.10   Google Image Search Results for [San Luca Bologna]
Source: Google Search

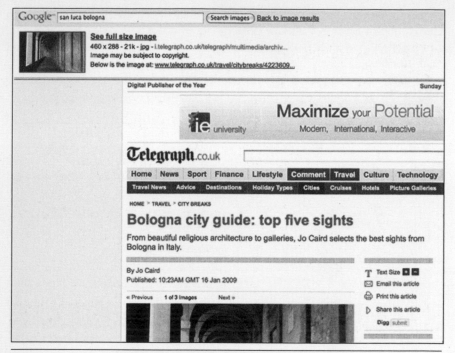

Figure 5.11 Acquisition from Google Image Search Results

Source: Google Image Search

Even though I didn't know I was looking for them, the images caught my attention first (even though I had been specifically thinking I was looking for a map!). I clicked on one of the images and came across a *Telegraph* article about Bologna, which in turn led me to some great information about local hotels, restaurants, and shops (Figure 5.11).

And so, blended search and public relations have joined together with search to bring more visitors to the businesses of Italy. (See Chapter 9 for more information on how PR can work together with search for better visibility.)

From there, I clicked "Back to image results" and then to another image found on virtualtourist.com (Figure 5.12).

I continued to explore "off the beaten path" tips, and just like that, Virtual Tourist gained a user.

As you can see from Figure 5.13, Google has continued to enhance their search results. The same search in early 2012 still shows a map, images, and web pages (the same list of web pages, in fact), but significantly more information is available on the search results page than before.

Of course, tourism isn't the only industry that can gain search acquisition from images. One of the bigger industries image searches can lead customers to is e-commerce.

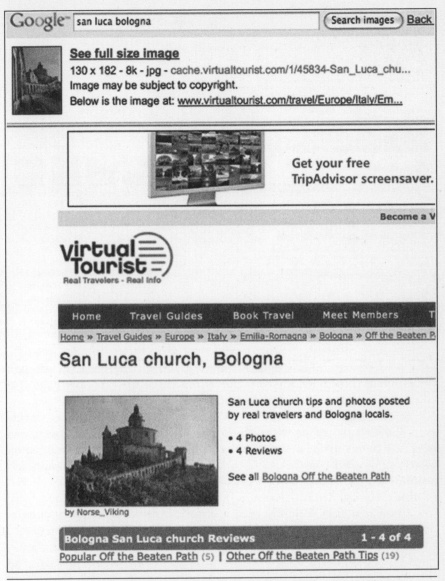

Figure 5.12 Google Images Search Results for Long-Term Acquisition
Source: Google Image Search

Let's say, for instance, that I'm looking for blue and white plates. The easiest way to research them may be to simply do a search, which gives me the results in Figure 5.14.

I can start my shopping on NexTag or Amazon, but if I'm not sure yet exactly *which* blue and white plates I want to buy, the image results seem like a

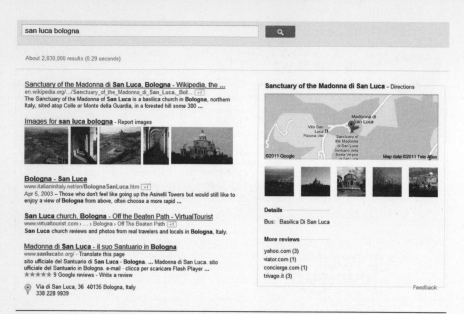

Figure 5.13 2012 Google Search Results for [San Luca Bologna]

great place to start. If I dive into the full list of images, not only can I see all of the different choices (critical for a purchase such as this one), but I can also choose between auctions, set replacements, and new retail.

As you might imagine, the search conversion workflow becomes critical here. If the site design doesn't take into account a visitor from an image search who may come directly to the page that contains the image, vital information about the site, its navigation, and how to order may not be present, and many visitors may be unsure how to proceed and might go back to the search results.

The Drayton Hall site provides a great experience for a visitor coming from an image search. The site, its value proposition, the overall navigation, and the item price and path to purchase are readily apparent (Figure 5.15).

On the other hand, the Yoko Webster page provides no information at all (Figure 5.16).

In addition to blended search opportunities for images, searchers conduct more than 1 billion image-specific searches a month, indicating that image optimization definitely shouldn't be overlooked.[15]

How can you best take advantage of this? Make sure your site includes images where they're useful, particularly if you're selling products. And ensure your Web development team implements images in a search-friendly way. (Chapter 7 talks a bit more about image optimization.)

Figure 5.14   Google Image Search Results for [Blue and White Plates]
Source: Google Search

■ BLENDED SEARCH: VIDEO

Video provides another big opportunity for search acquisition. Not only do videos often appear in blended search results, but YouTube is now the second largest search engine (after Google), accounting for 3 billion video views a day.[16] A Cisco study estimates that by 2012, more than 50 percent of consumer Internet traffic will be online video.[17] You can now submit product videos

Figure 5.15   Google Image Search Results for E-commerce Acquisition
Source: Google Image Search

to Google Product Search[18] as well, so clearly video opportunity continues to increase.

In October 2011 online video viewing was at an all-time high.[19] Of online Americans, 85 percent (184 million of us) viewed online videos more than 42 billion times (on average of 21.1 hours per viewer), up from 26 billion video views two years earlier.[20]

Introduction of new devices—faster mobile phones with larger screens and tablets such as the iPad—have accelerated our consumption of online video. Those viewing video on a tablet watch 28 percent more video content than desktop viewers.[21]

A 2011 study by Ooyala,[22] which provides an online video platform, noted "viewer engagement was generally higher on mobile devices than on desktops—even for long term videos."

People love videos. Tutorials, for instance, provide a great opportunity for video as a complement to textual instructions.

Assess your site for video opportunities, create a YouTube channel for your videos, and make sure that as with web pages, you use descriptive text that uses the language of your target audience (Figure 5.17).

Figure 5.16   Each Page Should Provide a Next Step

Source: Google Image Search

■ HOW DO UNIVERSAL RESULTS IMPACT SEARCHER BEHAVIOR?

Enquiro Research's eye-tracking studies found that when an image or video is present in the top half of the search results, the searcher seems to start the page scan there, rather than the top left[23] (Figure 5.18).

In a text-only set of results, searchers begin in the top left corner, scan right, and then down, and they tend to chunk the page into result sets of three to four results and evaluate those one by one. If searchers don't find the answer in the first chunk, they move on to the next one.

In results that contain multimedia, such as video and images, searchers started with the multimedia result as the first chunk and then scanned above it for the second chunk and below it for the third chunk (Figure 5.19).

Margarita Cocktail Recipe - **How to Make a Margarita**
cocktails.about.com/od/.../r/marg_cktl.htm `+1`

 ★★★★☆ 2 reviews - 3 mins
Cocktail recipe for a **Margarita**, a popular refreshing tequila and lime drink for summer.

How to Make a Margarita - wikiHow
www.wikihow.com/Make-a-Margarita `+1`

5 days ago – **How to Make a Margarita**. There's no "perfect" margarita--we can't even pin down the origin of this popular drink! However, many a cocktail ...

How to Make a Margarita Cocktail - YouTube
 www.youtube.com/watch?v=afl4SZIjUiU `+1`
Aug 12, 2008 - 4 min - Uploaded by epicuriousdotcom
Mixologist Eben Freeman, of Tailor restaurant in New York City, demonstrates how to prepare a ...

How to make a margarita cocktail - Margarita recipe - YouTube
 www.youtube.com/watch?v=uDOtcVtxURc `+1`
Jan 31, 2008 - 3 min - Uploaded by HowdiniGuru
http://www.howdini.com/howdini-video-6706937.html **How to make a margarita** cocktail - Margarita recipe ...

More videos for **how to make a margarita »**

Cooks.com - Recipes - **How To Make Margaritas**
www.cooks.com › Recipes `+1`

Results 1 - 10 of 101 for **how to make margaritas**. Result Page: 1 2 3 4 5 6 7 8 9 10 11 Next. 1. ... To salt the Margarita glasses, pour a single ... in the salt. ...

Figure 5.17   Video Results in Google Search
Source: Google Search

Similarly, when a local Onebox is on the page, searchers tend to evaluate the local listings as a separate chunk.

Clearly, optimizing for images and video is useful not only because it provides additional ranking opportunities but also because it enables you to stand out to searchers over the competition.

■ INTERNATIONALIZATION

A notable influence on personalized results is regional location. Location-tailored results can be a substantial part of the relevance calculation. At a basic level, all results are personalized based on location. A searcher in the United

Figure 5.18   Eye-Tracking Heat Map: Video Search Results

Source: Enquiro Research

States will get more results from U.S./English-language websites than a searcher in Italy, who will get more results from Italian websites written in Italian. In addition, certain queries have additional location-based relevance factors. For instance, someone searching for [pizza] in Seattle is likely to see Seattle-based restaurant results, and someone searching for [pizza] in Boston will likely see Boston-based restaurant results.

Regional relevance factors are particularly important to businesses that are local in nature (such as pizza restaurants) and those that serve particular countries (for example, British Telecom would like its site to be surfaced to British searches; HP would like its Spanish site to be served to Spanish searchers). These factors get trickier as the intent becomes more complicated. What about U.S. searchers who are looking for vacation accommodations in Croatia? Or a French speaker on vacation in Italy who is looking for information about trains in Poland? And how should businesses target the European Union? Or how should a business target researchers in Mexico, rather than in Spain, with Spanish content?

Internationalization for search acquisition is beyond the scope of this book, but check marketingintheageofgoogle.com for resources.

Figure 5.19 How Searchers Interact with Multimedia Results

Source: Enquiro Research

■ CONTINUED ENHANCEMENTS TO THE SEARCH RESULTS PAGE

Google and Bing continue to evolve the search results display. Since the first edition of this book was published, for instance, Google began showing maps listings for queries with local intent.

In the search results shown in Figure 5.20 for [best cocktail bar], all but the first result are pushed down to make way for listings from Google Places.

(See Chapter 6 for more on how local businesses can maximize searcher engagement.)

As for November 2011, Google began testing something called sources. (See Figure 5.21.) Google says this module, shown on the right side of search results, which pulls in data for a variety of sources, is one of many experimental features.[24]

■ GETTING TECHNICAL: HOW IT ALL COMES TOGETHER

Now, for the technical part. But don't worry! I'm not asking you to go make changes to the servers yourself! Chapter 7 contains more details about best cocktail bar

About 31,800,000 results (0.21 seconds)

The 25 **Best Cocktail Bars** in America: Restaurants + Bars: GQ
www.gq.com/food-travel/...and-**bars**/.../**best-cocktail-bars**-in-america [+1]
They are the great American invention. And there has never been a better time to drink
them than now. We traveled 34462 miles and sipped 400 gin fizzes, ...

Places for **best cocktail bar** near SeaTac, WA

The Zig Zag Café	A	1501 Western Avenue #
zigzagseattle.com		202
★★★★★ 71 Google reviews		Seattle
		(206) 625-1146
Tini Bigs	B	100 Denny Way
www.tinibigs.com		Seattle
★★★★★ 16 Google reviews		(206) 284-0931
Yo's Bistro	C	205 Southwest 152nd
www.yosbistro.com		Street
3 Google reviews		Burien
		(206) 244-4084
Feedback Lounge	D	6451 California Ave SW
www.feedbacklounge.net		Seattle
★★★★★ 11 Google reviews		(206) 453-3259
Mistral Kitchen	E	2020 Westlake Avenue
mistral-kitchen.com		Seattle
★★★★★ 25 Google reviews		(206) 623-1922
Sambar **Bar** & Lounge	F	425 NW Market St.
www.sambarseattle.com		Seattle
★★★★★ 11 Google reviews		(206) 781-4883
Tavern Law	G	1406 12th Avenue
www.tavernlaw.com		Seattle
★★★★★ 43 Google reviews		(206) 322-9734

More results near SeaTac, WA »

Figure 5.20 Google Places

working with Web developers and ensuring that they're using search-friendly
best practices.

➤ Crawling

Before a search engine can evaluate the content on your site to determine
whether it's relevant for a searcher's query, the engine has to know the page
exists and extract that content from the site for analysis.

Figure 5.21   Google Sources

1. *Discovering the pages:* Search engines find out about pages on the Web generally by following links from other sites on the Web and by following a site's internal links. The most important thing to remember about the discovery process is that you should build a great site that makes others want to link to it and that you should have a comprehensive site navigation structure. Of course, you'd want both of these things on your site even if search engines didn't exist.

2. *Crawling the pages:* Once a search engine such as Google learns about pages on the Web, it uses a "bot" to crawl those pages. Your goal is likely to have your entire site crawled, which can be hindered by crawling inefficiencies and by infrastructure issues that make URLs inaccessible to the bots.

3. *Extracting content:* Once a crawler has accessed a page, it has to be able to extract the content from that page and store it. As with crawling, a number of obstacles may keep a search engine from extracting content from your pages. Common issues include all-Flash sites, pages full of multimedia such as videos and images with no textual markup, and sites built on technologies such as AJAX that search engines can have trouble parsing. A good rule of thumb is that if you develop the site using progressive enhancement techniques[25] that

make it accessible for visitors with disabilities[26] (who are using devices such as screen readers to access your site) and on mobile devices, search engines can generally access the content as well.

➤ *Indexing*

Once the crawler has accessed the pages and extracted the content, the search engines make a decision about whether to store that content. They'll generally not store pages if they determine that those pages are mostly empty, are duplicates of pages they've already stored, or have little value (for instance, the pages may be an aggregation of content that exists elsewhere on the Web). One common cause of duplicate content is syndication. (See Chapter 7 for more information.)

➤ *Ranking*

Crawling and indexing issues tend to be technical in nature. It can be vital for Web developers to understand these parts of the process to ensure the site's technical infrastructure isn't blocking the search engine bots. Ranking, on the other hand, is primarily dependent on how relevant a page is for the given query. If you build searcher personas and incorporate search data into your product development processes, you are already taking the important steps toward ensuring your pages are as relevant as possible to the searchers you are targeting. As noted previously, relevant, authoritative links also help search engines understand the value of your site's pages, and those come naturally with useful content and a successful marketing strategy.

According to leaked 2008 Google quality guidelines, utility (how helpful the page is for the searcher based on intent) "is the most important aspect of search engine quality."[27]

Once you start to think about personalization, differing results based on searcher location, and blended search results that may cause the searcher's attention to focus on a result other than the top-ranked site, you start to realize why ranking reports don't provide much actionable insight. (We'll look at that more closely in Chapter 8.)

Chapter
6

Implementing an
Effective Search Strategy

In previous chapters, we learned how to use the intersection of search data and business needs to identify effective website content strategies, as well as a little about how search engines work. How can we bring this information together into our organizations so that our content strategies are effective for search?

At a high level, in order to effectively use organic search as an acquisition channel, companies should ensure their websites can:

- Be discovered by search engines so that their pages can be added to the list the crawler uses to traverse the Web.
- Be accessible to the crawler (build the site architecture so that it doesn't introduce obstacles).
- Have extractable information (ensure content isn't inaccessible).
- Be relevant and useful to searchers.

Sounds easy, right? The good news is that the path to success is fairly straightforward. But as you might imagine, the devil is in the details. The practice of ensuring that sites implement all of these things in a way that searchers can find them is known as search engine optimization (SEO).

However, as we've seen, for a business to be effective online long term, it has to think of search as a key part of all aspects of its organization, and not as a separate activity. And the term *search engine optimization* is a bit of a misnomer because it implies that you're optimizing your site for search engines when in reality you're optimizing your site for your audience (who often are searchers) and ensuring your site is built to be successful in an online environment.

You may, in fact, need a point person to ensure that search acquisition best practices are being built out within your organization, particularly if your organization is in the early stages of building out that process.

This book isn't about how to tactically implement SEO. A number of books, conferences, and sites exist about tactical SEO implementation.

> If you are interested in the tactical details of SEO, check out Search engineland.com (where I'm an editor) and the Search Marketing Expo conferences.[1] More information is located on my resources page at MarketingintheAgeofGoogle.com.

This book is about how to think strategically about search and how your business fits into a search-based culture. With that in mind, this chapter talks about what's required to implement search best practices within an organization, and the following chapter talks about working with developers.

■ WOULD YOU LIKE TO EXCHANGE LINKS WITH MY SITE BUY-CHEAP-VIAGRA-WHILE-YOU-PLAY-POKER-ONLINE-AND-FILE-A-MESOTHELIOMA-CLASS-ACTION-LAWSUIT.INFO?

The phrase *search engine optimization* tends to bring up bad memories of e-mails asking you to trade links and web pages with repeated words but no real information and no place to click but on ads.

SEO implies optimizing a site for search engines, but understanding how search fits into your business isn't really about that at all. It's about operating your business effectively within the current landscape. If you have retail stores, you likely have a real estate specialist scouting out locations. If your product appeals to teenage girls ages 13 to 17, you'll want to do market research to find out what they like. As we've seen, search strategy is no different.

But still the term *SEO* is often more associated with buy-cheap-Viagra-while-you-play-poker-online-and-file-a-mesothelioma-class-action-lawsuit.com than it is with customer engagement, usability, product strategy, and more sales.

Consider this posting on a tech start-up e-mail list (emphasis mine):

> *We are in dire need of a customer experience/consumer experience expert. . . . Does anyone have any suggestions for partners/firms/consultants to reach out to in order to try to find adequate partners to assure that the consumer's needs and issues are addressed? (**Not SEO experts**— usability or consumer experience experts for e-commerce).*

And yet the description is exactly what good SEO should be: understanding and improving the customer experience.

On an entrepreneur forum, someone posted that 95 percent of SEO is useless. He went on to write:

Some of the tactics I've seen "SEO professionals" sell are:

1. *Link farms—This goes into my pile of 95 percent of the SEO tactics that shouldn't be used.*
2. *Code all content within H1 tags.*
3. *Code all content within anchor tags.*
4. *Put title attributes on all content.*
5. *Make the content as verbose and wordy as possible.*
6. *Put your top 20 keywords in all image & file names.*
7. *Paying forum/blog . . . spammers.*

Yet, nothing he's listed there is an "SEO tactic." All of these items are spammer tricks (and not even ones that are generally used anymore). What he's said is similar to saying that 95 percent of what painters do is a scam, and then listing as that 95 percent things like substituting cheaper paint and charging you for the expensive stuff, painting only one wall when you paid for all four, and spraying graffiti rather than painting the room.

Any legitimate painter would have good cause to protest that none of those things are painting tactics.

Let's take a look at just a few more viewpoints on SEO found on the Web:

1. "Many of the so-called 'SEO professionals' are not much more than modern snake oil salesmen. They game and manipulate the system for their own intentions."[2]
2. "Everyone uses Google for search, and therefore online businesses need to be found on Google, which means you need to do Search Engine Optimization. SEO is the worst thing ever invented. It's destroying good Web application development."[3]
3. "I actually despise being labeled an SEO. Why? SEO's are like the 21st century car salesmen. Most are slimy and have no clue what they are talking about. They tell you [that] you just need to put spammy keywords in your title tag, keyword tag, and write a spammy as hell description metatag."[4]
4. "Search Engine Optimization is not a legitimate form of marketing. It should not be undertaken by people with brains or souls."[5]

The perception of the SEO profession may have hit one of its lowest moments in August 2009, when Fox News published a story titled "Top Online Marketing Jobs to Leave You Friendless." The article states:

> *Job-hunting? Think about becoming an e-mail spammer . . . or a website spammer . . . or a search engine optimizer. Here's a great opportunity to become part of a team of Web-savvy professionals who clog the Internet with unwanted ads and sell users' personal information to the highest bidder. Not only are these jobs legal, they can be downright lucrative. Here are some of the top online marketing jobs that will make you money . . . and leave you alone and friendless.*
>
> *Search Engine Optimizer*
>
> *Ever wonder why "nonsense" websites sometimes turn up in your search results on Google or Yahoo!? That's because search engine–optimizing scammers work full-time to create thousands of other websites that link to the spam site.*[6]

Of course, that doesn't actually describe a search engine optimizer. It describes a Web spammer.

■ BEYOND SEO

I don't know if the term *SEO* can be reclaimed. Although the negative perception about SEO is inaccurate, it is the case that a subset of those who practice SEO tend to narrowly focus on rankings, rather than customer experience. This certainly isn't true of all who practice SEO, but it's hard to distinguish when we're using the same name to describe both types of practices. And, as mentioned earlier in this chapter, the term *SEO* doesn't describe well the whole picture of integrating a search acquisition strategy into a more comprehensive business strategy.

- Using search data to build a comprehensive and effective product and content strategy.
- Understanding searcher behavior and building searcher personas that maximize customer satisfaction and conversions.
- Realizing the customer acquisition funnel often begins with the search box, not your website.
- Integrating organic search with other marketing efforts.
- Ensuring the technical architecture of the site can be properly crawled and indexed by search engines so that it can be visible to searchers.

When I look at organic search acquisition, I'm looking from a point of triangulation. I understand that searchers want the best result as quickly as possible. I understand that search engines want to understand the Web so that they can deliver the most relevant results. And I understand that site owners want to market their content effectively to the right audience.

We've talked about using search data, building a comprehensive strategy, creating searcher personas, and engaging with customers. But what do your product marketers, content writers, and Web developers need to know about their roles in ensuring your search strategy is effective?

➤ *Web Architecture*

- Web development teams should build websites in such a way that they can be easily crawled and indexed by search engines. (We talk about this in Chapter 7.)
- Upper management should provide the necessary support for making infrastructure search engine–friendly.
- Upper management should state requirements in terms of functional outcomes (an easy-to-navigate menu system) rather than implementation (a Flash menu).
- The content management system and content modification process should easily allow for nontechnical staff to update important content sections of the site, such as the title, headings, and paragraphs.

➤ *Strategic Development*

- Those doing market research, determining product features, building a product road map, or developing a company vision should understand the value of search data and how to effectively make use of it.
- All marketing goals should be shared, and all marketing silos (such as offline advertising, online advertising, and e-mail marketing) should share data and understand how one channel impacts the rest.

➤ *Content Development*

Content writers should understand keyword research, searcher behavior, and how to build searcher personas. No one should build a page without knowing the answers to these questions:

- What is the goal of this page? What is the conversion event and call to action?
- Why would a visitor land on this page? What would he or she want to get from it?
- Why would that visitor then want to follow the call to action?

➤ *Advertising Initiatives*

- Any offline campaigns should include an organic search component. What searches might this campaign drive, and what is the searcher experience?
- Any ad agencies building Web content to support offline campaigns should have search friendliness as a default requirement.

■ BECOMING TOO FOCUSED ON SEO

As already noted, this book is not about how to tactically implement SEO. This book is about how to think strategically about search and how your business fits into a search-based culture.

There is, however, one point of tactical SEO that is important to convey to your organization. If you read search blogs, attend search conferences, and otherwise follow the search industry, it's easy to get caught up in the particulars of the search engine algorithms. How many times should a particular word be repeated? How many links should any given page have? How many words should be on any given page? Chasing the answers to these questions can have vast opportunity cost and little gain. The search engine algorithms are in a constant state of flux. Search engine engineers tweak settings every day to see how they can make results a little more relevant. If you spend your time optimizing your site for these algorithmic particulars, you'll never have time to do anything else.

A much better strategy is to focus on what the search engines are trying to achieve with all of those algorithm tweaks—showing the most relevant results for a given query. Ensure your technical team gets the foundational infrastructure elements right (as described in Chapter 7) and ensure your marketing and product teams build the right features and content. Not only will this result in you ranking well, but it will help you achieve what you're really after—which is not rankings, but customers.

■ SEARCH ENGINE GUIDELINES AND PENALTIES

The search engines have published guidelines.[7] Violate any of those guidelines and you risk having your site demoted in ranking or removed from the index. The spirit behind the search engine guidelines is that the search engines reserve the right to take action on any sites that intentionally try to manipulate their ranking algorithms—which makes sense, since core to the search engines is the relevance of their results. If sites are manipulating those results and making them less relevant and useful to searchers, the engines have methods of pinpointing that and adjusting for it.

Search engines (Google in particular) have published a number of examples of what might constitute results manipulation. Generally, these are pretty straightforward and likely sound very similar to the spammy tactics the SEO naysayers incorrectly attribute to SEO. But the examples also serve as a check for those who aren't spammers who may have lost sight of what's really important about search acquisition in their focus on rankings.

■ BUILDING SEARCH INTO THE PROCESS OF THE ORGANIZATION

By now, you know that a successful search acquisition strategy relies on weaving search best practices throughout the organization. This becomes difficult as business activities can be segmented from each other, departments may have political reasons for not collaborating with others, and some organizational processes simply aren't built for this type of cross-department collaboration.

The key is support from the top down. If upper management provides a central search goal that can be shared by all parts of the organization and provides the resources necessary for search integration, individual departments are motivated and empowered to embrace search best practices.

Following are some best practices to consider weaving into the organization.

➤ Content Architecture

We've seen, at a high level, how search engines work and how searchers interact with results. Beyond what topics you choose to include on your site, which clearly have a significant impact on the audience you attract, what should you think about when building content?

- *Ensure the site has useful information architecture*. Do multiple pages have similar content? Will visitors be confused about which page to access to get the information they want?
- *Ensure the content uses the language of the customer*. Make sure anyone writing copy understands keyword research (see Chapter 2) and uses it as part of the writing process. And make sure the organization has a process in place that keeps track of this research. Too often, I see companies spend significant time and energy researching customer language and crafting engaging messaging, only to have another department or outside agency later revise the content without realizing the work that had been done and removing all of those carefully researched words.

  One potential method for keeping track of the words customers use to search is to indicate the ones chosen for the page focus in the meta keywords tag[8] of the page. The contents of this tag aren't used by search engines for organic search, but they can be helpful for internal communication. Depending on the content management system your organization uses and what internal processes you have in place, determine best practices for communicating these types of details on a page level.

- *Use standard HTML components on the page.* Once you've determined the key content for the page (for instance, "natural arthritis treatments"), ensure that content appears in the page's title, primary heading, and textual content. Remember that based on how searchers skim search results pages, you should put the most important keywords in the far left of the title. And you should qualify phrases as fully as possible without being overwhelming ("Canon X54T Digital Camera with Zoom" rather than "X54T"). (See Figure 6.1.)

- *Remember that every page of the site is a potential entry page for visitors.* As we discussed in Chapter 4, every page should:

  ⇒ Clearly indicate the primary topic.

  ⇒ Help the visitor complete a task.

  ⇒ Provide orientation and contextual information about the site.

  ⇒ Motivate the visitor into the acquisition funnel with a compelling call to action. As we discussed, every page needs a clear call to action. Pages can suffer from no call to action or too many calls to action. Without a clear call to action, all the work to get the page crawled, indexed, and ranked was for nothing.[9]

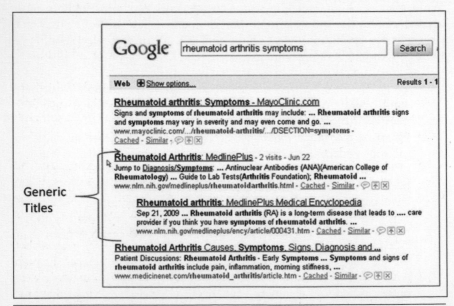

Figure 6.1   Google Search Results for [Rheumatoid Arthritis Symptoms]

⇒ *Answer visitor questions*. Remember the list of questions we generated using the Wordtracker Keyword questions tool in Chapter 2? The type of phrasing searchers use can be important to keep in mind when building content, particularly for sites that provide a collection of answers or FAQs about their business. For instance, answers.oreilly.com provides information about the most commonly asked questions in technology. The company would attract far greater acquisition from search if it worded its headings as questions, much as people would search for them, rather than as answers. So, for instance, "How Do I Set Up a Relational Database with Rails" rather than "How to Set Up a Relational Database with Rails."

- *Ensure the site has a good internal linking structure*. This is vital for an easily crawlable site. At least one link should exist to every page (a good HTML site map helps provide this, as well as gives visitors a browsable architecture), and the links should use descriptive anchor text.

It's important to think about what to link to from your home page. This is the page that most visitors will see, so it makes sense that you would want your most important pages to be linked to it. Search engines know this too, so they can use this link architecture as a signal of importance.

Sites can go overboard with this, though. As soon as someone starts thinking about how to structure links solely in terms of how the search engines might interpret them and not in terms that make sense for visitors, the usability of the site declines and search engines (which are on to these tactics) can no longer use these signals to determine relevance.

■ MARKETING, ADVERTISING, AND PUBLIC RELATIONS

We know that organic search should be integrated into other marketing activities—everything from market research to Super Bowl commercials. What do the marketing, advertising, and public relations departments need to know about search?

- *Your customers are also searchers*. For any advertising campaign you undertake, ensure organic search is part of the planning process. What taglines and products are you promoting? What might your advertising efforts cause your audience to search for? Do you have pages on your website devoted to those things, and can search engines access them?
- *Searchers are also your customers*. The people you are trying to attract through search are the same people you are trying to attract through e-mail campaigns, other online and offline advertising campaigns, press releases, and other channels. Share data and you may be amazed at how much more complete a picture you can get of your audience and

how much better you will be able to provide them with a compelling, consistent experience.

- *Be wary of all-Flash sites and microsites.* We'll talk about this a bit more in Chapter 7, but advertising agencies sometimes build microsites and Flash sites as part of a campaign. There's nothing inherently wrong with either tactic, but both require a bit of extra attention to ensure their content can be easily found by search engines. Make sure your ad agency knows that searchability is part of the project requirements.
- *Understand online reputation management.* When someone searches for your brand, what types of results appear? Ensuring your site is easily visible can help minimize any negative results about your brand. (See Chapter 9 for more on this.)
- *Links are valuable.* Any online marketing, public relations, or social media effort generally includes links back to the site. These links can be a valuable acquisition channel. Relevant links can also be valuable for helping search engines understand the value and context of the page.

Marketing, social media, and public relations can help your link profile considerably. Use social media to spread awareness about your great content, and you're likely to get bloggers to pick up on it and write about you. Once your public relations team understands the importance of search and links, the team will do its part to make search acquisition effective by linking to specific pages (rather than just the home page) with descriptive anchor text in its press releases to increase the chances that news outlets will use those links and anchor text.

■ MARKET RESEARCH AND PRODUCT DEVELOPMENT

We've already seen just how valuable search data can be for market research, product development, and audience analysis. From an organizational standpoint, determine how use of search data can effectively be integrated into existing processes. This may be as easy as simply getting departments to share data. If the advertising department is already doing keyword research for paid search campaigns, it may be able to just share its findings with product development. If you are not currently using search data, user research, market research, or other departments, you may need to learn how best to do keyword research and incorporate searcher personas into existing audience analysis and market research.

■ METRICS AND ANALYTICS

Use analytics data to augment search data and better understand your customers. (We'll talk more about analytics in Chapter 8.) You can learn what they're searching for that leads them to your site, what pages they find most useful, and what pages other sites find more valuable based on referral data. You can also use analytics to track your organic search efforts. Are you getting qualified traffic from the queries that you have targeted for your searcher personas? And are those searchers finding those pages useful?

■ CUSTOMER SUPPORT

We know that, as user behavior changes, more customers will turn to online support mechanisms. Customer support can take advantage of search in a number of ways, including:

- Using search data to find out what problems customers are having and what they're searching for.
- Ensuring that searches for frequently asked questions bring up relevant answers from the company.
- Reaching out to any disgruntled customers who have posted negative information about the company (generally findable by doing brand searches).

■ HOW SEARCH IMPACTS LOCAL BUSINESS

Search engines have become the new Yellow Pages. Local search volume accounts for 13 percent of all searches (and was up 16 percent in 2011 vs. 2010).[10] Increasingly, local and mobile search are blurring. Nearly 21 million of us search for local information via mobile browsers.[11]

This book is all about ensuring that your website solves the right problems for your customers, but local businesses have additional opportunities to reach potential customers by claiming their listings on the search engine maps.

Google,[12] Bing,[13] and Yahoo![14] all let you provide your business details for free. Completing this information not only ensures that potential customers searching their maps and local listings can find you but also prevents your listings from having inaccurate information. Don't forget to include details such as your hours of operation.

- Include your business description, hours of operation, and any other relevant information.
- Add photos, your website address, phone number, and other contact information.
- Be sure to include all of the relevant categories for your business.[15]

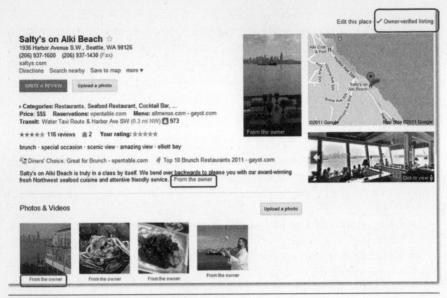

Figure 6.2   Google Places Listing

Source: Google Places

For instance, take a look at the Salty's listing (a restaurant near me) on Google Places (Figure 6.2). The owner has verified the listing and has added a description, photos, and videos.

Take a look at what local directories rank well for queries you care about (such as your brand and topic area) and make sure that you've claimed your listings there if that's an option.

For instance, when I search for [salty's alki] on Google, the restaurant's Urbanspoon listing displays prominently (Figure 6.3).

The restaurant owner can claim ownership of the restaurant and, just as with the business listings on the major search engines, can ensure all of the business details (such as hours of operation, website link, and physical address) are accurate. (See Figure 6.4.)

Salty's on Alki - West Seattle - Seattle | Urbanspoon
www.urbanspoon.com › Seattle › City of Seattle › West Seattle +1
★★★★★ Rating: 75% - 400 votes - Price range: $25 on up per entree
Salty's on Alki, Seafood Restaurant in West Seattle. See the menu, 8 photos, 7 critic reviews, 7 blog posts and 33 user reviews. Reviews from critics, food blogs ...

Figure 6.3   Urbanspoon Listing in Google Search Results

Source: Google Search

Figure 6.4 Urbanspoon Restaurant Page

Source: Urbanspoon

As a local business owner, you should also pay attention to ratings and reviews, as described in Chapter 9.

As discussed in Chapter 10, a mobile strategy is becoming more important for local businesses as well. Google reports that a third of Google searches on mobile devices have local intent (Bing reports that number at around 50 percent)[16] and that 61 percent of users who have looked up local businesses on their smartphones have called the business and 59 percent have visited the store.[17] Local search on mobile devices has been growing at 50 percent each year since 2009 (from 1 billion U.S.-based local searches in 2009 to 3.45 billion predicted local searches in 2012).[18]

■ GOOGLE'S CHANGING ALGORITHMS

Since the first edition of this book was published, Google has launched several substantial algorithm changes, notably the "Mayday" update of May 2010[19] and the series of "Panda" updates, beginning in February 2011.[20]

In addition, search itself has evolved. As described earlier in this book, Google Instant suggests queries as a searcher types. Maps, website previews, interactive elements, and other additions beyond links are increasingly being incorporated into search results.

Many people have asked how I would change the advice in this book based on these types of high-impact changes to search. My answer? I wouldn't change any of my strategic advice. The best strategy is always to solve your audience's problems. Build websites that meet customer needs, not ones that match some perceived set of algorithms. Certainly, from a tactical perspective, as new types of media are displayed in search results and Web technologies improve, you can take advantage of those improvements (see more on this in Chapter 7).

But Google's latest algorithms aren't a shift in focus—they aren't now valuing different types of pages and content. Rather, Google (and other search engines) are getting better at identifying the types of pages they've tried to display for searchers all along—those that best meet searcher needs.

Google's Panda algorithm in particular received a lot of attention in 2011. Google has said that it "was designed to improve the user experience by catching and demoting low-quality sites that did not provide useful original content or otherwise add much value. At the same time, it provided better rankings for high-quality sites—sites with original content and information such as research, in-depth reports, thoughtful analysis and so on."[21] In other words, Google is getting better at identifying the pages that best meet searcher needs as described throughout this book.

Should you be worried about building a marketing strategy that includes organic search when Google's algorithms keep changing? Not if that strategy is based on creating a high-quality site for your audience.

► *How Google's Panda Algorithm Works*

Google's Panda algorithm (named after an engineer who worked on it) differs from previous ranking changes in that it's site-based rather than page-based.

Google evaluates the percentage of the site that provides a high-quality experience (including content, navigation, and usability) for the searcher—in short, all of the things discussed throughout this chapter.

Since this is a site-wide evaluation, the major difference with Panda versus other Google ranking algorithms is that if a site receives a low Panda score, the rankings for the entire site might be lowered (resulting in overall lower search traffic for the site), even for the high-quality pages of that site.

Google engineers noted in an interview with *Wired*[22] that they used this set of questions when testing how this algorithm flagged sites:

> *We wanted to keep it strictly scientific, so we used our standard evaluation system that we've developed, where we basically sent out documents to outside testers. Then we asked the raters questions like: "Would you be comfortable giving this site your credit card? Would you be comfortable giving medicine prescribed by this site to your kids?"*
>
> *. . . everything from. "Do you consider this site to be authoritative? Would it be okay if this was in a magazine? Does this site have excessive ads?" Questions along those lines.*
>
> *And based on that, we basically formed some definition of what could be considered low quality.*

Google's Matt Cutts described the problem Panda was intended to solve: "The problem had shifted from random gibberish, which the spam team had nicely taken care of, into somewhat more like written prose. But the content was shallow."

Google notes, "Our goal is simple: to give people the most relevant answers to their queries as quickly as possible."

Their recommendations continually stress this:[23]

Give visitors the information they're looking for: Provide high-quality content on your pages, especially your homepage. This is the single most important thing to do.

They follow this philosophy themselves:[24]

Focus on the user and all else will follow. *Since the beginning, we've focused on providing the best user experience possible. Whether we're designing a new Internet browser or a new tweak to the look of the homepage, we take great care to ensure that they will ultimately serve **you**, rather than our own internal goal or bottom line.*

It can be difficult to look at the content on your site purely in the context of the best visitor experience, without considering business goals, technical obstacles, monetary realties, and resource restrictions, but that is the type of evaluation that Google does when determining which pages to rank (and which pages to flag as low quality as part of a Panda calculation).

If you suspect Google's Panda algorithm has negatively impacted your site's traffic, take a close look at both the uniqueness and quality of the content on the site.

In a post on the Google Webmaster Central Blog, Google Fellow Amit Singhal provided a detailed checklist of items they use when evaluating sites.[25] These include:

- What is the primary question/task a visitor to this page has?
- Does this page answer that question/task better than any other page on the Web?
- Is the information trustworthy/authoritative?
- Is the content well-edited and researched?

If you find that the quality of your content has been constrained by your resources, you may need to make some hard choices and radical changes in overall strategy and in tactical execution. Obviously, this is not an easy undertaking, but it can lead to long-term benefit, not only in search visibility, but in audience engagement and conversion as well.

CHAPTER 6 CHECKLIST: INTEGRATING SEARCH INTO AN ORGANIZATION

Web Architecture

- ❐ Web development and information technology (IT) should build sites to be search engine–friendly (described in Chapter 7).
- ❐ Upper management should support a development life cycle that includes time for incorporating search best practices.
- ❐ The site infrastructure should easily allow for content updates without code changes.
- ❐ The site should have useful site architecture with little duplication and clear navigation.
- ❐ Web pages should use standard HTML components, such as unique title tags, H1 tags, and unique meta descriptions.
- ❐ Web pages should be accessible and render well on devices such as screen readers and mobile browsers.

Strategic and Content Development

- ❐ Business, product, and marketing goals should incorporate search data and organic search acquisition.
- ❐ All content should use the language of the customer, not that of the organization.
- ❐ Customer support should use search data to learn about problems before they escalate.

Advertising and Marketing Initiatives

- ❐ All offline campaigns should include requirements for brand visibility in organic search.
- ❐ Agencies should be given search friendliness as a requirement for Web design and advertising campaigns.
- ❐ Public relations should understand the value of external links and ensure press releases are crafted to generate these effectively.

Checklist for Hiring an In-House Search Engine Optimizer

❏ Project management experience

❏ Ability to collaborate and work well with cross-functional teams

❏ Good understanding of usability, conversion funnels, Web analytics, Web design, and information architecture design

❏ Experience working with Web developers and a firm understanding of technical requirements of organic search

❏ Good writing skills and competent HTML skills

❏ A similar approach and philosophy about organic search as yours

Checklist for Hiring an Organic Search Agency

❏ Avoid firms that promise specific rankings.

❏ Avoid firms that provide rankings reports as a main deliverable.

❏ Avoid firms that don't disclose to you what actions they are taking on your behalf and what changes they are making to your site.

❏ Avoid firms that don't disclose their methods for link building or that perform link building by buying links or via link exchange campaigns rather than by building long-term valuable content or engaging with the community.

❏ Ensure the firm has experience working with paid search agencies (if your organization uses paid search), Web developers, and Web designers.

❏ Ensure the firm has a good understanding of usability, conversion funnels, Web analytics, Web design, and information architecture design.

❏ Ask about the firm's approach to organic search acquisition. It should align well with your company's philosophy and goals.

❏ Ask how the firm feels about Google's Webmaster guidelines.

❏ Evaluate the firm against Google's SEO agency recommendations.[26]

Chapter 7

Working with Developers

How to Turn Business Strategy into Tech Speak

As noted in Chapter 6, a site's technical infrastructure is a vital part of search acquisition. If the search engine bots can't crawl and extract content from a site's pages, that site has little chance of ranking well in search engines for relevant queries. In addition, changing a site's content management system or server setup, merging sites after an acquisition, building microsites, and engaging in other common activities can greatly impact search acquisition.

Web developers should understand the principles of searchability and build them into the infrastructure, and they should have a set of best practices for modifying that infrastructure and troubleshooting problems. This chapter provides an overview of the technical issues involved with search acquisition. (You can find more detailed discussion at MarketingintheAgeofGoogle.com.) Either you can give this chapter directly to your Web developers, or if you're interested in the technical details, you can use it to help you better understand the technical issues, which will allow you to have productive conversations with the development team about how best to build search best practices into the development process.

For search best practices to be successfully implemented in Web development, the development team needs executive support. This means the developers need to be given the training to expand their core skill set into understanding how to make Web infrastructure searchable, they need time to test searchability in addition to functionality, and they need to be provided context about why they are being asked to make changes. Web developers know how to make sites functional and might be suspicious if you ask them to make changes that don't seem to improve functionality. But if you explain that both 301 and 302 redirects transfer the visitor from one page to another, but only a 301 tells search engines to index the new page instead of the old one, you'll get the developers on your side much more quickly.

As noted in Chapter 5, the path to a site being found in search engines includes crawling, indexing, and ranking. Following are more technical details on each of these components.

■ CRAWLING

The crawling process consists of several components. First, search engines have to learn about the pages. Then, they need to have enough time during the period they've allocated to the site to crawl those pages. Finally, they have to be able to technically access the pages.

➤ Discovery

The first step in crawling is discovery. How does the engine find out about pages on the Web? Generally, this happens in one of the following ways:

- By finding links to the pages from other sites on the Web
- By finding links to the pages from within your site
- From an XML Sitemap

➤ Crawl Allocation

Search engine bots have resources to crawl every page on the Web, and they are also mindful of not overcrawling a site and causing an undue burden on the server. For these reasons, search engine bots spend only a limited period crawling each site. The following factors can aid in a more comprehensive crawl:

- *Fast server response times:* If the server is slow to respond to requests, the search engine bots may slow down their crawl to ensure they aren't overloading the server.
- *Fast page load times:* The faster each page loads (server-side), the more pages search engines will likely be able to crawl during their allocated

---

What's an XML Sitemap?[1] It's a file in a particular format that contains a list of all the URLs on a site. Google and Bing use this file to augment their discovery processes. Submitting a Sitemap can help search engines know more comprehensively about your site. See sitemaps.org for more information.

---

crawl period. You can monitor page load times for Google in Google Webmaster Tools. If you see a spike in page load times when you haven't made significant changes to your site (such as added substantial multimedia content), there may be a problem with the server (Figure 7.1).

- *Unique content:* If much of the content appears to be duplicate or empty (this can happen, for instance, with directory sites that have regions, categories, or entries that don't yet have content), the search engine bot may stop crawling.
- *Accessible URLs:* URLs may be inaccessible to crawlers for a number of reasons, such as redirects set up on the URLs that inadvertently create an infinite loop (so URLs redirect back and forth to each other) or that create a long redirect chain.[2] You can see a report of any URLs that Google's bots couldn't access via Google Webmaster Central.[3]
- *Crawl efficiency:* If the crawler spends all its time on pages that you don't need to have indexed (such as registration pages and contact forms), less time will be available to crawl the pages you do want indexed. You can block content you don't want indexed using robots.txt.[4]

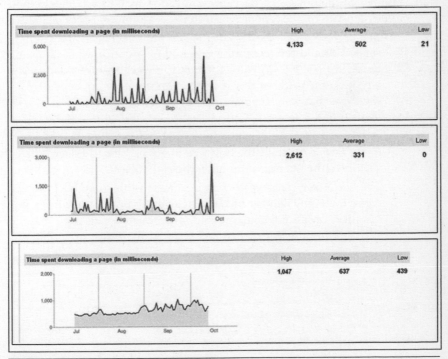

Figure 7.1 Google Site Crawl Report

Source: Google Webmaster Tools

- *Server efficiency:* You can reduce the resources the search engine bot consumes per page by enabling compression and if-modified-since on the server. Compression serves pages to the bot in a compressed format and the if-modified-since response returns a 304 (not modified) to the bot when it requests a page that hasn't changed since the last request rather than the entire contents of the page.[5]
- *Bot speed control:* You can slow down the crawl of Yahoo!'s and Microsoft's bots by using the crawl-delay setting in robots.txt.[6] If either of these bots seem to be crawling your site particularly slowly, check the robots.txt file to see if this entry exists. You can slow down Google's crawl of the site in Google Webmaster Tools. If Google is limiting its crawl because it's not sure if your server can handle a higher load, Google Webmaster Tools will present a "faster" option that you can specify as well (Figure 7.2).
- *Canonicalization:* Canonicalization is the process of consolidating all duplicate URLs to one original, or "canonical," version.[7] If multiple URLs exist that all lead to the same page, then search engine bots may spend a considerable amount of time crawling the same page over and over via different URLs and not have time to get to unique pages. A number of methods exist for canonicalization of URLs.[8] The method to use depends on the canonicalization issue. Common issues include:

⇒ *The www and non-www version of the site both resolve.* Ideally one version should redirect to the other.[9] For instance, when someone types in mysite.com, you can set the server to redirect to www.mysite.com. Without this redirect, an entire second copy of your site exists that search engines will try to crawl.

⇒ *The URL structure has changed, so content exists on both the old pages and the new pages.* In this situation, a 301 redirect from the old pages to the new is generally the best way to go, particularly since it helps visitors to the old pages end up in the right place.

⇒ *The URL structure generates infinite URLs.* With some URL implementations, any number of URLs may bring up the same page. For instance, on an e-commerce site, a product listing page may be available in different sort orders (ranked by lowest price, highest

Figure 7.2   Google Webmaster Tools: Requesting a Faster Crawl

Source: Google Webmaster Tools

rated, etc.), but the content in each case is the same (just ordered differently). For instance, mystore.com/shoes.php?sort=lowest, mystore.com/shoes.php?sort=best, and mystore.com/shoes.php?sort=newest might bring up the same list of products.

Another common way this happens is if the system is set up so that the marketing department or ad agency can append tracking codes to the URLs to keep track of marketing campaigns. For instance, the marketing department might send information about the new shoes page out in an e-mail newsletter with the URL mystore.com/shoes.php?source=email and might let bloggers know about the new shoes page, hoping they'll blog about it with the URL mystore.com/shoes.php?source=blog. Both of these URLs bring up the same page. Session IDs appended to URLs can also cause infinite URL issues. If possible, store session information in cookies (and make sure those visitors who don't have cookie support—such as search engine bots—can access the site).

When a crawler detects that a page can load from infinite parameters, it may stop crawling that site to avoid being caught in what's known as a spider trap. Another problem with this type of structure is that since the crawler has limited resources to spend on a site, time spent crawling the same page over and over from different URLs means that less time is available for crawling unique pages. In this situation, the canonical meta attribute[10] or the Google Webmaster Tools parameter handling tool[11] are good options.

⇒ *Pages are blocked by the robots exclusion protocol.*[12] The robots exclusion protocol enables you to block search engines from crawling parts of your entire site via either a robots.txt file located at the root of your site or via a meta tag on the source code of your pages. Many valid uses of this protocol exist, but it's easy to mistakenly block search engine bots from pages you do want to be indexed. If you find that your site isn't indexed as well as you'd like, check that the bots aren't accidentally being blocked out.

■ INDEXING

Once a search engine bot has crawled a page, it attempts to store the contents of that page in the search engine index. Common reasons a search engine may not store the contents of a page include:

- *Redirects are incorrectly implemented.* Most of the time, when you move content, you are moving it permanently. In those cases, implement redirects using the 301 HTTP status code. This code signifies that the change is permanent. Commonly, redirects default to the 302 HTTP status code, which signifies that the change is temporary. From a search engine perspective, this difference is important because if you've moved content (for instance, when changing domains or URL structure), you want the search engines to replace the old URLs with the new ones in the index. If possible, avoid JavaScript and meta refresh redirects.

- *The content is locked behind registration.* If you require registration to view your content, search engine bots can't access it. A number of options exist for balancing search acquisition needs and registration requirements. For instance, you can provide abstracts of content outside of registration or you can participate in Google's First Click Free program.[13] This is discussed further at marketingintheageofgoogle.com.

- *The content is hidden in Flash or Silverlight.* Search engines have gotten better at crawling Flash pages, but a number of problems remain. You can find a list of resources on making Flash accessible to search engines at marketingintheageofgoogle.com.

- *The content is blocked by AJAX or JavaScript.* As with Flash, search engines are getting better at crawling other types of rich content such as AJAX and JavaScript, but only if developers implement these technologies in a search-friendly way. This type of implementation not only makes the content more accessible to crawling but also makes it more accessible to visitors on mobile phones, screen readers, and older browsers. You can find a list of resources on making JavaScript accessible to search engines at marketingintheageofgoogle.com.

- *Little extractable text is available.* If the pages are full of video and images, search engines have little text with which to understand what those pages are about. At their core, we're still dealing with text-based search engines that return pages based on a searcher's text-based query. There are a number of ways you can ensure search engines can have some information about multimedia on your pages, such as images and videos:

  ⇒ *Images:* Major search engines such as Google continue to be, at their cores, text based. They can't understand images without textual content. To ensure your site's images can be properly indexed and ranked by search engines, use descriptive ALT text, make image filenames descriptive (for instance, yellow-goldfish.jpg rather than image123.jpg), use descriptive text around the image (in captions, headings, and titles), and use high-resolution, high-quality images whenever possible. Be cautious about using images for navigation and avoid putting text into images.[14]

  ⇒ *Video:* In October 2011, Americans watched 42.6 billion videos online. YouTube is the second largest search engine in the United States.[15] Your best bet for ensuring your video can be found may be to simply host it on YouTube. If you host it elsewhere, ensure the

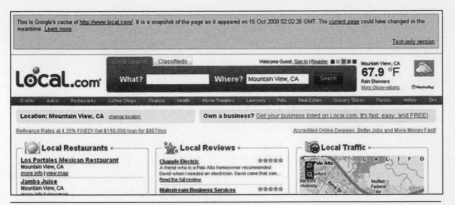

Figure 7.3   All Regional Content Should Load on Unique URLs

Source: Local.com

host is feeding Google an XML Video Sitemap.[16] You should also provide transcripts, if possible, and use descriptive headings and descriptions for your videos.

- *Multiple sets of content are associated with a single URL.* If the site is set up so that the URL doesn't change when the content changes or it is based on a single URL rather than allowing different users to be served regional content based on where they're located, search engines will see only one version of that URL. This often happens when the page is dynamically generated based on a visitor's location, for instance. A better strategy is to redirect to a separate URL with that regional content. For instance, local.com has a dynamically generated home page with local business information. Because the URL is the same no matter what content is loaded into the page, when I entered the URL, Google has indexed it with content from Mountain View, CA (where many Google bot computers crawl from) (Figure 7.3).

Local.com could avoid this issue by redirecting the visitor to a URL such as local.com/mountain-view-ca or mountain-view-ca.local.com and displaying the local content there.

■ RANKING

As we've seen throughout this book, ranking is based on what pages search engines have calculated to be most relevant to what they have determined the searcher is looking for. You can't influence how the engines interpret searcher intent, but you can ensure your pages are as relevant as possible for target queries. The bottom line, of course, is to understand your customers and what they are looking for and provide exactly that. But on a more tactical level, relevance is based in large part on your site's content and on external links. We discussed both content and links in Chapter 6, but following are technical implementation details about the content.

► *Page Components*

In the section on content architecture in Chapter 6, I talked about the importance of including primary keywords in the page components. These components include page titles, meta descriptions, and heading tags, as described next. Key to making this work within an organization is ensuring that these components can be easily changed without requiring code change or launch. The content management system or other mechanism for building content should enable marketers, content writers, and others to easily change this text.

Page Titles   The page title is what's contained in the element in the source code and appears in the browser title bar. This text is important because it's what appears as the default title of a bookmark and generally is the title of the page in the search results. When possible, this tag should be formatted as follows:

Most important keyword in compelling phrase + Brand

For instance,

How to Rollerblade—eHow.com Video Series

In the search results in Figure 7.4, for [how to rollerblade], the first two results have titles that do a good job of describing what the page is about, although the first result doesn't make it clear what site the page is on (which could make that result seem less credible). The third result doesn't match the query, so searchers may skip it as they skim the page (although more people search for inline skating than rollerblading, so the fact that the title of this page doesn't match the query we're looking at isn't reason enough to modify the text). The fourth result may not seem as relevant as the title implies that the page is for an advanced user rather than a beginner.

Each page should have a unique title that focuses on the core topic for that page (ideally using the phrase with the higher search volume). The page title is likely the most important element on the page.

Meta Description   The meta description attribute is contained in the page's source code and is often used as the description below the title in the search results.[17] This is your chance to provide a targeted marketing message to

How to Rollerblade: 9 steps (with video)
www.wikihow.com › ... › Individual Sports › Inline and Roller Skating +1
Jun 22, 2011 – **How to Rollerblade**. **Rollerblading**, or inline skating, is a popular
activity presumed to have started as an alternative to ice skating during warm ...

How to Rollerblade: Video Series | eHow.com
www.ehow.com › Sports +1
Learn tips and techniques on **how to rollerblade** from putting on the skate to
controlling speed and tricks like jumping off curbs.
▶ 0:50   Skating Backward: Tips & Techniques: Learn How ...   May 5, 2008
▶ 0:42   Bicycle Move for Rollerblading: Learn How to ...   Oct 29, 2009

Learn How to Inline Skate
inlineskating.about.com/.../Inline_Roller_Skating_Tutorials_Learn_H... +1
Inline Roller Skating Tutorials - Learn **How to Rollerblade** ...
Motivational Practice Sayings for Inline and Roller Skaters   Learn how ...
Inline Skating Instruction and Coaching Experiences and Tips   Lessons ...

Rollerblade Tricks and Techniques
simon27.tripod.com/ +1
Rollerblade Tricks. I have been skating for over 5 years and have accumulated quite a
few tricks that I would like to share with you. I would right away like to ...

Figure 7.4   Google Search Results for [How to Rollerblade]

Source: Google Search

engage with potential customers. It should be unique to each page and should give context to the content of the page. Since the search results description real estate is limited be concise, provide a compelling value proposition for the page and use the primary keywords you've chosen for the page. However, don't make the mistake of repeating the keywords; this doesn't help ranking and can make the result look spammy. The words from the search query are bolded, which can draw the searcher's attention to your listing.

Search engines don't always use the meta description in the results. Based on the query, other text from the page may be deemed more relevant and may be shown instead. Search engines will also pull this text from elsewhere if the meta description text is too short.

Let's take a closer look at the [how to rollerblade] results.

The eHow.com result has an informative and compelling description. From the source code, we can see that this text comes directly from the meta description (Figure 7.5).

```
<meta name="description" content="Learn tips and
techniques on how to rollerblade from putting on the
skate to controlling speed and tricks like jumping off
curbs." />
```

Figure 7.5   A Compelling Meta Description

Source: eHow.com

However, the result for wikihow.com isn't quite as succinct or compelling.

It wastes valuable real estate by repeating the heading of the page (which is already evident in the title), it is cluttered by ellipses and unfinished phrases, and it doesn't describe what the page is about (learning how to rollerblade). It appears instead to be about the history of rollerblading, which is not what the searcher is looking for.

Looking at the source code, the problem is clear. It appears the site is dynamically generating the meta description tag, which is not a problem generally, except that the description is simply pulled from the first set of words on the page.

This practice can be a scalable way to create unique meta descriptions for a large number of pages, but when implementing a technical solution like this, review the finished product and experiment with ways to dynamically generate descriptions that are more compelling and descriptive.

Headings   When possible, pages should use semantic markup for clearer meaning for both search engines and devices such as screen readers. Headings are marked up in HTML using <H> tags. Generally a page has one tag, a few more tags, and so on, much like numbering an outline. Headings are important for a couple of reasons. Search engines *can* use the text in them to determine relevance, although how much weight they're given may vary. More important, a descriptive heading can provide context to searchers to let them know they're on the correct page. As you recall from the page content phase of the searcher workflow, this context is important for anchoring visitors and ensuring they don't bounce back to the search results.

Content   Each page should contain enough text to provide valuable information to the visitor. This text should use the language of the visitor (based on keyword research).

➤ *Syndication*

There are good reasons for syndicating content. Syndication can bring traffic, exposure, and sales.

If you're a blogger, you might syndicate your posts to get wider distribution. If your posts are seen by a bigger audience, you might gain some of those readers for yourself. If your site provides authoritative resources, you might have a partnership with other sites that want to include that content. And if you sell products, you might provide affiliates with content feeds, which in turn brings in additional revenue.

But What Should Rank?   But from a search engine perspective, syndication can cause a bit of a conundrum. If what you wrote is a relevant result for a search, the search engine wants to show it to the searcher—but not show it twice (or three times, or maybe even a thousand times in the case of an affiliate feed). And that makes sense. If you're searching for something, you don't want multiple results that all lead to the same content, even if that content is on different sites.

So what's a search engine to do?

Search engines generally identify duplicate results and filter out all but one. They have lots of ways to decide which version to show. They try to figure out which one is the "original" by looking at things like which version was published first and which has the most links pointing to it.

Your content may appear on other sites at times other than when you syndicated it (such as when your RSS feed has been scraped), and search engines try to account for that too by looking at things like which site is more authoritative.

How Can You Make Sure Your Site Ranks First? So what do I suggest you do if you're syndicating content but want your original version to rank above the syndicated ones?

- Create a different version of the content to syndicate than what you write for your own site. This method works best for things like product affiliate feeds. I don't think it works as well for things like blog posts or other types of articles. Instead, you could do something like write a high-level summary article for syndication and a blog post with details about that topic for your own site.
- Always include absolute links back to your own site in the body of the article. This is particularly helpful when your content is scraped.
- Ask your syndication partners to block their version of your article (via robots.txt or a robots meta tag or the rel=canonical attribute that points back to your site). If you are able to, put together a syndication agreement that states they get your content as a benefit for their readers, not as a way to acquire search traffic for that content; then you can keep control of ranking for what you've written and they can provide a benefit to their audience.

Maintain Control If search is not yet a large acquisition channel for your site, then you may not mind if another site ranks for your material as you may get more traffic from the syndicated site (so make sure you at least have a link back to your site). But as your site starts to stand on its own and search traffic starts growing, you will want to have more control. So think of your longer-term strategy when you negotiate syndication partnerships and don't give up all of the control of the content you work so hard to create to others.

As noted in Chapter 6, syndication issues have gotten trickier with the launch of Google's Panda algorithm. If Google's algorithms find that a site is composed of a lot of syndicated (nonunique) content, they may lower the ranks of the entire site based on the Panda score.

➤ Content That's Not Unique

Syndication isn't the only instance in which duplication can cause ranking problems. Another common issue comes up with e-commerce sites. Many companies use manufacturer databases or product feeds to describe products for sale. After all, it may not be reasonable to write unique product descriptions for millions of products. But remember that thousands of other sites may be using those identical product descriptions. How do search engines decide which to rank?

You can try to outrank every site that uses the same product descriptions, but a better strategy may be to add unique value on top of that content. For instance, you can aggregate information to provide comparisons between products or brands. You can also enable user-generated content so that visitors can provide reviews, ratings, and comments. This information adds value to the page beyond the boilerplate description. (See Chapter 9 for more on this.)

■ SEARCH ENGINE TOOLS FOR WEBMASTERS

Both major search engines have tools and educational resources for site owners. These tools provide great diagnostic reports, as well as statistics, and ways of providing input to the engines. You can find these tools at:

Google Webmaster Central: google.com/webmasters

Microsoft Bing Webmaster Center: webmaster.bing.com

CHAPTER 7: WEB DEVELOPMENT CHECKLIST

Crawlability

❑ Every page on the site should have at least one internal link. The site should be easy to browse.

❑ Every page on the site should be listed in an XML Sitemap, which should then be submitted to the major search engines.

❑ The site should be well linked throughout the Web.

❑ Each URL should be accessible and not create infinite versions or redirect loops.

❑ Multiple versions of a URL shouldn't resolve to the same content, and if they do, canonicalization techniques should be implemented.

❑ If the URL structure changes, implement 301 redirects from the old URLs to the new ones.

❑ Ensure the site or parts of it aren't inadvertently blocked with robots.txt.

❑ Ensure you are using the tools from the major search engines to be alerted of any crawling issues.

Crawl Efficiency

❑ The server should quickly respond to requests.

❑ Pages should load quickly.

❑ Each page should contain substantial unique content.

❑ The server should use compression and should return a 304 not modified response when content hasn't changed.

Indexability

❑ Ensure redirects are implemented via 301 and not 302 (or through JavaScript).

❑ Ensure all content you want indexed is available and not blocked behind a login.

❑ Ensure all content is extractable. If the site is implemented using Flash, Silverlight, JavaScript, or AJAX, ensure those technologies are implemented in a search-friendly way.

❑ Ensure all multimedia, such as images and video, are implemented in a search-friendly way.

❑ The same URL shouldn't serve up different content. For instance, if you want to serve different content based on region, redirect visitors to a separate URL for each set of content.

❑ Ensure each page's title element, meta description tag, and H1 tags contain the vital keywords for the page and include them in a compelling way for visitors.

❑ Ensure that all content is unique across the Web. If you syndicate content or publish content that's syndicated, ensure you have a strategy to avoid duplication issues.

Chapter

8

How to Cut through the Data and Get the Actionable Metrics You Need

There's no shortage of analytics data available. In fact, that tends to be the problem. So much information exists that it can be difficult to figure out what's important and actionable. Particularly from a search perspective, the key is remembering those goals you defined when building searcher personas. What metrics give you insight into how well you are reaching those goals? And just as importantly, what can you do with the data you're tracking?

■ CONVERSION RATES

Businesses are finally starting to break out conversion rates from search. But too many of them start and end there. At a tech event in Seattle, Glenn Kelman, the chief executive officer (CEO) from Redfin noted that Redfin's conversion rate from search is low.[1] But "from search" is like calculating a conversion rate from TV ads with no interest in whether the commercials aired during a Friday night monster truck rally or a Saturday morning cartoon or tracking only the conversion rate for "advertising," when that might include TV, radio, print, and online.

Conversion rate is absolutely important to understanding how well a site is performing, but it's much more actionable when viewed by acquisition segment. Even better is if you can tie visitors to future behavior. Do visitors who come in through message boards talking about eco-friendly materials read an average of three articles on the site, share those links on two social media sites, which in turn bring in 12 visitors who convert?

Avinash Kaushik, Google's analytics evangelist and author of *Web Analytics: An Hour a Day* and *Web Analytics 2.0: The Art of Online Accountability and*

Science of Customer Centricity, suggests rolling all conversion data into one metric: task completion rate by primary purpose.[2]

He suggests finding out the core reasons why visitors come to your site. One way is to display an optional survey that asks, "Why are you visiting the site today?" and then determining whether each visitor segment was able to complete the task. Another way is to simply ask.

He suggests that this metric is more valuable than conversion rate to your business goal (selling something, etc.) because not all visitors are there for that purpose and, therefore, will never convert in the way you are measuring.[3] Some percentage of visitors is looking for company information, product support, or other information. You want to find out all the reasons that bring visitors to your site and if you are meeting their needs. In some cases, understanding this can help increase satisfaction of existing customers and improve customer lifetime value; in other cases, this can help increase engagement of potential customers and improve the likelihood that they will return to purchase later. But, just as important, by segmenting those visitors who are not there to purchase today (or do whatever task is mapped to your conversion goal), you have better insight into how well you are converting those visitors who do have purchase intent.

■ DEFINING GOALS

Define your goals before setting up metrics for your search acquisition strategy. When I ask people what their goals are for a particular site or page, I hear answers like "to rank well" and "to get more traffic." But those aren't business goals. You want to rank well only so you can attract visitors to your site, and you want to attract visitors to your site only if you have a reasonable chance of converting them.

A 2011 Econsultancy/SEMPO survey found that by far the most common metric for search engine optimization (SEO) success is site traffic (Figure 8.1). But of course, untargeted site traffic isn't valuable to your bottom line, and focusing on that number alone can be misleading and misguide your search investment.

■ WHAT'S NOT IMPORTANT

Look at many Web analytics and SEO reports and you'll see things like the following:

- Rankings reports that list hundreds of keywords and how the site ranks for them
- Indexing reports that show the change in the number of indexed pages over time
- Absolute traffic numbers

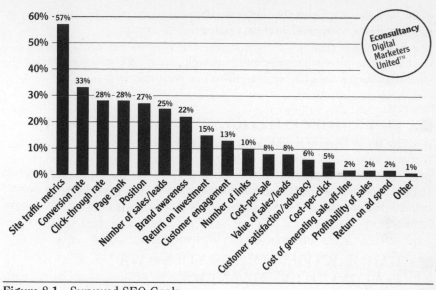

Figure 8.1 Surveyed SEO Goals
Source: Econsultancy/SEMPO[4]

- Overall percentage of traffic from organic search and overall conversion rate from organic search
- Page views
- Daily unique visitors
- Top entry and exit pages
- Visitor screen resolutions and browser versions

But these numbers tell us little if anything about the performance of the site. Who are these visitors? What are they looking for? Are they the visitors we are trying to attract? Did we engage them?

Better metrics would focus on goals and actionable insights:

- What's the organic search traffic breakdown for query categories we are targeting, and how are those visitors behaving on the site? (Are they converting? Engaging? Abandoning right away?)
- What query categories aren't performing as well as we'd like? Is the performance breakdown at the search result (resulting in lack of traffic for those queries to the site) or at the site level (resulting in early abandonment or low conversion rates)?
- What are the primary reasons visitors are coming to the site, and what are their task completion rates?
- What referring links are bringing the most traffic, and how well are those visitors performing on the site? If they're performing well, this may be an audience you should spend time cultivating.

The specific metrics that help you measure your business are unique to your site, but always evaluate them against the following:

- Do they give you insight into how well you are meeting your goals?
- Are they actionable? What will you do with this data?

■ COMPETITIVE INTELLIGENCE AS A BENCHMARK TO HOW WELL YOU'RE REALLY DOING

Benchmarking data can be a valuable data point about how well you're really doing. It can help you know if an increase in search traffic is due to an overall trend of higher search volumes for your industry or is at the expense of your competition.

■ HAVING ACTIONABLE ANALYTICS DATA IS A COMPETITIVE ADVANTAGE

By some estimates, only 23 percent of sites have an analytics package installed, and only 1 percent are doing A/B or multivariate testing.[5] By simply having these data at hand, you're well ahead of most of your competition.

■ ATTRIBUTION

Attribution issues make metrics even more complicated. As we've seen, searchers don't always follow a straight path from search to purchase. They not only may search for several different things (with subsequent queries triggered in part by results they saw in earlier queries) but may also search over more than one session. One study found that 56 percent of purchases occur in a search session later than the first one.[6] Another found that only 43 percent of purchasers make that purchase within an hour of the site visit.[7] For some categories, the lag times can be substantial, such as shown in Figure 8.2.

eBay, which we'll learn more about shortly, handles the attribution issue in its metrics by using cookie data to store visitor information and attributing a conversion to search if it happens within 24 hours. The numbers tell us that this method isn't perfect, but it's better than attributing conversions only at the point of searching.

In addition to the time lag element of attribution, there's the triggering element. We can see this in a hypothetical example for Volvo. In this example, we'll consider entering a zip code to find the nearest dealer a conversion (Figure 8.3).

Looking at these hypothetical numbers separately, branded search converts significantly better than nonbranded search or display ads. With display

Figure 8.2 Travel Search Conversion
Source: DoubleClick

ads, 20,000 people saw the ad, but only 1,000 of those clicked on it; and of that 1,000, only 50 converted. But with branded search, 10,000 people clicked on the Volvo result after searching for it and 6,000 of them converted. In isolation, it seems clear that we should stop our display advertising spend, stop optimizing for nonbranded searches, and put all of our energy toward branded search. Or should we?

Let's take a closer look. In this example, 50,000 people did nonbranded searches (such as for "fuel-efficient cars" and "safe cars"). Of those 50,000, 30,000 visited the site and 30,000 × 0.15 converted, but all 50,000 saw the Volvo brand in the results. Of the 20,000 people who saw the display ad, only 1,000 clicked through to the site, but all 20,000 saw the Volvo brand.

Of the people who saw the Volvo ad, 1,000 later searched for [Volvo] and clicked through to the site, and 5,000 of the people who did nonbranded searches and saw the Volvo result later searched for [Volvo] and clicked through to the site.

So without the display ads and nonbranded search results, we'd be left with only 4,000 visitors. Study after study[8] has found that most prepurchase

	A	B	C
1	Entry Point	Monthly Volume	Conversion Rate
2	Display ads	1,000 visitors (20,000 impressions)	5%
3	Non-branded search	30,000 visitors	15%
4	Branded search	10,000 visitors	60%

Figure 8.3 Conversion Metrics from Multiple Channels

activity involves generic terms and that brand searches tend to happen only close to purchase (Figures 8.4 and 8.5).

Clearly the generic searches are providing insight into brands or the searchers would simply begin with brand searches. Many searches don't search for brands at all before purchasing.

But how do you track searcher behavior across multiple sessions? Several companies are trying to solve this problem. Some of them store information in a user's cookie when a display ad is served, for instance, and later can determine what users saw the display ad and then later did searches that led those users to the site (and what those searches were). These technologies aren't able to tell when a searcher has seen an organic result and not clicked on it. (The only way to currently get organic impression information is via Google Webmaster Tools, and those data are only in aggregate, not per visitor.)

You can track visitors by IP address as well, although this method isn't 100 percent reliable either, since many people search at work and buy at home or search in one location and then e-mail their spouse the link for later purchase.

Figure 8.4   The Importance of Generic Searches
Source: DoubleClick

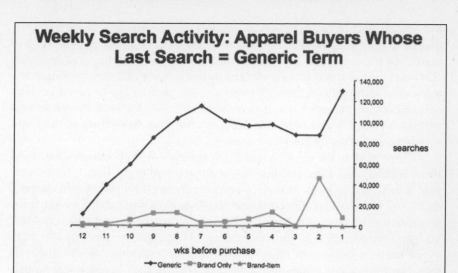

Figure 8.5 Generic Search Behavior
Source: DoubleClick

For more in-depth discussion of attribution in Web analytics and possible approaches, see *Web Analytics 2.0: The Art of Online Accountability and Science of Customer Centricity* by Avinash Kaushik.

■ HOW EBAY USES ANALYTICS TO INFORM WHAT THEY SHOULD DO, NOT JUST SHOW WHAT THEY'VE DONE

eBay has one of the largest websites in the world and, judging by the paid search ads served up with nearly every query, is one of the largest bidders on keywords. Between the paid search data about what people are searching for and what they click on and information about how visitors navigate the site, eBay has one of the largest data sets on user behavior of any site on the Web. A few short years ago, those at eBay threw most of that information away after only six months. In 2006, they realized they had a gold mine of data that could help them better understand their customers, build better buying and selling experiences, and improve eBay. Now, they protect that data vigilantly and have realigned business processes and goals to prioritize analytics throughout the organization.

According to Greg Fant, vice president of customer insights and marketing, analytics data don't just tell eBay how it has done; they tell what it *should* do. Decisions that used to take weeks of one person's opinion versus another are now data-driven. The site's testing platform helps confirm the decisions.

Using data to drive strategy was an organizational shift in solving problems that didn't come easily. But the benefits were huge. Fant says those at eBay used to be blind to problems but now they can see issues as they pop up. Issues that used to take three to four months to track down can now be found in a week. And shifting from financial metrics to site metrics has helped them better connect with customers and maximize happiness for both the buyer and the seller. They found that data were so vital that they changed their site infrastructure to get the data they needed.[9]

Those at eBay are quick to stress that search and Web analytics data help them with all decisions, not just marketing-related ones. Both organic and paid search data help them discern searcher intent, find patterns in queries, and learn broader classifications and interests than what they can get from just monitoring on-site behavior. They pay close attention to what queries searchers are pairing with the word "eBay." What problems are they having? What are they looking for eBay to provide? By identifying "silent sufferers," they can learn about issues and solve them before they become widespread pain points.

Segmenting by query type has helped those at eBay identify different loyalty points, learn about ways different segments are motivated, and begin to better understand the analytics holy grail that is customer lifetime value.

How has eBay been able to transition to a data-driven organization, build search data into product strategy, and break down data silos? It has been a long process. Those at eBay credit support from the top: board-level agreement led to an organizational shift and analytical platform from which to base decisions. And the rest of the company came on board through a common set of metrics and a vision across the entire company. When everyone is working toward the same goal and is measuring the same things, sharing data becomes significantly easier. For eBay, that common metric is purchases per week. Analytics used to be spread out under multiple divisions. They've now centralized. They focus on data that are practical and actionable.

They go after low-hanging fruit for quick wins along the way while they work on longer-term initiatives such as new infrastructure and an A/B testing platform. They build some things on a separate infrastructure for faster implementation and less impact to the primary site. They prioritize (based, of course, on data). And they've built an in-house organic search team that is focused on understanding how Google crawls, indexes, and ranks. Dennis Goedegebuure, who until recently was eBay's senior manager of SEO, made it his mission during his years there to build a centralized organic search team and develop search-friendly best practices throughout the organization.

Fant talks about a new breed of data-driven marketers and leadership teams who are ushering eBay into a new era of audience analysis, market research, and product strategy. At eBay, everyone understands that the user experience often begins on Google, and they spend a lot of time working to understand what Google searchers are really looking for.

Both intent and attribution are issues that eBay spends a lot of time on. A sample customer interaction on eBay is shown in Figure 8.6.

In this example, the searcher initially looks for [Google Android] and clicks on eBay's paid search ad. This brings the searcher to an eBay page that lists items related to Google Android, including phones, phone covers, and chargers. The searcher later goes back to Google and this time remembers both that eBay had relevant information and that the previous search hadn't been specific enough to bring back only phones. So, the second search is for [eBay Android G1]. This time, the searcher clicks eBay's organic result and lands on another search results page that still isn't quite specific enough. The searcher then searches within eBay to better refine the results and ultimately clicks an item listing.

In this scenario, if eBay tracked only the search that led to the click on the item listing, they would know only that the visitor had searched for [G1 HTC Android phone] within eBay. Had they followed the path back only one level, they would know that being visible in organic results is

Figure 8.6   A Sample eBay Search Session

Source: Google Search and eBay

important, but they wouldn't know that the paid search ad was important for branding and caused the searcher to include the word "eBay" in that search. By following the visitor all the way to the initial search, eBay knows that the word "google" was initially an important component, dropped later only to make room for more specific keywords. The complete picture is much more helpful in formulating customer understanding than just the final query.

But this very common navigation path raises hard attribution questions. Who gets credit for the sale? Paid search? Organic search? Internal site search? In truth, they all contributed to the customer's path to conversion. Without any one of them, the sale may never have happened.

When eBay started revising their product pages based on user data such as this, traffic from search went down. eBay couldn't be more pleased. Why? Because eBay has higher quality, more descriptive pages in the search results, the quality of the traffic now is substantially better. Searchers who are genuinely interested in buying and selling are the ones clicking through the search results and visiting the site. And the pages they are visiting are the pages most likely to convert. eBay no longer has as much unqualified traffic to pages that have low conversion value. eBay has learned that traffic alone is meaningless. More traffic isn't necessarily better.

By incorporating search data throughout their organization, eBay makes better business decisions, builds more effective product strategy, connects more closely with customers, and knows about problems before they escalate. It has created a more efficient working relationship between teams, and ultimately, it has increased purchases per week.

■ CAN SOFTWARE ACCURATELY CALCULATE ATTRIBUTION?

Many analytics companies have been working to address the issues of attribution and return on investment (ROI) metrics for organic search. Can these tools help eBay with its attribution problem? Maybe. Richard Zwicky, founder of Enquisite, which had been working on this problem, said they had looked at using persistent and session-based cookies to understand the full visitor path, not simply the last click. They tracked what the visitor searched for before the last search, and they could weigh the value of the clicks themselves. They also attempted to relate value across channels. Just how valuable was that paid search ad in influencing the searcher's decision to later do a brand search and ultimately purchase from eBay?

ClearSaleing is one of the many companies that have looked at tackling the attribution issue. Their *Attribution Management Buyer's Guide* outlines their approach to calculating attribution across online channels, including both paid and organic search.[10] As they note,

. . . many conversions are the result of multiple forms of advertising. For example, a banner impression leads someone [to] click on a paid search ad, then an organic search, and then they convert. If the solution you're using is only able to capture paid search, it would be oblivious to the fact that the banner impression is what introduced that person to your brand, and that the organic listing is what eventually closed the deal.[11]

■ WHAT ABOUT OFFLINE ATTRIBUTION?

Of course, ideally, attribution tracking would include offline channels as well (both for bringing in customers and for the conversion). How can you track a billboard that leads to a search that leads to a sale, such as the case of the movie *2012*? What about a search that leads to a phone call that leads to a sale? We know that television advertising triggers search[12] and we know that searches are often the first step to offline purchases,[13] but can we track that?

A number of at least partial solutions exist for offline attribution, but the key is understanding that a relationship exists, sharing data between departments, and devoting resources to learning how these relationships work for your customer base.

For instance, dynamic number insertion[14] can help track phone calls based on different search ads. You can use a different phone number online than in printed materials so that you can track online and offline channels. You can provide online coupons to be used for offline purchases. You can even display different coupons based on what search led the visitor to the page. At a more basic level, you can track the change in offline purchases as your site becomes more visible in organic search (noting other factors, such as advertising and seasonal fluctuations that may impact this).

Companies are working to both provide better offline metrics and integrate offline and online data into a comprehensive customer picture. Euclid Elements, for instance, professes to offer "online analytics for the offline world." They seek "to enable retailers and business owners with physical locations to measure things like foot traffic by time of day, average customer time in store, loyalty and lift of online promotions, as well as the effectiveness of window displays and other metrics" by tracking customers via their smartphones (Figure 8.7).[15]

Path Intelligence is offering similar technology, piloted by U.S. malls during the 2011 holiday shopping season:[16]

Options include tracking response to mailers and other advertising by providing the equivalent of Web metrics like unique visitors, "page impressions" (measuring how many people walked past a display or advertisement), and "click-through" (determining how many people who passed an advertisement then visited the store associated with it).[17]

Figure 8.7   Euclid Elements Offline Tracking
Source: Euclid Elements

■ THE TROUBLE WITH DATA

The trouble with data on the Web is that they're impossible to measure with absolute accuracy.[18] This is true of data everywhere, of course; it's just more measurable on the Web. Cities hire car-counting firms to track how busy intersections are to make decisions about new traffic signals, and although it's likely the counters miss a few cars here and there, the city can still be fairly confident in the conclusions. We track how many people are watching particular television shows by relying on a sampling of viewers to accurately log their viewing habits. They don't, of course, but it's still the best signal we've got. With Web analytics data, it's much easier to tell just how far off the numbers are. If you run two Web analytics programs on your site in parallel (and many sites do), you will come up with two sets of data that can never be reconciled. But that's okay. Rather than spend your time trying to reconcile them, just know that they are about as accurate as Nielsen data or car counting and can be used for overall trends and measurements, if not exact counts.

■ THE VALUE OF AN EXPERIENCED IN-HOUSE WEB ANALYTICS EXPERT

Accurate, actionable data are critical in today's online environment. And with so much information available—much of it confusing and not actionable—the best way to cut through to what really matters is to ensure you have a skilled Web analytics expert on staff who can cull through the hundreds of data points and give you the top five metrics that show you how the business is going and help you make business decisions.

Avinash Kaushik wrote on his blog about the top things to look for in a Web analytics manager. The person should:

- *Have passion.* "You have to love the Web, you have to love its life changing power, you have to believe that at some level you, yes you, have the power to change people's lives by killing reports that show, in 8 font, conversion and visitors stats and replacing them with analysis that will fundamentally improve the experiences of your customers and ease their stress."
- *Love change.* "The Web changes and grows and morphs like an alien being. You just got used to prefetching and here is Google trying to guess searcher intent (and now 'personalized search' where even your awesome organic listing might not result in your being number one) and then come RIAs and Ajax and then will come something else and, like a tidal wave, it keeps coming. Ask for one thing they know of that will mess up the analytics world in the next 180 days. If they have an answer, you have a winner."
- *Question data.* "The core problem with all the tools today is that they rely on data that usually tells you little. [Good analysts] question the data and analysis and bring a new and different perspective and can overcome cool recommendations from the latest consultant."
- *Believe in customer-driven innovation.* "True innovation and sustainable competitive advantage will [often] come from actions that are Customer Driven. What this translates into is a Manager who has had exposure to Testing and Usability and Surveys and Site Visits and Field Studies or Market Research . . . someone who can bring to bear their experience to find the right ways for you to apply the power of analytics and research to find the right answers for your customers."

Data are tricky. You need to make sure the underlying data are solid so that you know you can trust your conclusions. You need to measure the right things. And you need to focus your investments on analyzing data that are actionable. A great Web analytics manager, particularly one who understands that all acquisition channels bring the same customers, can ensure that you are looking at the right data and taking full advantage of it.

Chapter 9

Social Media and Search

W e've seen how valuable it can be to appear in search results when searchers are looking for what you have to offer, and we've seen the important role that links play in helping your site rank well. We've also seen how keyword research can provide insight into how your potential customers are thinking about your brand, your industry, and your competition.

Social media can help on all of these fronts, working as a brand amplifier and customer support extension to deepen engagement with your customers.

Search and social media became even more entwined in 2011 with the launch of Google+. In November 2011, Google made brand pages available for Google+, presenting a new opportunity for organizations to connect with audiences. Google has increasingly been incorporating social data and content into its Web search results, and Bing has been doing the same (particularly based on its partnership with Facebook).

Over the past year, I repeatedly heard the same question: Should an organization invest its resources in search or social? But that's the wrong question. As discussed in Chapter 6, you have one set of customers (not separate customers who use e-mail versus ones who use search versus ones on social media). Learn where your customers are and meet them there.

As discussed more deeply in Chapter 10, it's not the case that consumers are abandoning search engines for social networking sites (90 percent of us use search engines versus 47 percent of us who use social media).[1] As we saw in Chapter 1, search volume continues to increase every year. We, as online consumers, are augmenting our search activity with social media activity, not replacing it.

In addition, although search can often be a more effective way to reach buyers, social media can be a great way to improve brand perception and increase support reach.

■ WHAT IS SOCIAL MEDIA?

Lately, when people hear the term *social media*, they tend to think of the fairly new developments of sites such as Facebook and Twitter, but in reality, social media has been around as long as we have been social and have used media. Letters to the editor in traditional print newspapers are an example of social media.

Online social media, in turn, has been around as long as we've been online. Before what we now know as the World Wide Web, people were connecting all over the world via bulletin board systems (BBS) and later in chat rooms on platforms such as Prodigy and CompuServe. Today, even multiplayer online games such as World of Warcraft are social media—they are yet another way that people connect online. Online social media, as defined for the purposes of this book, includes:

- *Discussion sites:* These sites include general and topic-specific message boards.
- *Content-sharing sites:* These include any sites that enable users to share what they've created with one another, such as photo-sharing sites (such as Flickr), blogging platforms (such as Blogger and WordPress), and microblogging platforms (such as Twitter). For the purpose of this book, social bookmarking sites, such as Delicious and Digg fit into this category as well.
- *Social networking sites:* These include places that exist specifically to facilitate connections between people. For instance, Facebook began as a way for college students to stay in touch and now enables friends, families, and colleagues to share contact information, photos, and a variety of details about their lives.
- *Review sites:* These are most often seen as stand-alone sites, such as TripAdvisor, which focuses on sharing information about travel, but they can also be part of larger sites. Amazon, for instance, is an e-commerce site but has a large social review component.

Of course, you can see that many of these categories overlap. Digg and Slashdot both enable users to share content they've found, as well as discuss that content with one another. Flickr is primarily focused on sharing photos, but users often get into lengthy discussions and form groups around particular topics.

Involvement in social media can be beneficial to companies for a number of reasons, but for this book, we'll focus on how social media can benefit you as it relates to search.[2]

■ OTHER TYPES OF MEDIA

Being involved in other types of media (such as press) can be beneficial from a search perspective for many of the same reasons as social media, so it's included in this chapter as well. Other types of online media include online newspapers and magazines (and blogs as well, although those can also be considered a type of content-sharing social media), press releases, syndicated or original articles published on sites other than your own, and interviews (given to traditional press or others).

■ BEING VISIBLE IN SEARCH RESULTS

As we've seen, if your brand doesn't appear in search results for queries related to your industry or product, searchers are unlikely to consider you and you'll often lose that potential customer to the competition. One way to appear in search results, of course, is by ensuring your own site appears, but social media sites give you nearly infinite opportunity to show up for any number of queries that use language you may not even realize your customers are using.

In addition, many people are now searching social media sites directly. You can get twice the visibility (in both Web searches and social media searches) with one investment.

In the past couple of years, Google and Bing have begun incorporating content shared on social networks into personalized results. This means, for instance, if someone you are friends with on Facebook has "liked" an article, then you might see that article in Bing search results (when it otherwise wouldn't be listed), and if someone you subscribe to in Google Reader posts an article, you might see it listed in Google search results.

A site with content that a lot of people share on various social networks then has a significantly increased opportunity to be seen by searchers. This is described in more detail in Chapter 10.

The most important thing to realize is that potential customers are looking for authenticity. Attempts to blanket social media sites with positive mentions of your brand are likely to backfire. Much better tactics include:

- Ensuring you have a voice in places your customers are talking about you.
- Facilitating discussions online with your customers and potential customers.
- Providing useful and targeted content (in the form of press releases or other resources, articles, and interviews) to interested content creators. (This means not sending out press releases to an untargeted mass distribution list, but identifying those reporters and bloggers who care about your industry and sending them customized e-mail that describes why you think they're interested and what you're willing to provide to them.)

Monitor the likely places where people could be talking about your brand, product, or industry (you can do this manually or by engaging a service), and build up a brand presence in those locations. Contribute to the conversation whenever useful (by providing additional resources or information, clarifying details, and fixing problems).

The trick is to be helpful rather than overly promotional. Keep in mind that people aren't spending time on these sites to be marketed to. However, they are interested in your product or industry and welcome solutions to their problems, inside information, and avenues for providing feedback.

How does this relate to search? Say you run a printer business and you've started contributing to printer forums in threads where users have been troubleshooting issues. For instance, in one thread, a customer who owns the Acme 1250 color inkjet may be asking if he can print photos, and if so, how he can produce the best prints. You reply with details on the best paper to use, the settings to configure, and how to change the options for 3×5 versus 5×7 prints. The customer is ecstatic and tells all his friends about the great service he received.

In the days before the Web, he may have simply asked his friends or the local print shop for help and your company would never have had the opportunity to help him. Or, he may have called your 800 number, gotten great service, and told all his friends.

The difference now is that at least 10,000 people a month are searching for information on how to print photos.[3] If the discussion thread that you've provided such useful information for appears on the first page of results for these queries, you've helped open a whole new avenue for customer acquisition. As a bonus, the discussion will be slightly different on each site. Some people will ask how to print digital photos, others will wonder how to print pictures, and still others will ask if they can print pictures from their digital cameras. If you run a printer business, you'll want to include a page on your website that describes digital printing, but it's unlikely you'll be able to account for all the various ways people will search for the topic. By contributing to discussions throughout the Web that ask questions about digital printing, you'll have many more opportunities to rank for related queries, no matter how they're worded.

These discussions may also help your brand be seen by people doing more generic searches, such as those researching what type of printer to buy. If even a small subset of those searchers are in the market for a printer and see a discussion in which your brand has shown itself to be helpful and responsive to customer needs, you've gained an advantage in competitive analysis those searchers may be doing.

■ THE SYNERGIES OF SEARCH AND SOCIAL MEDIA AND PUBLIC RELATIONS

Consider that the public relations (PR) you do or social media you become involved with will live well beyond the initial publication or post.

For instance, consider a restaurant. In years past, a positive write-up in a newspaper or magazine might result in filled tables the next weekend. One neighbor recounting a delicious meal to another neighbor while walking the dog might get the restaurant an additional reservation that week.

But consider how things have changed with our increasing reliance on search. When visiting Bologna, Italy in 2009, I decided to venture into the town for lunch. How did I pick a location in a city famous for its food? With the help of a search engine, of course. Searching for "best place to have lunch in Bologna Italy" brought up an article in *The Guardian* called "24 hours in Bologna: Foodie Heaven" that listed five promising choices. These five restaurants didn't only get the lift in visibility during the week that article initially ran in the paper or among regular readers. The article was written in 2000 and was still showing up on the first page of search results—thanks to one positive customer review.

I did the same search in December 2011 and that article is still not only listed on the first page of the search results, but is also now ranking even higher than in 2009. That's 11 years of payoff for one piece of public relations.

Also in the top five was a discussion of Bologna restaurants from the message board Chowhound.com (Figure 9.1).

Businesses spend a great deal of time and energy on getting that one positive mention in mainstream press, that one good interview, that one well-placed signal of support, even though that publicity can be fleeting and untargeted. But let PR and social media work for you in search and capture a far more receptive audience (one who is specifically searching for what you offer) for years to come.

■ ONLINE REPUTATION MANAGEMENT

If you've been around for any length of time, it's likely that someone out there doesn't like you. If you're absent from search, it could be your detractor's site that shows up when potential customers search for you. Generally, there's not much you can do about this. Search engines such as Google merely index the Web and don't evaluate the contents for lack of criticism or even truthfulness.

But if your brand has positive mentions throughout the Web via social media sites, press, and other avenues, those mentions could rank highly and push negative mentions of your brand lower in the search results, decreasing chances that searchers even see them.

For instance, Seattle patent lawyer Adam Philipp has been able to ensure the entire first page of search results for his name are positive by completing social network profiles that rank well and taking advantage of YouTube video (not that I'm implying any negative results for his name exist, of course). See Figure 9.2.

As you can see, the first (and fairly easy) step is just to make sure that you have a presence on relevant social networks so that your profile from those locations is available to show up in relevant search results.

Figure 9.1 Google Search Results for [Places to Have Lunch in Bologna Italy]

Source: Google Search

➤ Lessons from the TSA

We can see this in action with an incident involving the U.S. Transportation Security Administration (TSA). A mom wrote a scathing blog post in which she accused the TSA of taking her baby from her and walking away with him during a routine security check at the airport. The story caught fire, and the Google search results for [tsa takes baby] were filled with recounting of the story. The TSA responded the very same day on their blog with video footage showing that, in fact, the baby was never separated from the mother and sat in his stroller beside her during the screening. The content of the Google search results quickly changed. A search for [tsa takes baby] became filled with stories about the TSA blog post and the original stories included updates with the TSA's side of the story (Figure 9.3).

What could have been a public relations disaster for the TSA was quickly averted, and anyone searching for information on the story was presented with both sides. The TSA didn't stop there. They monitored the story and updated their post with answers to questions and additional video footage.

adam philipp seattle

About 7,890,000 results (0.24 seconds)

Adam Philipp — AEON Law
aeonlaw.com/attorneys/adam-l-k-philipp/
Adam L.K. **Philipp**. 1218 3rd Ave., Suite 2100. **Seattle**, WA 98101. Phone:
. 206.217.2200 . Fax: 206.217.2201. Email: **adam@aeonlaw.com** · Download
Adam's ...

Seattle Patent Attorneys and High Technology Intellectual Property ...
aeonlaw.com/
Seattle patent and IP attorneys at ÆON Law provide great high-technology ...

⊞ Show more results from aeonlaw.com

Adam Philipp (@mypatents) on Twitter
twitter.com/mypatents
Sign up for Twitter to follow **Adam Philipp** (@mypatents). High-tech patent attorney in
Seattle. ... Get short, timely messages from **Adam Philipp**. Twitter is a rich ...

Lawyer **Adam Philipp** - **Seattle** Attorney - Avvo.com
www.avvo.com/attorneys/98101-wa-adam-philipp-31663.html
Read 4 client reviews. Compare **Adam Philipp** to other Patent Application attorneys in
Seattle. Write a review. Read professional ratings.

Adam Philipp | LinkedIn
www.linkedin.com/in/adamphilipp
Greater **Seattle** Area - Founder of ÆON Law
View **Adam Philipp's** professional profile on LinkedIn. LinkedIn is the world's ... Founder
of ÆON Law. Location: Greater **Seattle** Area; Industry: Law Practice ...

Protecting IP Part #1 with **Adam Philipp** AEONLaw - **Seattle** Startups ...

www.youtube.com/watch?v=SU0rJEckSaQ
Sep 26, 2011 - 12 min - Uploaded by seattlestartupsnet
In this episode Toddy Mladenov from **Seattle** Startups Network talks with
Adam Philipp from ÆONLaw, a **Seattle** law firm ...

Protecting IP Part #2 with **Adam Philipp** AEONLaw - **Seattle** Startups ...

www.youtube.com/watch?v=48Dg-_0Q9Uc
Sep 25, 2011 - 13 min - Uploaded by seattlestartupsnet
In this episode Toddy Mladenov from **Seattle** Startups Network and
Adam Philipp from ÆONLaw discuss patents in detail ...

More videos for adam philipp seattle »

Figure 9.2   Social Media Sites in Search Results
Source: Google Search

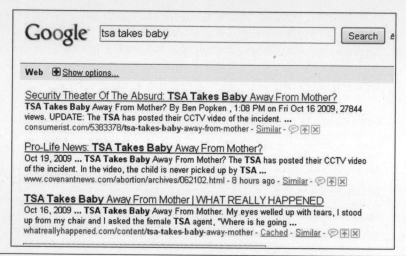

Figure 9.3 Google Search Results for [TSA Takes Baby]

Source: Google Search

➤ *Lessons from the 2012 Presidential Republican Primary Race*

In November 2011, presidential candidate Herman Cain was accused of sexual harassment. Searches for the topic skyrocketed (Figure 9.4).

Cain's campaign realized potential voters were searching on this and related topics on both Google and Twitter and bought paid search ads to tell their candidate's side of the story.[4]

Figure 9.4 Google Search Interest for [Cain Accuser]

Source: Google Insights for Search (October 30, 2011–November 12, 2011)

Michael Johnson, director of new media for the Cain campaign, said, "It is always important to control the message and when there is so much noise online, it is important for us to get in front of it and put our message out there."

■ HELPING YOUR COMPANY SITE TO RANK WELL

As mentioned in Chapter 6 relevant external links to your site are an important factor in how search engines decide how to order search results. By raising awareness about your brand and product on a site such as Digg or Flickr, you increase the chances that others will mention (and link to) you in blogs, forums, and social networking sites. The key is targeting an interested audience. Although Digg has a large audience, it may not include very many people who are interested in your industry and who are likely to, in turn, blog about it.

■ MARKET RESEARCH

In Chapter 2, you learned about how to use keyword research tools to find out what your potential customers are most interested in. You can also use search itself to find out what they're saying about you, your competition, and your industry. The advantage of adding social media search to your market research tool set is that you'll get close to real-time information that can help alert you to any upcoming public relations issues, get a head start on the competition about coming trends, and get much richer detail than a list of generated keywords from search data can provide.

You're already keeping track of where you're being talked about online and becoming involved in the conversation as described previously. Now you can simply take the next step and use this information for market research.

■ FINDING OUT WHERE PEOPLE ARE TALKING ABOUT YOU ONLINE

The first step to finding out where the conversations of interest to you are happening online is compiling a list of sources. Next, compile a list of topics to search for (you might use standard keyword research to augment this): generally your brand, your competition, your products, and industry-specific topics. Then, conduct the searches and save the results. In many cases, you can set up alerts so that you are notified right away when a conversation is taking place.

You have many options for this process—from completely manual (and free) to engaging an expensive service that not only conducts the searches but analyzes the information and creates reports on it.

Following are some suggestions on where to start when embarking on this task manually.

- *Use Google search*. With Google advanced options, you can restrict searches to a specific timeframe (such as the past 24 hours) and can even search through only reviews or only discussion forums. You can also use Google Blog Search to search through only blogs and Google News to search through only news (Figure 9.5).
- *Use Google Alerts*. Google Alerts enables you to set up automated searches for news, blogs, video, groups, and Web search and have the results delivered via e-mail or RSS as they happen, once a day, or once a week.
- *Use vertical search engines*. Take advantage of the search built into many sites. Twitter, YouTube, and Flickr, for instance, all have fairly robust search capabilities. Some sites even let you subscribe to results so that you can be alerted to new discussions as they happen.
- *Seek out reviews*. If you sell a product or service, chances are good that someone, somewhere, is reviewing what you have to offer. If you provide a product, check out e-commerce sites, such as Amazon, that encourage reviews. And look for targeted review sites (such as TripAdvisor for travel and Epinions for everything else).
- *Find targeted communities*. Nearly every topic has an enthusiast community and many brands do as well (Figure 9.6).

Check Flickr, for instance, for groups, discussions, and photos (Figure 9.7).

Figure 9.5 Google Search Results for [Taryn Rose]
Source: Google Search

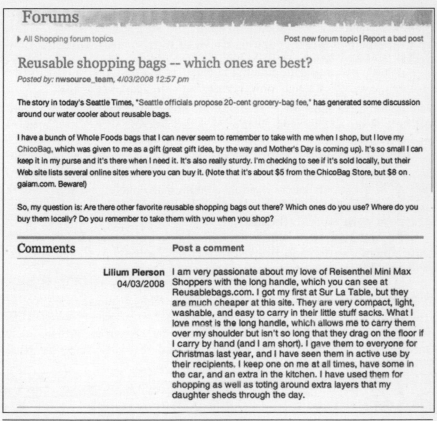

Figure 9.6 A Community for Every Passion

Source: Personal screen capture

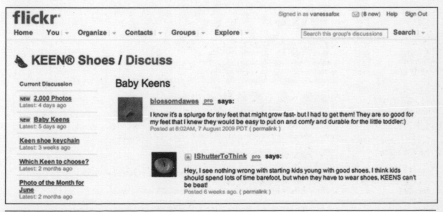

Figure 9.7 Photo Communities

Source: Flickr

■ AVERTING A PUBLIC RELATIONS DISASTER

Up-to-the-minute focus groups via search of social media chatter not only provide long-term insight into future product direction and customer engagement but can alert you to an issue before it becomes a crisis.

When Motrin launched its "baby wearing" campaign, they didn't need to commission a customer survey to find out how viewers perceived it. They had to look no further than Twitter, a microblogging service that enables anyone to post short thoughts on the Web (Figure 9.8).

A quick search the day after the campaign launched revealed that many moms were offended by the campaign; in fact, they created the #motrinmom hashtag (a grassroots categorization system that enables users to cluster their posts together under a single topic) to compile their grievances. The negative posts rose quickly (Figure 9.9).[5]

The *New York Times* noted that within hours of the campaign launch, #motrinmom was the most tweeted subject on Twitter.[6] A YouTube video sprung up that showcased the posts (Figure 9.10).[7]

Motrin may have had a misstep with the campaign, but they had instant access to amazing consumer feedback. Did they take advantage of it? Not at first. In fact, Motrin didn't appear to even realize their customers were talking about them online until a blogger called their agency to ask about the uproar. Once alerted, they took down the ad and said that they "take feedback

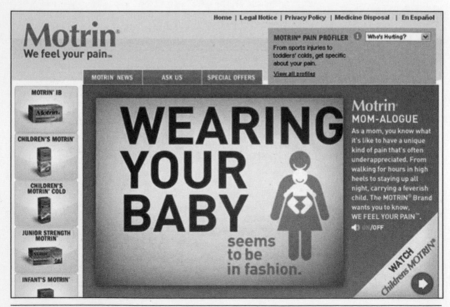

Figure 9.8 Motrin Ad: "Baby Wearing"
Source: Motrin

Figure 9.9   [Motrin] Trends on Twitter

Source: Twitscoop.com

seriously." And, after the incident, I imagine they are doing a better job of understanding where they might find that feedback in our online world.

■ GARNERING SUPPORT

Remember the Occupy movement search interest from Chapter 2? The movement has used social media to keep those searchers informed, rally their troops, and keep people interested.[8]

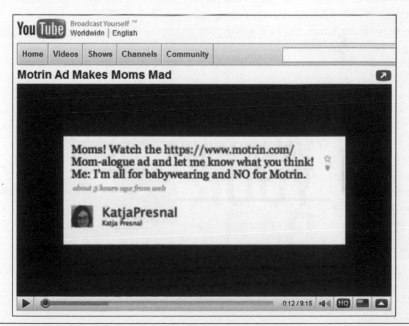

Figure 9.10   Mom's Take Their Motrin Anger to YouTube

Source: YouTube

@Adbusters
Adbusters Magazine

Dear Americans, this July 4th dream of insurrection against corporate rule http://bit.ly/kejAUy #occupywallstreet

4 Jul via TweetDeck

Figure 9.11 The Tweet That Started the Occupy Wall Street Movement
Source: Twitter

"I think the online component was critical—the ability to stream video, to capture the images and create records and narratives of sacrifice and resistance," said Yochai Benkler, a professor at Harvard Law School and codirector of the Berkman Center for Internet and Society at Harvard.

The movement started on Twitter in July 2011 with a tweet[9] calling for a march in Manhattan in September. (See Figure 9.11.)

Videos, such as one showing police pepper spraying students at the University of California, Davis, spread on YouTube and helped keep the movement's momentum going (see Figure 9.12). As of late November 2011, 1.7 million videos have been tagged on YouTube with "occupy" and collectively have been viewed 73 million times.[10] As of early December 2011, the video from the University of California, Davis, alone had been viewed 1.4 million times.

■ BUT WE WANT TO CONTROL OUR BRANDING!

Many companies are understandably hesitant to enter the new world of social media. After all, historically, only those with media and PR training made official statements on behalf of companies for good reason—an entire brand can be at risk with one wrong comment. And legal and marketing departments the world over have spent substantial resources developing branding guidelines and messaging requirements.

But the truth is that the world has changed. And not participating in the conversation is a loud statement of its own to your customer base. You can't control your branding message in any case because your customers are already talking about you online. The best you can do is to participate.

And the advantages of search alone (through increased visibility in search results and up-to-the-minute market research) make entering this space

Friday, Nov. 18th 4:54PM:

Police pepper
spray students who
refuse to move out of
the way.

0:01 / 1:25

Like   + Add to ▾   Share

1,461,670

Uploaded by asucd on Nov 18, 2011
Friday Nov. 18th at 4:54 PM

3,576 likes, 531 dislikes

Figure 9.12   Occupy Wall Street Movement Viral Video
Source: YouTube

worthwhile, not to mention the added benefits of better engaging with customers, providing an efficient customer support mechanism, and opening a whole new acquisition channel. (Those latter topics of course, are excellent material for another book.)

But it's smart to be wary of jumping into social media. You want to go about it in the right way, and since you're engaging directly with consumers, you don't want to abandon your efforts halfway through to rethink your strategy.

Here are a few options for getting started:

- *Start with market research.* Find out where your current and potential customers are talking about you, your competitors, and your industry online and just listen for a while. Gather the information and get a sense of the overall perception, how your competition is getting involved, what your customers need the most, and what data are most valuable. This alone can provide great insight into your business.
- *Train your PR and marketing staff on social media.* They already have media and PR training and have experience speaking publicly on behalf of the company. They can combine these skills with an understanding of how social media communities work, the importance of authenticity online, and how to respond online.
- *Train your customer support staff on PR and marketing.* Your customer support team already is skilled in dealing with customers (particularly the unhappy ones) one-on-one. You can extend these skills by training them in how to speak publicly on behalf of the company so that they

can begin treating questions posed on social media sites in a similar way as those posed to them directly over phone or e-mail.

- *Start a blog.* A blog is a great way to start a conversation with your customers. You can use the market research about how your customers are talking about your industry to identify a list of topics to talk about. See a discussion speculating on the next edition of your two-door coupe? Interview the engineer who designed the new dashboard and add a few pictures. Read a blogger's post questioning the safety record of your competition. Take the initiative and post your own safety record, with backup documentation. In this way, you can begin engaging the community, but at a much smaller scale and with much greater oversight than if you let every employee post on behalf of the company on any social media site they happened upon. Allow for comments to the blog, which will evolve this conversation and give a select group of employees the ability to gain experience replying directly online.

- *Create a set of commonsense guidelines and let your employees spread the company message.* This suggestion is a scary one, and certainly, it doesn't work for every company. But the truth is that most people are online, and it's easy to identify where people work (by virtue of their social networking affiliations, blog bio, or random conversations). Create a set of guidelines about what kind of information not to discuss publicly (such as financial details and upcoming launches), how to speak on behalf of the company (don't promise things on behalf of another department, don't belittle customers), and what's within bounds (offering to pass on feedback, answering questions ["That purse also comes in green and in a larger laptop style"]). Since you've hired smart and capable employees who already likely serve as brand ambassadors for you to their friends and family, trust them to do so at a larger scale.

■ TACTICAL SUGGESTIONS

- Find out where your industry is being discussed to get insight into what potential customers are most interested in.
- Answer questions honestly and provide solutions to problems when you can.
- Provide "inside information" to enthusiasts on blogs or forums.
- When issuing press releases or other resources to bloggers, reporters, or others, ensure you include a URL in addition to a link, link directly to what you are highlighting (not just the home page), and use language that you would like to receive as anchor text.
- Consider adding a company blog so that you have a convenient source to link back to where you can provide more detailed information.

Figure 9.13 Twitter Search Results for [Obama from: Terrymoran]
Source: Twitter

- If you do add a blog, ensure it's located on your main company domain (at blog.mydomain.com or mydomain.com/blog, for instance) and that it uses backend infrastructure, such as WordPress, that makes it easy to implement search-friendly technical components.
- Understand that posting online is the same as giving an interview to the *New York Times*. And that once it's out there, you can't take it back. This is all commonsense stuff. If you're out at dinner with your spouse and mention that you're about to take your company public, someone at the next table might be a reporter who then could write it up as front-page news. The difference is that when you post online, *everyone* is at the next table and you can't say that you were misquoted. Consider the ABC reporter who posted an (alleged) off-the-record remark made by President Obama about the recent MTV Video Music Awards. The reporter deleted the comment soon after, but it lives on forever in searches and screenshots (Figure 9.13).

And deleting comments after the fact can start to look like a cover-up and only make matters worse (Figure 9.14).

You don't have to go any further than TripAdvisor to find examples of what works and what doesn't. Being apologetic and intent on fixing issues might make potential customers feel as though you care and are appreciative for the feedback (Figure 9.15).

Being defensive just makes you sound like a jerk (Figure 9.16).

■ THE VALUE OF USER-GENERATED CONTENT FOR SEARCH ACQUISITION

User-generated content—that content that you let visitors add to your site—can be valuable in a number of ways. It helps you have deeper engagement

Figure 9.14 You Can't Delete Social Media Interaction
Source: Twitter

with your customers (they feel a sense of ownership toward your brand), and you can more quickly build out content that helps visitors and provides more opportunities to rank in search engines.

But user-generated content is also a lot of work. You need to engage vocal users early and get them excited about the site. You need to give users a compelling reason to contribute. And you need to seed the site with content so that you don't launch empty. You also need internal oversight—someone in place to keep things moving along, making sure it's all headed in the right direction.

Management Response
NativoLodgeMGMT, Marcos Urtiaga, Front Office Manager
(Management representative)
Sep 24, 2008

We sincerely apologize about your second stay with us and we are concerened that we did not meet the same expectations that we did your first stay with us. The issues that you have addresses have been reported to the management team and we are working on the best solution to prevent them from happening again. Once again, we apologize and hope that we can get another chance to make your stay at the Nativo Lodge as enjoyable as the first.

Figure 9.15 Addressing Consumer Issues Online
Source: Tripadvisor.com

> **Management Response**
> **candymanager, manager**
> (Management representative)
> *Dec 4, 2008*
>
> Blame the websites not us. They overbook us we have no control over this. We tell them to stop selling but they still continue.
>
>
> Thank You
> Candy
> Have a Sweet Day!

Figure 9.16 How Not to Address Consumer Issues Online

Source: Tripadvisor.com

■ YOU CAN COMPEL VISITORS BY BEING COMPELLING

You need to compel users to spend time on your site and the only way to do that is to be compelling. How you do that depends on the type of site that you have. Think about (or talk with your users about) what it is you have that no one else does. Why do visitors need to come to your site rather than anyone else's? If you can't come up with anything, then you may need to work on your site a little before sending out the party invites.

Once you have some value to your site, you need to seed the content a bit before asking others to contribute. You can partner with other content sites (for instance, review sites) to get this content. Just keep in mind that this puts you back into the nonunique content space, and those pages are unlikely to rank in search engines. They still may be valuable for seeding purposes, though, so you may find that they're valuable for your needs. Or perhaps you can create a mash-up of content that adds unique value on top of each separate component. You can also hire writers to write content for you, although in that case, you should consider how to disclose it (if the writing is for something like reviews). One way is REI's model of both expert and user reviews—each on their own tab (Figure 9.17).

You can also launch with an invite-only test and get a small group to seed the content for you. The difference between launching publicly with no content and launching to a small invite-only group with no content is that the invited group expects that the site will be empty and they'll know that it's their job to start testing things out. They'll much more happily post to empty pages.

How do you go about an invite-only test? Identify the early adopters and influencers in your niche. Often these are bloggers who are fairly easy to find. You can also check out local or topical forums and find those who post early

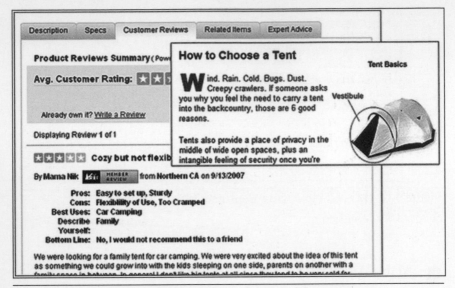

Figure 9.17 Combining Expert and User-Generated Content

Source: Rei.com

and often. For instance, I live in West Seattle. The West Seattle Blog[11] is run by bloggers who are completely engaged with the local community. They know everything, and they blog it all. If I were looking to jump-start user-generated content on a Seattle community site, they would be the first ones I would try to get involved. You can find testers like this everywhere: on social networking sites, at conferences, on Wikipedia, and so forth.

These are your users who are the most knowledgeable and therefore most likely to provide the best contributions, contribute the most, and spread the word about your site to others.

Once you've got a group, pull them in with flattery. Let them know how great they are and how they can help you with the site. Let them have input during the test phase, and encourage them to contribute lots of content. You may want to leave the test phase by asking your early testers to invite others, rather than opening the site up to everyone initially. This may get your testers talking about your site and providing a bit of buzz.

You also want to consider incentives for those who add content. Some sites have been successful with cash (such as discounts on future purchases) but that can encourage spam, so watch that closely. Better incentives can simply be things like reputation points, elite badges for top posters, and moderator positions. People tend to post online for the fame and glory.

Amazon does this with their top reviewers program. And for years, online forums have been rewarding top posters with special titles and icons.

Figure 9.18 Using Ratings and Reviews to Add Value to Pages

Source: Amazon

You should also consider your focus. Don't start too big. What's the core to your site? Start there and expand.

You also need internal oversight to keeps things going and ensure quality. You might be able to do this with outside moderators à la Wikipedia. Or you could allow the community to vote on content. Digg, of course, lets users either vote stories up or bury them. You may end up hiring someone internally. What works for you depends on your site.

Amazon does it by letting you rate the reviews, as, for example, was done for the Buffy DVD reviews in Figure 9.18.

You may want to participate in social networking on other sites, blog, comment on other blogs, or jump in and get involved in the community. You can get a better dialog going with users this way, but you have to be willing to let whoever does that for your company have honest voices.

Before you get all this going, you should definitely set up some goals and ways to measure them, and you should have a backup plan in case the best laid plans don't lead to the eternal spring fountain. You may need to adjust your site's value add, your incentives, or the group you're engaging. The most important question to ask is: Are you building what people need? That's the best way to keep them coming and coming back.

■ TAKING ADVANTAGE OF DIVERSIFIED ACQUISITION STREAMS

Although search is an important way that your potential audience researches and transacts, it's always a good idea for a business to diversify as much as possible. Social media can be a great way to engage audiences independent of the search-related value of doing so.

PlaidDoctrine Suzanne Park
@RPS_tweets we have an Eco-friendly laptop briefcase that fits a
17" MacBook pro
30 Jan

Figure 9.19 @PlaidDoctrine Twitter Reply Offering Helpful Information
Source: Twitter

On Cyber Monday 2011, for instance, visitors to retail websites from social networks generated 0.56 percent of all online sales. Facebook accounted for most of that traffic (86 percent).[12]

Looking more closely, it appears that consumers were using social media to find out about deals and coupons from social media when shopping.

The key is to not spam your audience with irrelevant advertising but instead offer them what they want when they want it. For instance, with Cyber Monday shoppers, those coming from social media sites were looking for deals and coupons.[13]

If someone is complaining on Twitter that they can't find an eco-friendly laptop bag, send them a link to yours (Figure 9.19).

If your followers are looking for deals, let them know what those deals are when Black Friday rolls around (Figure 9.20).

■ GETTING STARTED

How can you get started with social media? As noted earlier in this chapter, don't just look at number of users; look at where your users are and what they are doing. They may be spending more time on Facebook, but are they looking at photos of their nieces and nephews or asking their friends what car to buy? LinkedIn certainly has more users than Etsy, but if you want to reach serious knitters, Etsy is the place to start.

@SocialJulio
Julio Fernandez

So @DellOutlet has 1.5 million followers.
Last tweet was Nov 21. @DellHomeUS is
Tweeting to 74k followers. #BlackFriday
missed opportunity

Figure 9.20 @DellOutlet's Missed Twitter Opportunity
Source: Twitter

But at least for the social networks you likely hear about most, here are the numbers:

- *Facebook* is the largest social network in the United States as of late 2011, with more than 800 million total users and 600 million active each month. More than 50 percent of the U.S. population has an account (although more than 75 percent of Facebook users are outside the United States).[14]
- *Twitter* has more than 200 million users and more than half log in daily, for a total of 250 million tweets sent each day.[15]
- *LinkedIn* has more than 135 million users in more than 200 countries, and it predicts 4 billion searches for people on their network in 2011.[16]
- *Google+* had more than 40 million users as of the third quarter in 2011, just before opening the network up to business pages.[17]

■ GOOGLE+ BUSINESS PAGES

In 2011, Google launched Google+, their answer to Facebook. Google+ opened brand pages in November 2011.[18] You can see Pepsi's Google+ brand page in Figure 9.21.

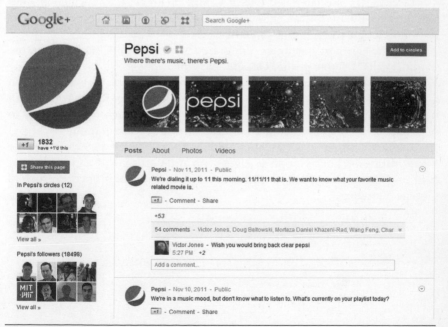

Figure 9.21   Pepsi's Google+ Page

Source: Google+

Google said:

For you and me, this means we can now hang out live with the local bike shop, or discuss our wardrobe with a favorite clothing line, or follow a band on tour. Google+ pages give life to everything we find in the real world. And by adding them to circles, we can create lasting bonds with the pages (and people) that matter most.

For businesses and brands, Google+ pages help you connect with the customers and fans who love you. Not only can they recommend you with a +1, or add you to a circle to listen long-term, they can actually spend time with your team, face-to-face-to-face. All you need to do is start sharing, and you'll soon find the super fans and loyal customers that want to say hello.

Is it important to establish a Google+ brand page? It remains to be seen if Google+ will become as ubiquitous as Facebook, but it makes sense to claim your organization name and set up integration with your Google+ page and your website. Right away, Google began integrating features from Google+ into search results (such as showing author photos and the number of people who have that author in Google+ circles) below listings in the search results display. In January 2012, Google launched "Search Plus Your World", which weaves Google+ throughout Google search results.[19]

Google has also launched Direct Connect (Figure 9.22), which enables searchers to simply type a + before an organization name to access that organization's Google+ brand page directly.

Google+ is also becoming integrated with YouTube as part of what Google calls "shipping the Google part of Google+."[20] You can play YouTube videos directly from Google+, and YouTube playlists are listed in Google+ search results. The next step is very likely integration between an organization's Google+ page and YouTube channel. Each feature seems to begin with consumer integration, followed by business integration.

Google has been experimenting with adding Google+ details to Google Places listings,[21] links Google+ pages with AdWords ads,[22] and is likely to continue weaving Google+ throughout all of its business properties (such as Google Shopping).

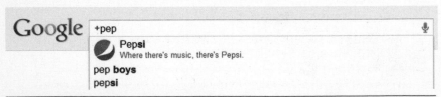

Figure 9.22 Direct Connect: Pepsi
Source: Google Search

How do you get started? At least initially, only one user account can administer the page. This means that you either want to set up a separate user account for the company (so multiple people can access it) or ensure whoever sets up the account will be the person posting to it.

You can select one of five categories for your business page (local, product/brand, company/organization, arts/entertainment/sports, and other). Local businesses have additional options available, but at least for now, these profiles aren't linked in any way to Google Places business pages (likely that will happen at some point).

You can "follow" people with a Google+ business account, but only after those people have followed you. This means that a company can't follow a lot of users as a way to spam them with advertising. Instead, if someone likes your brand and decides to put your Google+ page in a "circle," you can reciprocate.

Your organization can have several different Google+ profiles (for instance, one for each product), but be cautious about this. It may be easier to build up a following for one page than for multiple pages. If you are running a special promotion, you may be tempted to create a page specifically for that promotion, but it may be better to drive consumers to your main brand page. If you build up a lot of followers to a promotion page, what will you do with those followers once the promotion is over?

One feature of Google+ that organizations have already started taking advantage of is hangouts. These are group video chats that you can use to provide training, answer questions, or conduct feedback sessions. You can set up a hangout to be either broadcast or interactive.

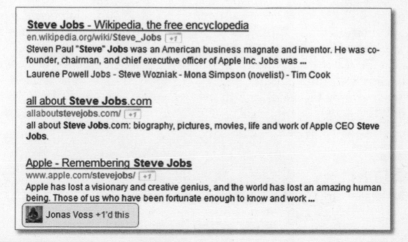

Figure 9.23   +1 In Google Search Results
Source: Google Search

Because Google+ is still a fairly new social network, use the Google+ badge[23] on your site to let people know about your page and cross-promote on other social networks you're active in.

Google has several steps you can take to "verify" that you're the business owner,[24] including linking to your website and adding a rel="publisher" attribute to the source code of your website that links to your Google+ page.

➤   *Google+ vs. +1 Buttons*

Google's +1 buttons are completely different from Google+, despite the common math symbol. A +1 button is similar to a Facebook "Like" button.

Figure 9.24   Pepsi's Facebook Page

Source: Facebook

In both cases, you can add the button to pages you think your visitors will like and share. As shown in Chapter 10, encouraging Facebook likes, Google +1s, or any other social sharing makes your content more visible not only on social networks but in search results as well (Figure 9.23).

It's too early to know how consumers will interact with Google+ brand pages, but we can look to what's happened with Facebook fan pages for clues. For the most part, we are on social networks like Facebook and Google+ to interact with our friends and family, versus the time we spend using search engines, which tends to be to accomplish specific tasks. We will, however, interact with pages that belong to brands that we like, and we will seek them out both for support and for promotions.

The first question organizations may have is how to balance Facebook and Google+ (and Twitter and . . .). In the case of Pepsi, its Google+ brand page is newly created, but the Facebook page has considerably more content available (Figure 9.24).

Should they post the same content in both places? Cater separately to each audience? The answer likely depends on the organization, but the right choice is likely not to create a page and then abandon it. At the very least, you should interact with those who post to the page and follow it.

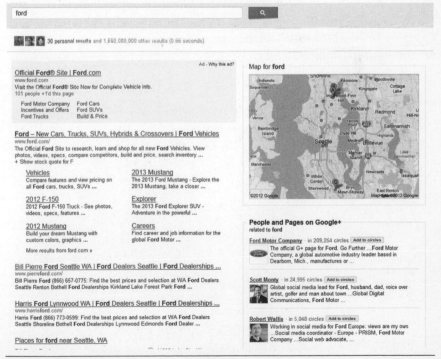

Figure 9.25 Ford vs. Chevy Search Results

Source: Google.com

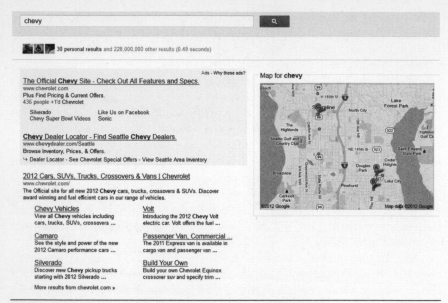

Figure 9.25 Ford vs. Chevy Search Results (*continued*)

As of early 2012, Google's "Search Plus Your World," the integration of Google+ has made Google+ brand pages on scale, as the search results pages are transforming differently when Google+ content is pulled into the results.

Chapter 10

What's Next?

Beyond Google and 10 Blue Links

We've already seen that search has progressed substantially from the days of text only. Search engines have started indexing images, videos, and Flash. And search results are reflecting the evolution of the Web by displaying news, videos, and images. What's next?

Google isn't going away. As we learned in Chapter 3, Google has become a habit for many searchers, and it works well enough that searchers don't have a reason to switch. These searchers have also come to expect search that works as well as Google everywhere they navigate online, including their in-site search. Even though Amazon is at its core a retail store, not a search engine, Amazon customers expect Amazon search results to be as relevant and useful to them as Google results are.

Our expectation of effective search everywhere will continue to influence new search engines that use input completely differently from Google's text box and that search over entirely different things. These new search engines won't replace Google. Rather, they'll be additional ways we search as part of everyday activities that may not currently involve search. Google itself will likely begin providing some of these nontext search interfaces over time.

When I originally wrote this chapter for the first edition of the book, I asked, "What's next?" But now, only two years later, this chapter really answers, "What's now?" In early 2012, it's still the case that doing text-based searches, using Google and Bing, typing in a few words and getting back a list of links—none of that has gone away, nor will it likely go away anytime soon.

Instead, we've begun incorporating search into more aspects of what we do, and the text-based search that we've come to rely on has expanded in more useful ways. This chapter is really no longer about what the future might hold but about ways you can get ahead of the crowd and take advantage of where things are going once you've incorporated the foundational elements covered in the earlier chapters of this book.

Imagine that you're driving in your car and it starts running low on gas, automatically checks the map for nearby gas station, and alerts you. You haven't actively done a search, and certainly not a text search, but search is core to that experience working seamlessly. All of the pieces of that functionality already exist. The future of search is search built into everything, without us even realizing we're searching.

So this chapter is really about what's now. What's after that? It's anyone's guess. Microsoft has noted that 80 percent of what Europeans do online today didn't exist in their lives just five years ago.[1] Consider this: a new device called Twine enables any object to talk to the Internet.[2] Soon, we may, in fact, be able to Google our lost car keys and eyeglasses.

They key to success is the ability to adapt as the world changes.

■ NEW SEARCH INTERFACES

What new search interfaces can we expect to see? Many of them exist already. Shazam is an iPhone application (now with more than 100 million users)[3] that enables the iPhone owner to hold the phone up to a speaker so that Shazam can "listen" to music and identify it. The Urbanspoon[4] iPhone application has a slot machine interface. Simply shake the iPhone and the application detects your location and spins up restaurant locations (Figure 10.1).

Figure 10.1   Urbanspoon iPhone Application
Source: Urbanspoon

Google Maps now lets you search indoors (such as within an airport, shopping mall, or store).[5]

And take a look at Siri, released with the iPhone 4S. Simply speak to your phone when you want something. Mark Rolston of frog design noted that it doesn't take much to think about combining voice technology, like the kind Apple has in Siri, with the kind of processing power we have now to create a computer that uses any available surface (a wall, a mirror, etc.) as a screen. "I can talk at it and wave at it, and maybe I have a keyboard or maybe there are screens or cameras around, but [the computers] compose in the moment as we need them."[6]

Jason Hiner wrote on ZDNet in November 2011:[7]

The revolutionary piece of Siri is what it does in Internet search. It's early and Siri is still imperfect, but there are moments when Siri drastically streamlines the search process and gives us a peek at the future. For example, I recently asked Siri for "the closest Mediterranean restaurant" and got a list showing 11 restaurants, their user ratings, and their distance from my current location. Clicking any of the selections in the list immediately took me to a map.

All of these new search interfaces are just early hints at where search is going. Do we think of standing in the middle of an unfamiliar airport and wondering where the closest Cinnabon is as search? Why not? We have a mobile phone that can pinpoint our location and has a layout of where we are—and therefore can tell us exactly which way to walk, exactly how long it will take to get there, if a coupon is available, not to mention how far it is from our gate, and if our flight is on time or if we have a few extra moments to linger over coffee. Search becomes an integrated experience into our everyday lives.

➤ *Image Search*

A 2009 episode of the television show *Better Off Ted*, about a research and development (R&D) company set 25 years in the future, featured a revolutionary new product. Ted, the R&D manager, explained, "We've been developing a new search engine, and unlike language-based search engines, this face-matching technology uses visual recognition."[8] Rather than type text into a search box, this search engine would enable searchers to scan a person's photo and would show all other photos containing that person.

Image search engine Face.com took issue with the 25 years in the future: "What appears to be science fiction to these guys is a mere reality for our Photo Finder users."[9] Photo Finder uses tagged photos of a person to find additional untagged photos.[10] Similarly, image search engine Polar Rose uses facial recognition to find photos of people across the Web.

Facebook and Picasa both now incorporate facial recognition to suggest which of your friends are in photos that you upload. Just confirm and the photos are tagged appropriately.[11]

With Google Goggles,[12] launched in December 2009, you can take a photo with your mobile phone's camera and Google will attempt to recognize the item in the photo and return relevant search results. For instance, you can take a picture of a landmark, work of art, or product.

In 2011, the future technologies envisioned in that *Better Off Ted* episode are coming to life. Smartphone application SceneTap uses facial recognition to provide bar patrons with information such as the average age of the crowd and the ratio of men to women.[13]

Immersive Labs detects demographic information about those walking by digital billboards and delivers targeted ads based on that information.[14]

Where's the value to organizations? Beyond potential reputation management issues (in the *Better Off Ted* episode, an executive is found to have a secret life as a magician's assistant through the powers of the image search engine), the most obvious application is e-commerce. I may want to find dresses of a particular color or shoes of a particular style.

With Google Images today, for instance, I can search for similar images. If I see a pair of shoes I like, I can click the "Similar" link below it and see shoes of a similar style and then click from the image to the website to buy them (Figure 10.2). I can even start with a photo I upload rather than a text search and can filter by color, image type, and more.

The product search capabilities in Google Goggles and similar technologies on our mobile devices have clear implications for companies. If I'm in a store and take a picture of something I'm thinking of buying but see it listed for a lower price in Google Goggles, I can just order it online via my phone instead (Figure 10.3).

In fact, on Black Friday 2011, we saw exactly this type of consumer behavior. The *New York Times* even noted that "Best Buy, already acquainted with the sting of online price-comparison apps, declines to display standard bar codes on some products so they cannot be easily scanned by smartphones."[15] (Of course, as we've already seen, shoppers can just snap a photo of the product instead.)

Google's YouTube video describing the Goggles service explains how it can be used for local search as well. You can point your phone at a local business, and Google will display the name of that business and enable you to view information about it. Now, when you walk by a restaurant you've never tried, you can simply aim your phone at the restaurant for instant access to reviews.

In Figure 10.4, you can see that you can simply take a photo of a book cover to access information about it, compare prices, and preview it.

Google's not the only company innovating with image search. TinEye, for instance, lets you upload any image and find out where that image came

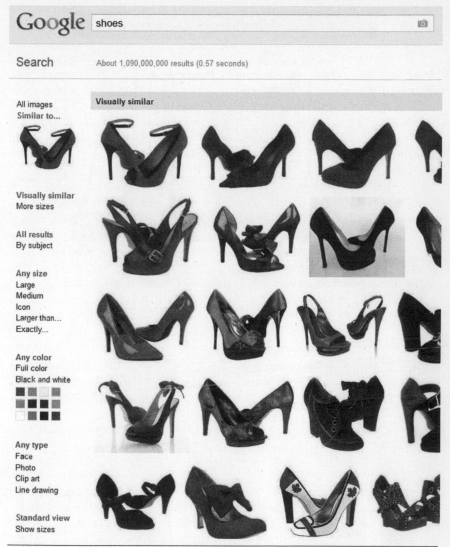

Figure 10.2 Google Similar Images

Source: Google Image Search

from. The company says it's "the first image search engine on the Web to use image identification technology rather than keywords, metadata, or watermarks."[16]

AirTight Interactive's Flickr Related Tag Browser[17] enables you to browse Flickr images semantically, providing connections between words, images, and ideas (Figure 10.5).

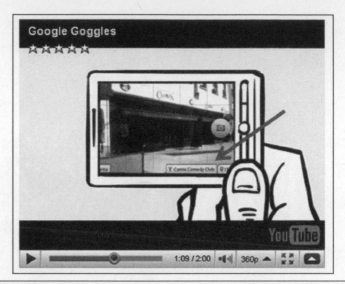

Figure 10.3 Google Goggles Local Search
Source: YouTube

➤ *Mobile Search*

Many companies, including Google, offer mobile applications that enable you to search via voice rather than text, although strictly speaking, this type of search is still text-based at its core. It's simply the input mechanism that has changed.

As you saw with Shazam, Urbanspoon, and Google Goggles, many of the new search interfaces hinge on mobile devices. The ubiquity of mobile devices

Figure 10.4 Google Goggles Book Search
Source: www.google.com/mobile/goggles/#book

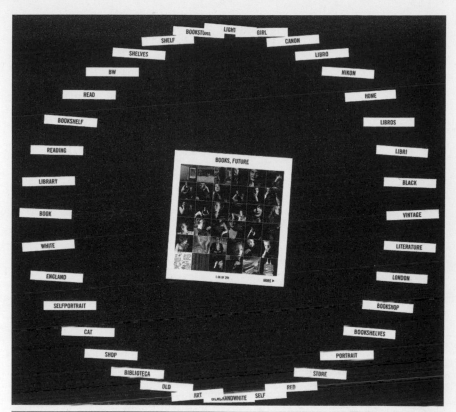

Figure 10.5 Flickr Related Tag Browser

Source: AirTight Interactive

(44 percent of U.S. consumers now carry smartphones)[18] means we can have search capabilities available wherever we are, for whatever needs we have (Figure 10.6).

comScore reported that "the mobile media user population (those who browse the mobile Web, access applications, or download content) grew 19 percent in the past year to more than 116 million people at the end of August 2011" and that in the United States and United Kingdom, around 7 percent of Internet traffic comes from non-PC devices.[19]

Tablets, with the iPad leading the way, have expanded search opportunities and have already changed how we consume and interact with information.

iPad adoption has grown quickly (Figure 10.7), and with new tablet devices such as the Kindle Fire taking off in popularity,[20] the number of consumers available to those organizations taking advantage of these types of devices continues to grow.

Putting aside for a moment all of the *new* ways mobile devices enable us to search, text-based Google searches alone on mobile devices grew fourfold

Figure 10.6 Smartphone Penetration by Age Group
Source: Nielsen[21]

between 2007 and 2011.[22] In September 2011, Google predicted that 44 percent of all holiday 2011 searches for last-minute gifts and store locations would be via mobile devices.[23]

And those searches turn into sales. We continue to increase how much we use mobile devices to research and buy (not only to research before we buy

Figure 10.7 iPad Adoption (Q2 2011)
Source: KPCB, Apple

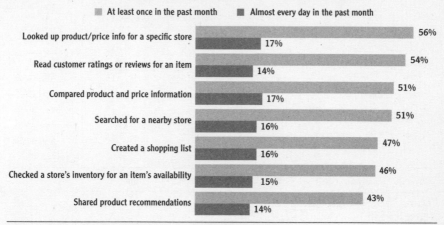

Q: How often do you perform these shopping activities on your tablet?
Source: comScore Tablet Advisor, U.S., September 2011

■ At least once in the past month   ■ Almost every day in the past month

Activity	
Looked up product/price info for a specific store	56% / 17%
Read customer ratings or reviews for an item	54% / 14%
Compared product and price information	51% / 17%
Searched for a nearby store	51% / 16%
Created a shopping list	47% / 16%
Checked a store's inventory for an item's availability	46% / 15%
Shared product recommendations	43% / 14%

Figure 10.8   iPad User Behavior, September 2011
Source: comScore

but to compare prices online while in a physical store).[24] On Cyber Monday 2011, 10.8 percent of Americans used a mobile device to visit a retailer site, up from just 3.9 percent in 2010. And 6.6 percent of those visitors made a purchase (versus 2.3 percent in 2010).[25]

In September 2011, more than 50 percent of iPad users reported looking up and comparing product or price information and searching for a nearby store[26] and nearly 50 percent reported making a purchase on their tablet over the past month (Figure 10.8).

Amazingly, even though we are increasingly using mobile devices to access the Internet, business owners aren't yet taking advantage of this effectively. Of Google's largest advertisers, 79 percent don't have sites optimized for mobile devices.[27]

Access your website on a smartphone browser. Can you easily navigate it? Read the text? Click links? Often, optimizing your site for mobile devices can be as easy as adding a mobile stylesheet to the site.

■ SOCIAL SEARCH

Social search[28] and *real-time search*[29] are buzzwords that have made their way into the search landscape. Both terms have at their core the rise of social networking sites, such as Facebook and Twitter. Initially, the hype was around recommendations from friends. Why search Google and get information from potentially unreliable strangers when you can search your social graph and get advice and recommendations from your personal social circle? So far, although we are using social networks more and more often for advice and

Figure 10.9 Search Volume 2009 vs. 2011

Source: comScore

recommendations, as noted in Chapter 9, we haven't started using search less often. This was true when I wrote the first edition of this book in 2009 and remains true now in late 2011. Search volume has continued to grow[30] (Figure 10.9) and is used by 90 percent of online Americans versus 47 percent who use social media[31] (Figure 10.10).

Much of the search-related value of social networks is focused on:

- *Real-time information (posts on social networks tend to be relevant for topical queries):* If you want to know how everyone else feels about Lady Gaga's latest outfit as she walks down the red carpet of the Grammy's, Twitter is the best first place to check.

Figure 10.10 U.S. Internet Usage

Source: PEW Internet & American Life Project

- *Additional ranking opportunities:* As noted in Chapter 9, your social media interactions (such as YouTube videos, Facebook page, and Yelp reviews) can rank in major search engines in addition to your website.
- *Signals of overall value:* Major search engines may determine that content shared a lot is more valuable than nonshared content.

Search engines such as Google have historically mined the Web and made the content from the Web easy to find. Social networks are creating new content, most of it about things that are happening right now, and then making that searchable. We know that events such as the Super Bowl or an actor's appearance as host on the show *Saturday Night Live* can trigger search spikes. Results on Google for those types of searches will generally provide a broad set of information, including a few listings that are fairly recent (such as news items and content from social networks). But search on the social networks themselves and you will see in real-time exactly what other people are saying. Think you just felt an earthquake? Grab your cell phone and search Twitter. It's likely you'll find out just where the earthquake was strongest and an initial report of damage before it even hits the news.

The major search engines such as Google have started incorporating real-time search into their results,[32] much as they did a couple of years ago for other types of information, such as images and videos.

In June 2011, Google's real-time search went missing, due to a lapsed deal with Twitter.[33] Google has since begun replacing the loss of this real-time data with Google+ and fresher news algorithms as noted in the previous chapter.

These days, Google uses data from social networks for personalization more than real-time data.

For instance Figure 10.11 shows that a Google search for [steve jobs] for a logged-in user differs in that two pages shared with that user on social networks have been inserted below the second search result.

Microsoft's Bing still has a deal with Twitter. For instance, a search for [Vanessa Fox Twitter] returns my Twitter profile and my most recent posts (Figure 10.12).

Bing also provides social search that searches only Twitter and Facebook[34] and provides the top shared links from both networks (Figure 10.13).

Bing also incorporates Facebook into its results, both by inserting a section called "Liked by your Facebook friends" into search results and by noting which results have Facebook likes (Figure 10.14).

What does the rise of social search mean for companies? Negative discussions about your brand may become more visible, but your involvement in proactively helping customers solve problems may become more visible as well. As discussed in Chapter 9, the most important step is to start paying attention to social media and how your organization might participate. You can learn about customer issues long before they escalate into public relations disasters and can address them proactively. You can also get involved in the

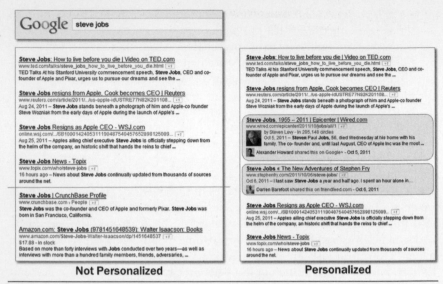

Figure 10.11 Google's Personalized Social Results

Source: Google Search

conversation. Be helpful. Offer useful information. Provide support. By getting involved now, you'll be ready as this type of search evolves.

Ultimately, the major search engines are looking to provide the most useful, relevant results for searchers. Incorporating real-time data and social information are just two of the many ways they are looking to improve how they do this.

Figure 10.12 Microsoft Bing Twitter Profiles in Web Search

Source: Microsoft Bing

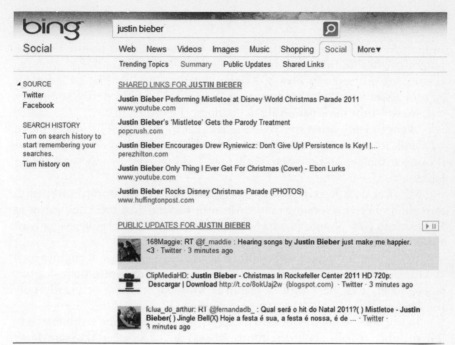

Figure 10.13   Microsoft Bing Social Search

Source: bing.com/social

Figure 10.14   Bing/Facebook Integration

Source: Microsoft Bing

■ SMARTER SEARCH

In late 2011, Wolfram|Alpha launched a real-time tracking feature that first pinpoints your location and then provides details on planes flying overhead (Figure 10.15). Seem futuristic? Maybe, until you use the Plane Finder AR app for iPhone and iPad2.[35] Just open the app, point your device at a plane, and see real-time information about the flight (Figure 10.16).

Want to know what star you're looking at in the sky? That query might be tough to type into a search engine, but all you need to do is point your iPhone at the sky and the Star Walk app[36] will tell you exactly what you're looking at.

Want to do a search for how to say "where's the bathroom" in Spanish next time you're vacationing on the Mexican Riviera? Just speak the words in English into your phone, and the Spanish translation will be spoken right back to you with Google's translation app.[37]

In the near future, we will continue to use text-based search engines such as Google and Bing, and both engines will continue to evolve their displays to be richer. But the future of search is wide open, and we've really only just begun.

In late 2007, a number of search experts and search engine representatives got together to talk about the future of search.[38] Google's Marissa Mayer stressed that Google is balancing the changing needs of searchers and the proliferation of new kinds of content with usability and simplicity. "The paradox of choice is real," she said.[39] She explained that Google continuously launches experiments to only a small percentage of searchers to help guide them toward a better interface rather than simply inundate searchers with choices.

Nearly everyone agreed that a core part of the near future of search was personalization (as was discussed in Chapter 5). Results will (and, in fact, have) become more local for searchers and more tailored to them. Mayer wondered aloud about the value of social search. When you ask friends what good movies they've seen lately, you're explicitly doing a search. How can search engines use that type of behavior to aid better search results? Can you take the social graph and combine it with search (and as we've just seen, Google has been doing just that)? Usability guru Jakob Nielsen chimed in that he believed that social networks were just too small to have positive influence on quality search results. However, as you can see, search engines are using social signals more and more.

How should companies prepare for the future? The most important step is to realize that search isn't going away. Potential customers will continue to research product and company information online, will expect to find customer support there, and will increase their online purchasing. Understanding the new customer behavior and buying patterns is vital to the success of any business—from start-up to global enterprise, whether an e-commerce site or

Figure 10.15 Wolfram|Alpha "Flights Overhead" Search

Source: Wolfram|Alpha

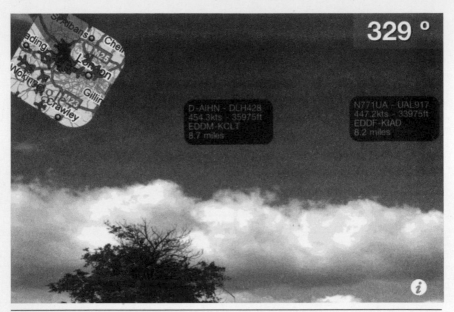

Figure 10.16 Plane Finder AR

Source: Pinkfroot

a business-to-business manufacturer. Media companies, local businesses, and traditional retail brands all can benefit from using search data for customer insights, product development, and business strategy. Organizations should incorporate organic search acquisition strategy into marketing initiatives and Web infrastructure.

Companies that evolve their internal processes and technical frameworks to incorporate organic search and all that it has to offer will have a substantial edge over the competition and will be in an ideal position to take advantage of any new search evolution.

Remember, the customers remain the same—they are simply adapting new behaviors to take advantage of the world of search. You're equipped with the knowledge from this book to adapt with them.

Notes

■ **CHAPTER 1**

1. www.pewinternet.org/Reports/2011/Search-and-email/Report.aspx.

2. www.comscore.com/Press_Events/Press_Releases/2011/11/comScore_Releases_October_2011_U.S._Search_Engine_Rankings.

3. www.comscore.com/Press_Events/Press_Releases/2010/1/Global_Search_Market_Grows_46_Percent_in_2009.

4. blogs.wsj.com/digits/2011/06/21/google-notches-one-billion-unique-visitors-per-month.

5. www.edelman.com/trust/2011/uploads/Edelman%20Trust%20Barometer%20Global%20Deck.pdf.

6. www.theinquirer.net/inquirer/news/1939459/people-trust-search-engines-company.

7. searchengineland.com/scoring-the-2011-super-bowl-commercials-for-search-visibility-and-visitor-engagement-63672.

8. Yahoo! internal search data.

9. googleblog.blogspot.com/2011/05/world-of-curiosity-peek-at-searches.html.

10. www.comscore.com/Press_Events/Press_Releases/2010/1/Global_Search_Market_Grows_46_Percent_in_2009.

11. twitter.com/#!/YahooSearchData.

12. eMarketer, July 2011.

13. Author interview with Steven Levy of *Wired* magazine (August 2009).

14. www.cim.co.uk.

15. stateofthemedia.org/2011/newspapers-essay/data-page-6.

16. A 2007 WebVisible/Nielsen study found that 74 percent of respondents used search engines to find local business information versus 65 percent

who turned to print Yellow Pages, 50 percent who used Internet Yellow Pages, and 44 percent who used traditional newspapers. AOL WalletPop (www.dailyfinance.com/photos/top-25-things-vanishing-from-america) called the Yellow Pages one of 25 things that were going extinct, along with outhouses and ham radios.

17. eMarketer, 2007: Eighty-five percent of online shoppers are also online buyers. JupiterResearch 2007: U.S. online retail sales will grow by 16 percent in 2007 to reach a total of $116 billion. Over the next five years, U.S. online retail sales will reach $171 billion. ThirdAge Inc. and JWT Boom 2007: Adults aged 45 years or older are more likely to shop online. Seventy-three percent of survey respondents indicate shopping is their top online activity.

18. www.census.gov/mrts/www/data/pdf/08Q4.pdf (accessed February 2009).

19. googleretail.blogspot.com/2010/11/online-is-key-during-holiday-season. html.

20. www.forrester.com/rb/Research/us_online_retail_forecast,_2009_to_ 2014/q/id/56551/t/2.

21. Google internal data, November 2011.

22. ow.ly/i/mqFk.

23. www.comscore.com/Press_Events/Press_Releases/2011/11/Black_Friday_ Boasts_816_Million_in_U.S._Online_Holiday_Spending.

24. www.latimes.com/business/la-fi-cyber-monday-20111127,0,5604987. story.

25. www.comscore.com/Press_Events/Press_Releases/2011/11/Cyber_ Monday_Spending_Hits_1.25_Billion?piCId=66028.

26. twitter.com/#!/Hitwise_US/status/141942274895515648.

27. http://searchengineland.com/ live-blogging-microsoft-searchification-day-2007-12283.

28. blog.comscore.com/2011/11/cyber_monday_work_computers.html.

29. www.comscore.com/Press_Events/Press_Releases/2007/07/Yahoo! _and_comscore_Online_Consumer_Study (accessed July 2007).

30. ir.comscore.com/releasedetail.cfm?ReleaseID=245287 (accessed March 2006).

31. Consumer electronics, toys and hobbies, video games and consoles, and music, movies, and videos enjoy more than 80 percent of conversions from online searches that take place offline.

32. www.mediapost.com/publications/?art_aid=99952&fa=Articles.show Article (accessed February 2009).

33. www.enquiroresearch.com/images/Eyetracking2-Sample.pdf (accessed June 2005).

34. Hitwise (accessed May 2009).

35. blog.comscore.com/2009/05/longer_search_queries_driving.html (accessed May 2009).

36. eMarketer studies found that 66 percent of searchers distrust paid ads and 29 percent are annoyed by them. An iProspect study found that 72 percent of Google searchers believe that organic results are more relevant to their queries than paid ones.

37. www.comscore.com.

38. papers.ssrn.com/sol3/papers.cfm?abstract_id=1491315 (accessed October 2009).

39. www.icrossing.com/sites/default/files/search-synergy-report.pdf.

40. googleretail.blogspot.com/2011/08/studies-show-search-ads-drive-89.html.

41. pages.enquiro.com/whitepaper-the-brand-lift-of-search.html (accessed May 2009).

42. eMarketer, June 2011.

43. Michelle Goldberg, a partner at venture capital firm Ignition Partners (September 2009).

44. blog.nielsen.com/nielsenwire/online_mobile/multitasking-at-home-simultaneous-use-of-media-grows (accessed September 2009).

45. 2007 iProspect/Jupiter Research study, www.iprospect.com/about/researchstudy_2007_offlinechannelinfluence.htm.

46. searchengineland.com/taking-on-arf-engagement-interruptive-advertising-and-whatever-else-youve-got-12598 (accessed November 2007).

47. www.useit.com/alertbox/banner-blindness.html (accessed August 2007).

48. sethgodin.com/sg/books.asp.

49. searchengineland.com/danny-sullivans-ad-age-column-fast-company-debate-10643 (accessed May 2007).

50. blog.comscore.com/2009/09/the_revenge_of_neglected_brand.html (accessed September 2009).

51. Author interview with Conrad Saam, Avvo (January 2010).

■ CHAPTER 2

1. Fourteen percent of searches are followed by a second, more specific search (called a refinement), and 24 percent result in a quick click back from the chosen site to the search results. Twenty-one percent of search sessions are longer than 10 minutes (Microsoft internal slides) (June 2009).

2. www.hitwise.com/us/about-us/press-center/press-releases/google-share-of-searches-66-percent-in-sept-2011/.

3. Miller, Geoffrey. *Spent: Sex, Evolution, and Consumer Behavior* (New York: Viking Adult, 2009).

4. Honomichl, Jack, and Laurence N. Gold. Honomichl Annual Industry Report (2007).

5. For more on these testing methods, see *Call to Action: Secret Formulas to Improve Online Results,* by Bryan and Jeffrey Eisenberg, and *Landing Page Optimization,* by Tim Ash.

6. www.newyorker.com/reporting/2011/11/28/111128fa_fact_schwartz.

7. blog.comscore.com/2011/11/occupy_wall_street_how_news_pu.html.

8. Google AdWords Keyword Tool, October 2011.

9. googleresearch.blogspot.com/2009/08/on-predictability-of-search-trends .html (accessed August 2009).

10. research.google.com/archive/google_trends_predictability.pdf.

11. google.com/insights/search.

12. google.com/googleblogs/pdfs/google_predicting_the_present.pdf.

13. www.washingtonpost.com/wp-dyn/content/article/2009/09/11/ AR2009091103771.html: (accessed September 2009).

14. www.google.com/insights/search.

15. adwords.google.com/select/KeywordToolExternal.

16. labs.wordtracker.com/keyword-questions.

17. compete.com.

18. spyfu.com.

19. www.alexa.com.

20. www.hitwise.com.

21. www.comscore.com.

CHAPTER 3

1. www.hitwise.com/us/about-us/press-center/press-releases/google-share-of-searches-66-percent-in-sept-2011.

2. www.seobythesea.com/?p=1021.

3. en.wikipedia.org/wiki/Bounded_rationality.

4. live.psu.edu/story/40091.

5. weblogs.hitwise.com/us-heather-hopkins/2009/08/only_70_of_canadian_searches_a.html (accessed August 2009).

6. www.iprospect.com/premiumPDFs/WhitePaper_2006_SearchEngine UserBehavior.pdf (accessed April 2006).

7. David Robins research, Louisiana State University, www.asis.org/annual-97/shifts.htm.

8. advertising.microsoft.com/small-business/adcenter-downloads/microsoft-advertising-intelligence.

9. Google AdWords Keyword Tool, December 2011.

10. www.google.com/trends/correlate.

11. searchengineland.com/google-correlate-more-search-data-to-mine-78560.

12. www.amazon.com/Why-We-Buy-Science-Shopping/dp/0684849143.

13. searchengineland.com/human-hardware-men-and-women-13614 (accessed May 2008).

14. www.searchengineguide.com/gord-hotchkiss/inside-the-mind-of-the-searcher-part-ii-search-behavior-explored.php (accessed June 2004).

15. Researcher Wendy Wood research, Duke University, www.duke.edu/~dneal/wood.neal.2007.pdf.

16. www.outofmygord.com/archive/2009/01/21/A-Cognitive-Walk-Through-of-Searching.aspx (accessed January 2009).

17. www.usercentric.com/news/2011/01/26/eye-tracking-bing-vs-google-second-look.

18. en.wikipedia.org/wiki/The_Magical_Number_Seven,_Plus_or_Minus_Two.

19. www.news.ucdavis.edu/search/news_detail.lasso?id=8592 (accessed April 2008).

20. searchengineland.com/human-hardware-searching-with-the-basal-ganglia-14578 (accessed August 2008).

21. www.enquiroresearch.com/Campaigns/Mapping-the-BuyerSphere.pdf.

22. www.iprospect.com/premiumPDFs/WhitePaper_2006_Search Engine UserBehavior.pdf (accessed April 2006).

23. www.jimboykin.com/click-rate-for-top-10-search-results (accessed August 2006).

24. ist.psu.edu/faculty_pages/jjansen.

25. www.schema.org.

26. searchengineland.com/yahoo-searchmonkey-enhanced-listings-available-to-searchers-14150 (accessed June 2008).

27. Lindgaard, G., C. Dudek, G. Fernandes and J. Brown. "Attention web designers: You have 50 milliseconds to make a good first impression!" *Behaviour & Information Technology* 25: 115–126.

28. Underhill, Paco. *Why We Buy: The Science of Shopping* (New York: Simon & Schuster, 2000).

29. For more comprehensive information about website usability and website optimization, refer to *Don't Make Me Think: A Common Sense Approach to Web Usability* by Steve Krug (www.useit.com) and to Jakob Nielsen's work.

■ CHAPTER 4

1. econsultancy.com/us/reports/sempo-state-of-search.

2. Persona definition courtesy of Tamara Adlin, author of *The Essential Persona Lifecycle: Your Guide to Building and Using Personas*.

3. Read *The Essential Persona Lifecycle: Your Guide to Building and Using Personas* to learn more about prioritizing personas based on their business value.

4. en.wikipedia.org/wiki/The_Long_Tail.

5. www.hitwise.com/us/datacenter/main/dashboard-10134.html.

6. Hitwise, September 2008.

7. www.slideshare.net/studentlamarketing/enquiro-white-paper-the-brand-lift-of-search (accessed January 2012).

8. www.iprospect.com/premiumPDFs/WhitePaper_2006_SearchEngine UserBehavior.pdf (accessed April 2006).

9. googleblog.blogspot.com/2009/10/managing-your-reputation-through-search.html (accessed October 2009).

10. www.flickr.com/photos/windo/3948998275.

CHAPTER 5

1. www.google.com/intl/en/corporate/tech.html.

2. Yahoo! began in the mid-1990s as a manual directory and transitioned into an automated search engine. Google launched in 1998. Microsoft launched a search engine of its own in 2004 (it previously licensed technology from other companies).

3. searchengineland.com/microsoft-yahoo-search-deal-simplified-23299 (accessed July 2009).

4. googleblog.blogspot.com/2008/05/introduction-to-google-search-quality.html (accessed May 2008).

5. googleblog.blogspot.com/2010/09/search-now-faster-than-speed-of-type.html.

6. searchengineland.com/jakob-nielsen-on-search-usability-11688 (accessed July 2007).

7. www.google.com/support/accounts/bin/topic.py?topic=14148.

8. searchengineland.com/just-behave-googles-marissa-mayer-on-personalized-search-10592 (accessed February 2007).

9. searchengineland.com/googles-matt-cutts-on-personalization-and-the-future-of-seo-10649 (accessed May 2007).

10. searchengineland.com/googles-personalized-results-the-new-normal-31290.

11. googlewebmastercentral.blogspot.com/2007/05/taking-advantage-of-universal-search.html (accessed May 2007).

12. searchengineland.com/qa-with-marissa-mayer-google-vp-search-products-user-experience-10370 (accessed January 2007).

13. searchengineland.com/up-close-google-squared-19313.

14. insidesearch.blogspot.com/2011/11/evolution-of-search-in-six-minutes.html.

15. searchengineland.com/google-adds-more-answers-info-to-search-results-34221.

16. www.youtube.com/t/press_statistics.

17. www.cisco.com/en/US/solutions/collateral/ns341/ns525/ns537/ns705/ns827/white_paper_c11-481360_ns827_Networking_Solutions_White_Paper.html.

18. searchengineland.com/get-youtube-videos-in-your-google-product-search-feeds-25576 (accessed September 2009).

19. www.comscore.com/Press_Events/Press_Releases/2011/11/comScore-Releases_October_2011_U.S._Online_Video_Rankings?piCId=66028.

20. www.comscore.com/Press_Events/Press_Releases/2009/10/TV_Season_Premieres_Spur_Continued_Gains_in_Online_Video_Viewing_as_September_Attracts_Record_Viewership.

21. www.ooyala.com/blogs/video-index.html.

22. http://techcrunch.com/2011/11/12/people-now-watch-videos-nearly-30-percent-longer-on-tablets-than-desktops.

23. searchengineland.com/eye-tracking-on-universal-and-personalized-search-12233 (accessed September 2007).

24. searchengineland.com/confirmed-google-testing-new-sources-display-in-search-results-100261.

25. Progressive enhancement is a way of building web pages that layers technology elements so that a visitor using any browser type (even those that don't support the latest technologies) can access the basic content.

26. searchengineland.com/the-google-quality-raters-handbook-13575 (accessed May 2008).

27. www.w3.org/WAI.

■ CHAPTER 6

1. http://www.searchmarketingexpo.com.

2. Seattle Tech Start-up Mailing List (accessed August 2009).

3. Alex Bosworth, www.ninebyblue.com/blog/seo-is-the-worst-thing-ever-invented (accessed March 2008).

4. Jeremy Schoemaker, www.shoemoney.com.

5. powazek.com/posts/2090 (accessed October 2009).

6. www.foxnews.com/slideshow/scitech/2009/08/17/marketing-internet-scams?slide=6 (accessed August 2008).

7. www.google.com/support/webmasters/bin/answer.py?answer=35769.

8. en.wikipedia.org/wiki/Meta_element#The_keywords_attribute.

9. Read *Call to Action: Secret Formulas for Improve Online Results*, by Bryan and Jeffrey Eisenberg, for more on this topic.

10. www.comscore.com/Press_Events/Presentations_Whitepapers/2011/State_of_Local_Business_Search.

11. www.orangesoda.com/blog/the-power-of-local-mobile-search-infographic.

12. www.google.com/local/add.

13. ssl.bing.com/listings/BusinessSearch.aspx.

14. listings.local.yahoo.com/basic.php.

15. searchengineland.com/double-your-traffic-using-optimal-category-names-44559.

16. Bing internal data.

17. www.mobilecommercedaily.com/2011/09/22/44pc-of-holiday-searches-will-happen-via-mobile-google.

18. www.orangesoda.com/blog/the-power-of-local-mobile-search-infographic.

19. searchengineland.com/google-confirms-mayday-update-impacts-long-tail-traffic-43054.

20. searchengineland.com/google-forecloses-on-content-farms-with-farmer-algorithm-update-66071.

21. www.google.com/competition/howgooglesearchworks.html.

22. www.wired.com/epicenter/2011/03/the-panda-that-hates-farms/2.

23. www.google.com/support/webmasters/bin/answer.py?answer=40349.

24. www.google.com/intl/en/about/corporate/company/tenthings.html.

25. googlewebmastercentral.blogspot.com/2011/05/more-guidance-on-building-high-quality.html.

26. http://support.google.com/webmasters/bin/answer.py?hl=en&answer=35291.

■ CHAPTER 7

1. sitemaps.org.

2. googlewebmastercentral.blogspot.com/2008/11/date-with-googlebot-part-ii-http-status.html (accessed November 2008).

3. www.google.com/webmasters.

4. janeandrobot.com/library/managing-robots-access-to-your-website (accessed December 2008).

5. googlewebmastercentral.blogspot.com/2008/11/date-with-googlebot-part-ii-http-status.html (accessed November 2008).

6. www.ninebyblue.com/managing-robots-access-to-your-website.

7. searchengineland.com/canonical-tag-16537 (accessed February 2009).

8. searchengineland.com/google-lets-you-tell-them-which-url-parameters-to-ignore-25925 (accessed September 2009).

9. googlewebmastercentral.blogspot.com/2007/09/improve-snippets-with-meta-description.html (accessed September 2007).

10. searchengineland.com/canonical-tag-16537 (accessed February 2009).

11. searchengineland.com/google-lets-you-tell-them-which-url-parameters-to-ignore-25925 (accessed September 2009).

12. www.ninebyblue.com/managing-robots-access-to-your-website.

13. www.ninebyblue.com/effectively-using-images-2–2.

14. www.prnewswire.com/news-releases/comscore-releases-october-2011-us-online-video-rankings-134602043.html.

15. googlewebmastercentral.blogspot.com/2010/12/sending-video-sitemaps-q-holiday-cheer.html.

16. googlevideo.blogspot.com/2008/05/video-sitemaps-how-we-find-great-videos.html (accessed May 2008).

■ CHAPTER 8

1. www.techcrunch.com/2009/07/09/the-naked-truth-2009-slides-show-me-the-money (accessed July 2009).

2. Kaushik, Avinash. *Web Analytics: An Hour a Day*. (New York: Sybex, 2007).

3. www.kaushik.net/avinash/2006/07/stop-obsessing-about-conversion-rate.html (accessed July 2006).

4. econsultancy.com/us/reports/sempo-state-of-search.

5. webanalyticssolutionprofiler.com.

6. ir.comscore.com/releasedetail.cfm?ReleaseID=245287 (accessed March 2006).

7. www.doubleclick.com/insight/pdfs/searchpurchase_0502.pdf (accessed February 2005).

8. www.comscore.com/Press_Events/Press_Releases/2008/01/Importance_of_Search_Engines (accessed January 2008).

9. Author interview with Greg Fant, August 2009.

10. www.clearsaleing.com/wp-content/uploads/2009/07/am-buyers-guide-handout-final.pdf (accessed July 2009).

11. www.attributionmanagement.com/2009/10/attribution-management-buyers-guide-part-2-and-3 (accessed October 2009).

12. www.iprospect.com/premiumPDFs/researchstudy_2007_offlinechannelinfluence.pdf (accessed August 2007).

13. www.emarketer.com/Article.aspx?R=1005971 (accessed February 2008).

14. searchengineland.com/attributing-value-to-phone-calls-dynamic-number-insertion-can-help-26339 (accessed September 2009).

15. searchengineland.com/euclid-offers-google-analytics-for-the-real-world-99982.

16. money.cnn.com/2011/11/22/technology/malls_track_cell_phones_black_friday.

17. arstechnica.com/business/news/2011/11/were-watching-malls-track-shoppers-cell-phone-signals-to-gather-marketing-data.ars.

18. www.kaushik.net/avinash/2006/06/data-quality-sucks-lets-just-get-over-it.html (accessed June 2006).

■ CHAPTER 9

1. pewinternet.org/~/media/Files/Reports/2011/PIP%20-%20Social%20networking%20sites%20and%20our%20lives.pdf.

2. For a more comprehensive discussion of social media strategy, see *Friends with Benefits: A Social Media Marketing Handbook*, by Darren Barefoot and Julie Szabo.

3. Google AdWords Keyword Tool, average global monthly search volume (accessed September 2009).

4. thecaucus.blogs.nytimes.com/2011/11/09/cain-camp-turns-accuser-searches-to-their-benefit.

5. www.marketingpilgrim.com/2008/11/motrin-faces-twitter-headache-over-new-video-campaign.html (accessed November 2008).

6. parenting.blogs.nytimes.com/2008/11/17/moms-and-motrin (accessed November 2008).

7. www.youtube.com/watch?v=LhR-y1N6R8Q (accessed November 2008).

8. www.nytimes.com/2011/11/25/business/media/occupy-movement-focuses-on-staying-current-on-social-networks.html?_r=2&pagewanted=all.

9. twitter.com/#!/Adbusters/status/88013043438600192.

10. www.nytimes.com/2011/11/25/business/media/occupy-movement-focuses-on-staying-current-on-social-networks.html?_r=3&pagewanted=all.

11. www.westseattleblog.com.

12. www.coremetrics.com/downloads/benchmark-2011-cyber-monday.pdf.

13. blog.nielsen.com/nielsenwire/online_mobile/black-friday-cyber-monday-2011-buzz.

14. www.facebook.com/press/info.php?statistics.

15. www.readwriteweb.com/archives/twitter_confirms_it_has_passed_200_million_account.php.

16. press.linkedin.com/about.

17. investor.google.com/earnings/2011/Q3_google_earnings.html.

18. googleblog.blogspot.com/2011/11/google-pages-connect-with-all-things.html.

19. http://searchengineland.com/googles-results-get-more-personal-with-search-plus-your-world-107285.

20. googleblog.blogspot.com/2011/11/shipping-google-in-google.html.

21. blumenthals.com/blog/2011/11/23/is-google-starting-to-integrate-google-plus-pages-with-places-search-results/.

22. searchengineland.com/google-pages-for-businesses-the-adwords-impact-100396.

23. searchengineland.com/google-badge-tool-now-makes-facepile-style-badges-1-counts-to-be-consolidated-101347.

24. www.google.com/support/webmasters/bin/answer.py?answer=1708844.

■ CHAPTER 10

1. www.180360720.no/index.php/archive/the-next-80-part-1-introduction/?mid=541.

2. techcrunch.com/2011/11/25/twine-foreshadows-a-future-where-all-objects-talk-to-the-internet.

3. techcrunch.com/2011/10/18/mary-meekers-2011-presentation-on-internet-trends-slides.

4. www.urbanspoon.com/blog/27/Urbanspoon-on-the-iPhone.html (accessed July 2008).

5. googleblog.blogspot.com/2011/11/new-frontier-for-google-maps-mapping.html.

6. gigaom.com/2011/11/28/the-future-of-technology-means-making-the-computer-disappear.

7. www.zdnet.com/blog/btl/sir-why-apple-will-build-buy-or-partner-on-a-search-engine/64382.

8. abc.go.com/watch/better-off-ted/187472/228393/secrets-and-lives.

9. blog.face.com/2009/08/20/better-off-ted.

10. face.com/about.php.

11. picasa.google.com/support/bin/answer.py?answer=156272.

12. searchengineland.com/google-goggles-search-by-images-31364.

13. www.zdnet.com/blog/btl/siri-why-apple-will-build-buy-or-partner-on-a-search-engine/64382.

14. immersivelabs.com.

15. www.nytimes.com/2011/11/20/business/mobile-deals-aimed-at-black-friday-shoppers-stuck-in-line.html.

16. www.tineye.com/about.

17. www.airtightinteractive.com/projects/related_tag_browser/app/.

18. twitter.com/#!/Rafe/status/141936829141229568.

19. internet2go.net/news/data-and-forecasts/call-it-t-commerce-almost-50-ipad-users-have-made-purchases-past-month.

20. techcrunch.com/2011/12/02/kindle-fire-3-9-million.

21. blog.nielsen.com/nielsenwire/online_mobile/generation-app-62-of-mobile-users-25-34-own-smartphones.

22. techcrunch.com/2011/10/18/mary-meekers-2011-presentation-on-internet-trends-slides.

23. www.mobilecommercedaily.com/2011/09/22/44pc-of-holiday-searches-will-happen-via-mobile-google.

24. www.coremetrics.com/downloads/benchmark-2011-cyber-monday.pdf.

25. http://techcrunch.com/2011/11/29/the-final-tally-from-ibm-cyber-monday-online-spending-up-30-percent-from-last-year.

26. www.comscore.com/Press_Events/Press_Releases/2011/10/Smartphones_and_Tablets_Drive_Nearly_7_Percent_of_Total_U.S._Digital_Traffic.

27. www.mobilecommercedaily.com/2011/09/22/44pc-of-holiday-searches-will-happen-via-mobile-google.

28. searchengineland.com/the-impending-social-search-inflection-point-10885 (accessed April 2007).

29. searchengineland.com/what-is-real-time-search-definitions-players-22172 (accessed July 2009).

30. www.comscore.com/Press_Events/Press_Releases/2011/10/comScore_Releases_September_2011_U.S._Search_Engine_Rankings.

31. pewinternet.org/~/media/Files/Reports/2011/PIP%20-%20Social%20networking%20sites%20and%20our%20lives.pdf.

32. searchengineland.com/google-social-search-launches-gives-results-from-your-trusted-social-circle-28507.

33. searchengineland.com/as-deal-with-twitter-expires-google-realtime-search-goes-offline-84175.

34. www.bing.com/social.

35. itunes.apple.com/gb/app/plane-finder-ar/id390039844?mt=8.

36. itunes.apple.com/us/app/star-walk-5-stars-astronomy/id295430577?mt=8.

37. googleblog.blogspot.com/2011/02/introducing-google-translate-app-for.html.

38. searchengineland.com/search-in-the-year-2010–11917 (accessed August 2007).

39. Read Barry Schwartz, *The Paradox of Choice: Why More Is Less* (New York: Harper Perennial, 2004).

References

Adlin, Tamara, and John Pruitt. *The Persona Lifecycle: Keeping People in Mind throughout Product Design (The Morgan Kaufmann Series in Interactive Technologies)* (San Francisco: Morgan Kaufmann, 2006).

Albert, William, and Thomas Tullis. *Measuring the User Experience: Collecting, Analyzing, and Presenting Usability Metrics (Interactive Technologies)* (San Francisco: Morgan Kaufmann, 2008).

Ash, Tim. *Landing Page Optimization* (Hoboken, NJ: John Wiley & Sons, 2008).

Barefoot, Darren, and Julie Szabo. *Friends with Benefits. Online Marketing with Blogs, Facebook, YouTube, and More* (San Francisco: No Starch Press, 2009).

Berkman, Robert. *The Art of Strategic Listening: Finding Market Intelligence in Blogs and Social Media* (Ithaca, NY: Paramount Market Publishing, 2008).

Clifton, Brian. *Advanced Web Metrics with Google Analytics* (New York: Sybex, 2008).

Edwards, Douglas. *I'm Feeling Lucky. Confessions of Employee Number 59* (Boston: Houghton Mifflin Harcourt, 2011).

Eisenberg, Bryan, Jeffrey Eisenberg, and Lisa T. Davis. *Call to Action: Secret Formulas to Improve Online Results* (Nashville: Nelson Business, 2006).

Enge, Eric, Stephan Spencer, Rand Fishkin, and Jessie Stricchiola. *The Art of SEO (Theory in Practice)* (Sebastopol, CA: O'Reilly Media, 2009).

Godin, Seth. *Permission Marketing: Turning Strangers into Friends and Friends into Customers* (New York: Simon & Schuster, 1999).

Hunt, Bill, and Mike Moran. *Search Engine Marketing, Inc.: Driving Search Traffic to Your Company's Web Site*, 2nd ed. (New York: IBM Press, 2008).

Kaushik, Avinash. *Web Analytics: An Hour a Day* (New York: Sybex, 2007).

Kaushik, Avinash. *Web Analytics 2.0: The Art of Online Accountability and Science of Customer Centricity* (New York: Sybex, 2009).

Krug, Steve. *Don't Make Me Think: A Common Sense Approach to Web Usability*, 2nd ed. (Berkeley, CA: New Riders Press, 2005).

Levy, Steven. *In the Plex: How Google Thinks, Works, and Shapes Our Lives* (New York: Simon & Schuster, 2011).

Loveday, Lance, and Sandra Niehaus. *Web Design for ROI: Turning Browsers into Buyers & Prospects into Leads* (Berkeley, CA: New Riders Press, 2007).

Pink, Daniel H. *Drive: The Surprising Truth about What Motivates Us* (Riverhead Trade, 2011).

Qualman, Eric. *Socialnomics: How Social Media Transforms the Way We Live and Do Business* (Hoboken, NJ: John Wiley & Sons, 2010).

Ruby, Jeffrey. *The Handbook of Usability Testing: How to Plan, Design, and Conduct Effective Usability Tests* (Hoboken, NJ: John Wiley & Sons, 1994).

Schwartz, Barry. *The Paradox of Choice: Why More Is Less* (New York: Harper Perennial, 2005).

Scott, David Meerman. *The New Rules of Marketing and PR: How to Use News Releases, Blogs, Podcasting, Viral Marketing and Online Media to Reach Buyers Directly* (Hoboken, NJ: John Wiley & Sons, 2008).

Thurow, Shari. *Search Engine Visibility: Voices That Matter*, 2nd ed. (Berkeley, CA: Peachpit Press, 2007).

Weinschenk, Susan M. *Neuro Web Design: What Makes Them Click* (New Riders Press, 2009).

Index